A TEXT BOOK OF
MANUFACTURING TECHNOLOGY

For
S.E. SEMESTER – III

SECOND YEAR DEGREE COURSES IN MECHANICAL & AUTOMATION ENGINEERING

As Per New Revised Syllabus of Shivaji University Kolhapur.
(Effective From, 2014)

Dr. A. K. BEWOOR
B.E. (Mech.I), M.E. (Mech.) Ph.D. (Mech.)
Professor, Mechanical Engg., Deptt,
Cummins College of Engg. for Women's, Pune

S. M. SANAP
B.E. (Mech.), M.E. (Mech.)
Assistant Professor, Mechanical Engg. Deptt.
Sinhagad Academy of Enggineering
Kondhawa (Bk.) Pune

A. A. BHOSALE
B.E. (Mech.), M.E. (Prod.)
Assistant Professor, Workshop Deptt.,
Cummins College of Engg. for Women's, Pune

MANUFACTURING TECHNOLOGY (S.E. SEM. III MECH. & AUTO. – SU)   ISBN : 978-93-5164-225-1

First Edition :   August 2014

© :
The text of this publication, or any part thereof, should not be reproduced or transmitted in any form or stored in any computer storage system or device for distribution including photocopy, recording, taping or information retrieval system or reproduced on any disc, tape, perforated media or other information storage device etc., without the written permission of Authors with whom the rights are reserved. Breach of this condition is liable for legal action. Every effort has been made to avoid errors or omissions in this publication. In spite of this, errors may have crept in. Any mistake, error or discrepancy so noted and shall be brought to our notice shall be taken care of in the next edition. It is notified that neither the publisher nor the authors or seller shall be responsible for any damage or loss of action to any one, of any kind, in any manner, therefrom.

Published By :
NIRALI PRAKASHAN
Abhyudaya Pragati, 1312, Shivaji Nagar,
Off J.M. Road, PUNE - 411005
Tel - (020) 25512336/37/39, Fax - (020) 25511379
Email : niralipune@pragationline.com

Printed at
Repro Knowledgecast Limited
India

DISTRIBUTION CENTRES
PUNE

Nirali Prakashan
119, Budhwar Peth, Jogeshwari Mandir Lane
Pune 411002, Maharashtra
Tel : (020) 2445 2044, 66022708, Fax : (020) 2445 1538
Email : bookorder@pragationline.com

Nirali Prakashan
S. No. 28/25, Dhyari,
Near Pari Company, Pune 411041
Tel : (022) 24690204 Fax : (022) 24690316
Email : dhyari@pragationline.com
bookorder@pragationline.com

MUMBAI
Nirali Prakashan
385, S.V.P. Road, Rasdhara Co-op. Hsg. Society Ltd.,
Girgaum, Mumbai 400004, Maharashtra
Tel : (022) 2385 6339 / 2386 9976, Fax : (022) 2386 9976
Email : niralimumbai@pragationline.com

DISTRIBUTION BRANCHE

NAGPUR
Pratibha Book Distributors
Above Maratha Mandir, Shop No. 3, First Floor,
Rani Jhanshi Square, Sitabuldi, Nagpur 440012,
Maharashtra, Tel : (0712) 254 7129

JALGAON
Nirali Prakashan
34, V. V. Golani Market, Navi Peth, Jalgaon 425001,
Maharashtra, Tel : (0257) 222 0395
Mob : 94234 91860

BENGALURU
Pragati Book House
House No. 1, Sanjeevappa Lane, Avenue Road Cross,
Opp. Rice Church, Bengaluru - 560002.
Tel : (080) 64513344, 64513355,
Mob : 9880582331, 9845021552
Email:bharatsavla@yahoo.com

KOLHAPUR
Nirali Prakashan
New Mahadvar Road,
Kedar Plaza, 1st Floor Opp. IDBI Bank
Kolhapur 416 012, Maharashtra. Mob : 9855046155

CHENNAI
Pragati Books
9/1, Montieth Road, Behind Taas Mahal, Egmore,
Chennai 600008 Tamil Nadu, Tel : (044) 6518 3535,
Mob : 94440 01782 / 98450 21552 / 98805 82331, Email : bharatsavla@yahoo.com

RETAIL OUTLETS
PUNE

Pragati Book Centre
157, Budhwar Peth, Opp. Ratan Talkies,
Pune 411002, Maharashtra
Tel : (020) 2445 8887 / 6602 2707, Fax : (020) 2445 8887

Pragati Book Centre
676/B, Budhwar Peth, Opp. Jogeshwari Mandir,
Pune 411002, Maharashtra
Tel : (020) 6601 7784 / 6602 0855

Pragati Book Centre
Amber Chamber, 28/A, Budhwar Peth,
Appa Balwant Chowk, Pune : 411002, Maharashtra,
Tel : (020) 20240335 / 66281669
Email : pbcpune@pragationline.com

PBC Book Sellers & Stationers
152, Budhwar Peth, Pune 411002, Maharashtra
Tel : (020) 2445 2254 / 6609 2463

MUMBAI
Pragati Book Corner
Indira Niwas, 111 - A, Bhavani Shankar Road, Dadar (W), Mumbai 400028, Maharashtra
Tel : (022) 2422 3526 / 6662 5254, Email : pbcmumbai@pragationline.com

www.pragationline.com   info@pragationline.com

PREFACE

The book is written mainly for the Second Year Students of Mechanical and Automation Engineering for the subject **"Manufacturing Technology"**. It is strictly written as per the New Revised Syllabus of Shivaji University, Kolhapur, 2014.

New text book is written, taking in to account all the new features that have been introduced. All the entrants to the engineering field will definitely find this book, complete in all respect. Students will find the subject matter presentation quite lucid.

This book, **"Manufacturing Technology"** is primarily oriented to satisfy the specific needs of Second Year Mechanical Engineering, Production Engineering and Industrial Engineering students.

There has been rapid progress in various area of Manufacturing Processes. This book aims at exposing basic Manufacturing Technology as well as the new changes in this area.

Each topic is presented with necessary description of processes and technology, using schematic diagrams and actual photographs. Certain objectives for every chapter are planned and treatment of text is done accordingly. Special consideration is given to mention applications of every process described. Reference Material, Tables included in the book.

Our sincere hope is that the material presented in the book will be useful in understanding the subject as well as for attempting examination questions.

We take this opportunity to express our thanks to **Shri. Dineshbhai Furia** and **Shri. Jignesh Furia** and **Shri. M.P. Munde** for publishing this book in time.

We are also take this opportunity to express our thank all the staff members of Nirali Prakashan namely Mrs. Anita Kulkarni, Mrs. Shilpa Kale, Mrs. Sarika Wagh and Mrs. Pratibha Bele also Miss Sarika Shinde and Miss Rani Zinjade for their tremendous dedication and hard work in bringing out this book in an excellent form.

We are also thankful to **Mr. Virdhaval Shinde**, Branch Manager, Kolhapur Office and **Mr. Ashok Nanaware**, Branch Manager, Sangli District for their valuable help and efforts for promotion of my book.

Our special thanks to our family members, students and all those who directly or indirectly supported me in this project.

Any suggestions and feedback shall be appreciated and acknowledged.

September 2014   **Authors**

Pune

SYLLABUS

Unit I : Patterns and Pattern making (3)
Introduction to Foundry - Steps involved in casting, advantages, limitations and applications of casting process. Pattern types, allowances for pattern, pattern materials, color coding and storing of patterns.

Unit II : Moulding & Casting Processes (11)
Moulding : Methods & processes- equipment, Moulding sand ingredients, essential requirements, sand preparation and control, testing, core making. Moulding machines and core making machines. Design considerations in casting, gating and Riser - directional solidification in castings, solidification control devices: chills, ceramics bricks, directional solidification.

Casting : Sand castings, sand properties and their testing, pressure die casting, permanent mould casting, centrifugal casting, precision investment casting, shell Moulding, CO_2 Moulding, continuous casting-squeeze casting, electro slag casting.

Unit III : (A) Melting and pouring (6)
17 Types of fuel fired melting furnaces -Cupola furnace, crucible furnaces, Electric furnaces, - Metallurgical control in furnaces- Advanced Metal pouring equipments – Molten metal transfer and automatic pouring machines.

(B) Casting Defects : NDT tests, Machines and instruments used for identification of defects. Foundry layouts and mechanization – Use of automatic machines and robots for various casting processes.

Unit IV : Forming Processes (10)
(a) Forging : Forging principle, classification, equipments, tooling-processes, parameters and calculation of forces and power requirements during forging.

(b) Rolling : Principles of rolling processes, classification, types of rolling mills, rolling mill control, , effects of friction. Form rolling, rolling defects, causes and remedies

(c) Extrusion and Drawing Processes : Classification of extrusion processes-tools, equipments, and principle of these processes, rod/wire drawing-tool, equipment and principle of processes defects-Tube drawing and sinking processes.

Unit V : Basic Joining Processes (6)
Types of welding-gas welding, -arc welding,-shielded metal arc welding, GTAW, GMAW, SAW, ESW-Resistance welding (spot, seam, projection, percussion, flash types)-atomic hydrogen arc welding-thermit welding, Flame cutting - Use of Oxyacetylene, modern cutting processes, arc cutting

Unit VI : Shaping of Plastics (3)
Introduction to blow molding, injection molding, extrusion, calendaring and thermo forming
Note : The Workshop practice III should cover the practical based on this syllabus, the load of which shall be allotted to teaching staff.

CONTENTS

1. Patterns and Pattern Making — 1.1 – 1.18

2. Moulding and Casting Processes — 2.1 – 2.62

3. Melting and Pouring — 3.1 – 3.18

4. Forming Processes — 4.1 – 4.44

5. Joining Processes — 5.1 – 5.40

6. Shaping of Plastics — 6.1 – 6.20

Unit - I

PATTERNS AND PATTERN MAKING

1.0 INTRODUCTION TO FOUNDRY

Casting is the oldest and still most widely used process. A foundry is factory where casting of metal produced as per specified and required sizes. Metals are cast into shapes by melting them into a liquid by using furnace, pouring the metal in a desired mould, and removing the mould material or casting after the metal has solidified as it cools. The most common metals used for the casting are aluminium and cast iron. However, other metals, such as bronze, brass, steel, magnesium, and zinc, are also used to produce castings in foundries. In this process, parts of desired shapes and sizes can be formed.

Foundry bases itself on the founding or casting principles. Casting is one of the basic tools of shaping metals and alloys. The basic simplicity of the foundry proved to be a benefit for the growth of foundry industry and today a wide variety of products (or parts) such as complex shape and sizes, as well as difficult to machine material which can be easily casted in foundries. Recently domestic use to space vehicles are produced in foundries. Foundry may be defined as a commercial setup for manufacturing casting. Foundry may also be known as a collection of materials, fuel, fluxes and tools mahines to produced casted components. Foundry can shape parts weighing from a few grams to 100 of tons.

1.1 TYPES OF FOUNDRIES

Foundries are of many types according to, size of component, nature of work performed, material used in casting, and the frame work of the industry. Basically foundries categoriesd as follows:

- **Captive Foundry :**
  A captive foundry is an integral part of some manufacturing organisation; it makes casting for the same only and all the casting made in a captive foundry are consumed mainly in the products being manufactured by that industry. A captive foundry only produces castings for the operation that it is a part of.
- **Jobbing Foundry :**
  A jobbing foundry normally produced small number of casting of a given type for different customers. Such foundries, sometimes, also have facilities for mass production.
- **Production Foundry :**
  A production foundry is highly mechanised and can produce casting economically on mass scale

- **Semi production Foundry :**
  A semi production foundry is a combination of jobbing foundry and a production foundry as regards its nature of work is concerned. In other words, a semi production foundry accepts both production and job work.

1.2 FOUNDRY LAYOUT

The success of any manufacturing organization based on the ability to design and operate manufacturing facilities that can quickly and effectively adapt to changing technological. The below Fig 1.1 shows a typical foundry layout.

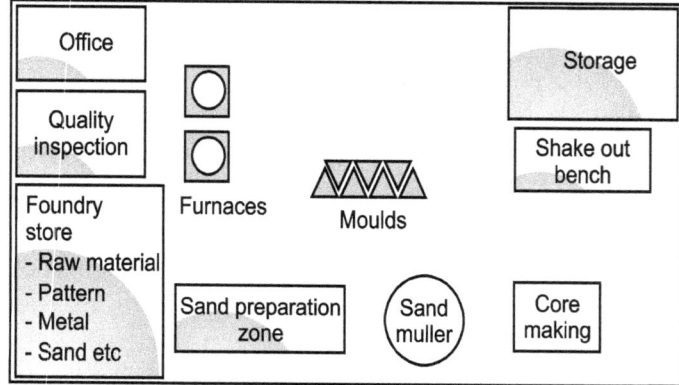

Fig. 1.1 : Foundry Layout

In a manual foundry, sand is prepared in a separate unit from where it reaches the hopper just above the moulding machine. Empty moulding boxes and transported on roller conveyor to the moulding machines where they are rammed, assembled and moved to pouring station. After the molten metal has solidified the moulds pass through cooling zone and ultimately at shake out station casting are taken out of the moulds. Casting go for felting and finishing where as empty cooled moulding boxes are roller conveyed to the moulding machines and the new casting cycle begins.

1.3 CASTING

Casting is one of the oldest methods of manufacturing of metal components. It is the primary manufacturing process. The principle of casting consists of the following major step; such as the metal is poured into a mould whose cavity is the mirror image or replica to the shape of the desired casting. As metal cools and solidifies in the mould a castings results. During its crystallisation and cooling in the casting mould, the metal acquires certain mechanical properties and service characteristic. The cooled and solidified casting removed from the mould, cleaned and subjected to further treatment if necessary. The Fig 1.2 shows the important step involved in casting.

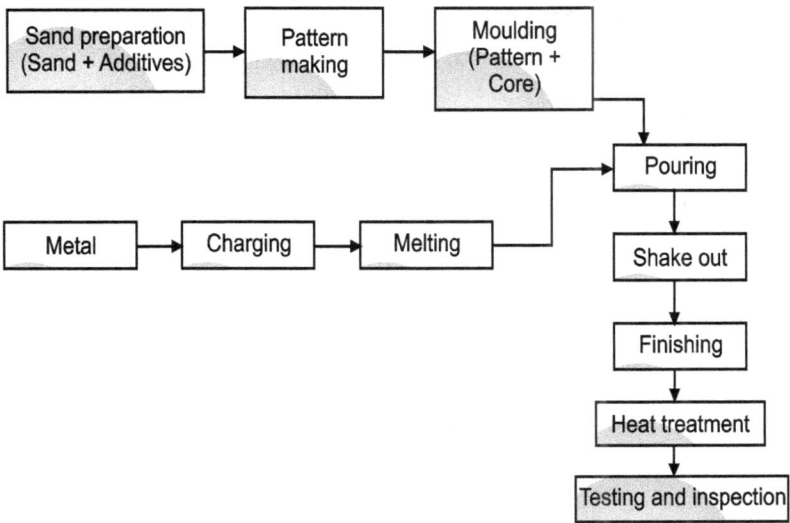

Fig. 1.2 : Steps involved in casting

The castings from metals and alloys find wide use as parts of machines and instruments turned out by the machine building and instrument making industries. The foundry practice most popular is the possibility of producing cast parts of complex shape with minimum machining allowances and good mechanical and service properties.

The basic moulding process is sand mould casting which accounts for 85% of the total output of cast products. The dimensional accuracy and surface finish of sand mould casting do not satisfy in many cases the requirement of modern machine building and instrument making industries. The steps for casting of components are as follows :

Pattern Making :

Pattern making is the first stage for producing a new casting. The pattern, or replica of the finished piece, is typically constructed from wood, metal, plastic, plaster or other suitable materials. These patterns are permanent so can be used to form a number of moulds. Pattern making is a highly skilled and precise process that is critical to the quality of the final product. Many modern pattern shops make use of computer-aided design (CAD) to design patterns. These systems can also be integrated with automated cutting tools that are controlled with computer-aided manufacturing (CAM) tools. Cores are produced in conjunction with the pattern to form the interior surfaces of the casting.

Mould Making :

The mould is formed in a mould box (flask), which is typically constructed in two halves to assist in removing the pattern. Sand moulds are temporary so a new mould must be formed for each individual casting. A cross-section of a typical two-part sand mould is shown in Fig. 1.3. The bottom half of the mould (the drag) is formed on a moulding board. Cores require greater strength to hold their form during pouring. Dimensional precision also needs to be greater because interior surfaces are more difficult to machine, making errors costly to fix. Cores are formed using one of the chemical binding systems. Once the core is inserted, the top half of the mould (the cope) is placed on top. The interface between the two mould halves is called a parting line. Weights may be placed on the cope to help secure the two halves together, particularly for metals that expand during cooling.

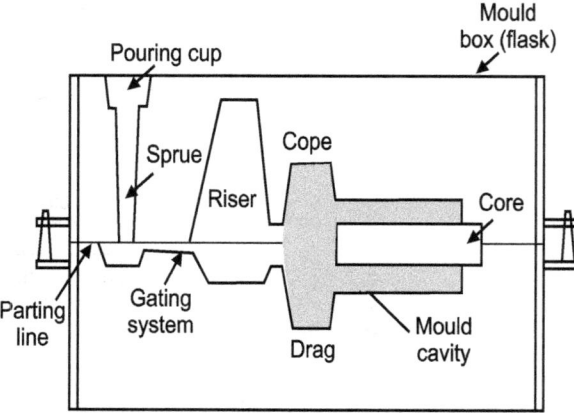

Fig. 1.3 : Casting

Mould designs include a gating system which is designed to carry molten metal smoothly to all parts of the mould. The gating system typically includes a sprue, gates, runners and risers. The sprue is where the metal is poured. Gates allow the metal to enter the running system. Runners carry the molten metal towards the casting cavity. Risers may have several functions including vents to allow gases to be released, reservoirs prior to the casting cavity to aid progressive solidification, and waste cavities to allow metal to rise from the casting cavity to ensure it is filled and to remove the first poured metal from the casting cavity, thus avoiding solidification problems.

Melting and Pouring :

Many foundries, use a high proportion of scrap metal to make up a charge. As such, foundries play an important role in the metal recycling industry. Internally generated scrap from runners and risers, as well as reject product, is also recycled. The charge is weighed and introduced to the furnace. Alloys and other materials are added to the charge to produce the desired melt. In some operations the charge may be preheated, often using waste heat. The furnaces commonly used in the industry are described below. In traditional processes metal is superheated in the furnace. Molten metal is transferred from the furnace to a ladle and held until it reaches the desired pouring temperature. The molten metal is poured into the mould and allowed to solidify.

Cooling and Shakeout :

Once the metal has been poured, the mould is transported to a cooling area. The casting needs to cool, often overnight for ambient cooling, before it can be removed from the mould. Castings may be removed manually or using vibratory tables that shake the refractory material away from the casting. Quenching baths are also used in some foundries to achieve rapid cooling of castings. This speeds up the process and also helps achieve certain metallurgical properties. The quench bath may contain chemical additives to prevent oxidation.

Sand Recovery :

Sand foundries recover a significant proportion of the waste sand for internal reuse. This significantly reduces the quantity of sand that must be purchased and disposed of sand is reclaimed mechanically; cores and large metal lumps are removed by vibrating screens and the binders are removed by the sand particles rubbing together. Fine sand and binders are removed by extraction and collected in a baghouse. In some systems metals are removed using magnets or other separation techniques. For operations using mechanical reclamation, the recycle rate is often limited to around 78%. This is due to the need to maintain a minimum sand quality. For large iron foundries, where sand quality requirements are less stringent, over 80% reclamation can be achieved by mechanical means. For many processes, mechanically reclaimed sand is not of sufficiently high quality to be used for core production. Thermal reclamation is becoming more widely used. This process heats the sand to the point where organic materials, including the binders, are driven off. This process can return the sand to an 'as new' state, allowing it to be used for core making. Thermal reclamation is more expensive than mechanical systems. Sand can also be reclaimed using wet washing and scrubbing techniques. These methods produce sand of a high quality but are not commonly used because they generate a significant liquid waste stream and require additional energy input for sand drying. The amount of internal reuse depends on the type of technology used and the quality requirements of the casting process. Reclamation processes, particularly mechanical ones, break down the sand particles and this can affect the quality of some metals. Also, for mechanical reclamation techniques, impurities may build up in the sand over time, requiring a proportion of the material to be wasted. Large iron foundries do not require a high sand quality so typically achieve the highest rate of reuse in the industry. Often sand cycles through the operation until it is ground down to a fine dust and removed by baghouses.

Cleaning Fettling and Finishing :

After the casting has cooled, the gating system is removed, often using band saws, abrasive cut-off wheels or electrical cut-off devices. A 'parting line flash' is typically formed on the casting and must be removed by grinding or with chipping hammers. Castings may also need to be repaired by welding, brazing or soldering to eliminate defects. Shot blasting propelling abrasive material at high velocity onto the casting surface is often used to remove any remaining metal flash, refractory material or oxides. Depending on the type and strength of the metal cast, the grade of shot may vary from steel ball bearings to a fine grit. The casting may undergo additional grinding and polishing to achieve the desired surface quality. The casting may then be coated using either paint or a metal finishing operation such as galvanising, powder coating or electroplating.

Testing and Inspection :

Finally, before the casting is despatched from the foundry, it is tested and inspected to ensure that it is flawless and conforms to the designed specification.

1.3.1 Advantages of Casting

Casting has several characteristic that clearly define their role in day to day life product, equipment used for transportation communication power agriculture construction and in industry. Cast metals are required in various shapes and sizes and in large quantities for making machine and tools. The metal shaping processes such as stamping, forming, welding, are of course necessary to fulfil a tremendous range of needs.

The main advantages of casting are :

- **Versatility in Production** : Metal casting is adaptable to all types of production, job as well as mass production.
- **Dimensional Accuracy :** Casting can be made to fairly close dimensional tolerance by choosing the proper type of moulding and casting process(**tolerance as close as ± 0.1 mm)**
- **Complexity :** The most simple or complex curved surface, inside or outside and complicated shapes, which would otherwise be very difficult or impossible to machine, forge can usually be produced by using casting process.
- **Fibrous structure :** Wrought metals have a fibrous structure, mainly due to stringer, like arrangement of the inclusions of non-metallic impurities. In cast metals, the inclusions are more or less randomly distributed during the solidification process.
- **Size :** Casting may weigh as much as 200 tons or be as small as a wire of 0.05 mm diameter.
- **Weight Saving :** As the metal can be placed exactly where it is required.
- **Production of prototypes :** The casting process is ideally suited to the production of models or prototypes required for creating new design.
- **Low cost :** Casting is usually found to be the cheapest method of metal casting.

1.3.2 Limitation of Casting
- Typically limited to one or a small number of moulds per box.
- Sand: metal ratio is relatively high.
- High level of waste is typically generated, particularly sand, baghouse dust band spent shot.

1.3.3 Application of Casting
Casting enables pieces to be combined into a single part, eliminating, assembly and inventory. Compared to machined parts, costs are much less. Virtually any metal that can be melted is cast. The size can be from a few grams (for example a watch case) to several tones (marine diesel engine) the shape from simple (manhole cover) to complex (6-cylinder engine block). Castings are used virtually everywhere. The transport sector and heavy equipment is the predominant consumer (for farming, construction and mining) taking up over 60% of castings produced. A sector wise casting consumption is given below which highlights the importance of casting in any industrial set up.
- **Transport** : Automobile, aerospace, railways and shipping
- **Heavy Equipment** : Construction, farming and mining
- **Machine Tools** : Machining, casting, plastics molding, forging, extrusion and forming
- **Plant Machinery** : Chemical, petroleum, paper, sugar, textile, steel and thermal plants
- **Defence** : Vehicles, artillery, munitions, storage and supporting equipment
- **Electrical Equipment Machines** : Motors, generators, pumps and compressors
- **Hardware** : Plumbing industry pipes, joints, valves and fittings
- **Household** : Appliances, kitchen and gardening equipment, furniture and fittings
- **Art Objects** : Sculptures, idols, furniture, lamp stands and decorative items

1.4 CASTING PATTERNS
In casting, a pattern is a replica of the object to be cast, used to prepare the cavity into which molten material will be poured during the casting process. When the pattern is removed the resulting cavity is the exact shape of the object to be cast. The pattern must be designed to be easily removed without damage to the mould. It must be accurately dimensioned and durable enough for the use intended. Either one time use or production runs. Patterns used in sand casting may be made of wood, metal, plastics or other materials around which sand is packed in the mould. Patterns are made to exacting standards of construction, so that they can last for a reasonable length of time, according to the quality grade of the pattern being built, and so that they will repeat ably provide a dimensionally acceptable casting.

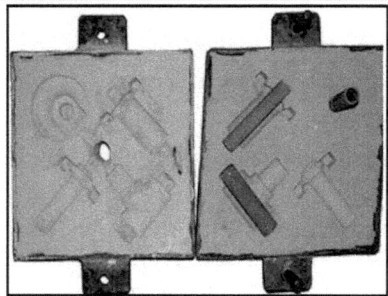

Fig. 1.3 : Casting

Fig. 1.4 shows top and bottom halves of a sand casting mould showing the cavity prepared by patterns. Cores to accommodate holes can be seen in the bottom half of the mould, which is called the drag. The top half of the mould is called the cope.

1.4.1 Pattern Making/Designing

The making of patterns, called pattern making (sometimes styled pattern making or pattern making), is a skilled trade that is related to the trades of tool and die making and mould making, but also often incorporates elements of fine woodworking. Each different item we wish to cast presents unique problems and requirements. In a large foundry there is a close relationship between the pattern maker and the moulder. Each is aware of the capabilities and limitations of his own field. Throughout the industry, pattern making is a field and an art of its own. The pattern maker is neither a moulder nor the moulder a pattern maker. Pattern makers (sometimes styled pattern makers or pattern makers) learn their skills through apprenticeships and trade schools over many years of experience. Although an engineer may help to design the pattern, it is usually a pattern maker who executes the design.

Following are some of the important aspects of pattern making.

(1) Various Allowances Provided on Pattern :

Pattern is having different size as compared to casting because it carries certain allowances due to metallurgical and mechanical reasons. The various allowances are

    (a) Shrinkage or contraction allowance.

    (b) Machining or finish allowance.

    (c) Draft or taper allowance.

    (d) Distortion or camber allowance

    (e) Shake or rapping allowance.

    (f) Mould wall movement allowance.

(a) Shrinkage or Contraction Allowance: As metal solidifies and cools, it shrinks and contracts in size. To compensate for this a pattern is made larger than a finished casting by means of a shrinkage or contraction allowance. Contraction is different for different metals.

(b) Machining or Finish Allowance: For good surface finish, machining of casting is required. For machining, extra metals are needed. This extra metal is called machining or finishes allowance. This allowance is given in addition to shrinkage allowance.

(c) Draft or Taper Allowance: At the time of withdrawing the pattern from the mould, the vertical faces of the pattern are in continual contact with the sand which may damage the mould cavity. This danger is greatly decreased if the vertical surfaces of pattern are tapered inward slightly. The slight taper inward on the vertical surfaces of a pattern is known as the draft.

(d) Distortion or Camber Allowance: If the shape of the casting changes then it is called distortion of the casting. A coasting will distort or warp if,

- It is of irregular shape.
- All its parts do not shrink uniformly.
- It has long flat casting.
- The arms pass unequal thickness.

(e) Shake or Rapping Allowance: When a pattern is rapped (shaped) in the mould before it is withdrawn, the cavity in the mould is slightly increased, so in order to compensate this, pattern is made slightly smaller than the actual. The allowance is called shaking or rapping.

(f) Mould wall Movement Allowance: Movement of mould wall in sand mould takes place because of heat and the static pressure exerted on the walls of the mould which comes in contact with the molten metal.

The shrinkage amount is also dependent on the sand casting process employed, for example clay-bonded sand, chemical bonded sands, or other bonding materials used within the sand. Following table shows typical pattern maker's shrinkage of various metals.

Table 1.1 : Typical pattern maker's shrinkage of various metals

Metal	Percentage	in/ft
Aluminium	1.0 – 1.3	1/8 – 5/32
Brass	1.5	3/16
Magnesium	1.0 – 1.3	1/8 – 5/32
Cast iron	0.8 – 1.0	1/10 – 1/8
Steel	2.5 – 3.0	3/16 – 1/4

(2) Sprues, Gates, Risers, Cores, and Chills :

The pattern maker or foundry engineer decides where the sprues, gating systems, and risers are placed with respect to the pattern. Where a hole is desired in a casting, a core may be used which defines a volume or location in a casting where metal will not flow into. Sometimes chills may be located on a pattern surface, which are then formed into the sand mould. Chills are heat sinks which enable localized rapid cooling. The rapid cooling may be desired to refine the grain structure or determine the freezing sequence of the molten metal which is poured into the mould.

(3) Demand :

Patterns continue to be needed for sand casting of metals. For the production of gray iron, ductile iron and steel castings, sand casting remains the most widely used process. For aluminium castings, sand casting represents about 12% of the total tonnage by weight (surpassed only by die casting at 57%, and semi-permanent and permanent mould at 19%; based on 2006 shipments). The exact process and pattern equipment is always determined by the order quantities and the casting design. Sand casting can produce as little as one part, or as many as a million copies.

- Following are some of the industrial types of patterns.

(A) Production Pattern :

In the case of our disc, say we are only going to make a casting from the pattern now and again one at a time, we dimension as above. The pattern is called a production pattern, one from which the actual castings are produced.

(B) Master Pattern :

Now, suppose we want to make one or more production patterns out of cast aluminium from which we intend to make production aluminium castings. In this case, we need a wood pattern from which to cast our production pattern. If we wanted as our finished or end product a cast aluminium disc, we would have to make our wood pattern with a double aluminium shrink rule or V_2 inch per foot shrinkage. As we are going to take V_4 inch shrinkage in going from our wood pattern to our cast pattern and another V_i inch to our end product, these rulers are called double shrink rulers. If we were going from a wood pattern to an aluminium production pattern to a brass casting as an end product the shrinkage allowance on your wood pattern would have to be 3/16 or 12/16 inch plus finish etc., if any. This type of pattern (the wood) is called a master pattern, a pattern from which the production pattern or patterns are made.

(C) Parting Line :

On our simple disc pattern, we note the upper face of the pattern is designated as the parting line or parting face. By this we mean a line or the plane of a pattern corresponding to the point of separation between the cope and drag portions of a sand mould. The parting may be irregular or a plane, as the mould must be opened, the pattern removed and then closed for pouring without damage to the sand. The parting line must be located where this can be accomplished. The portion of the pattern in the cope must be drafted so the cope can be removed and the same of the drag.

Any vertical portion of the pattern in either the cope or drag portion must be drafted or tapered. The junction or change of draft angle indicates the proper position of the parting line.

(D) Back Draft :
If the patterns were shaped and the mould parted at its upper face the back draft would prevent its removal without damage to the mould. Back Draft is a reverse taper which prevents removal of a pattern from the mould.

(E) Gated Pattern :
The gate is the channel or channels in a sand mould through which the molten metal enters the cavity left by the pattern. This channel can be made in two ways, one by cutting the channel or channels with a gate cutter, or by the pattern having a projection attached to the pattern which will form this gate or gates during the process of ramming up the mould.

(F) Set Gate Pattern :
If a pattern is made for a gate but not attached to a pattern but only placed against it while making the mould, this pattern is called a set gate pattern.

(G) Split Pattern :
This is a pattern that is made in two halves split along the parting line. The two halves are held in register by pins called pattern dowels. The pattern is split to facilitate moulding. The dowels hold the two halves of the pattern together in close accurate register, but at the same time are free enough that the two halves can be separated easily for moulding, like the pins and guides of the flask. The dowels are usually installed off centre.

(H) Medium Pattern :
A pattern that is used only occasionally or for casting a onetime piece is usually constructed as cheaply as possible. If it is a split pattern wood dowels are used for pins and fit into holes drilled into the matching half. This type of pattern is called a "Medium Pattern".

A core is a preformed baked sand or green sand aggregate inserted in a mould to shape the interior part of a casting which cannot be shaped by the pattern. When a pattern requires a core a projection must be made on the pattern, this projection forms an impression in the sand of the mould in which to locate the core and hold it during the casting. These projections are called core prints and are part of the pattern.

Sometimes it is possible to make a pattern in such a way that a core will remain in the sand when the pattern is removed. The pattern for a simple shoring washer is made in this way.

(I) Mounted Pattern :

When a pattern is mounted to a board to facilitate moulding, it is called a mounted pattern. In this case the mount has on each end guides which match up with the flask used to make the mould. The plate is placed between the cope and drag flask, the drag rammed and rolled over. The cope is now rammed and lifted off. The plate with pattern attached lifted off of the drag half, the mould finished and closed.

(J) Match Plate :

The match plate is the same as the mounted pattern with the exception that when you have part of the casting in the cope and part in the drag (split pattern), these parts are attached to the board or plate opposite each other and in the correct location so that when the plate is removed and the mould is closed the cavities in the cope and drag match up correctly. The moulding procedure is the same as a one sided mounted plate.

In most cases all the necessary gating runners, etc., are built right on the plate. The match plate might have only one pattern or a large quantity of small patterns.

(K) Cope and Drag Mounts :

In this case you have two separate pattern mounts, one fitted with female guides (for the drag) and one fitted with pins (for the cope). These must match up with the flask used.

The cope half of the pattern is attached to the cope mount and the drag pattern is attached to the drag mount. The cope and drag moulds are produced separately and put together for pouring. The usual practice is for one moulders to make copes and another to make the drags. Cope and drag mounts are quite common when making large and very large castings where a match plate would be out of the question due to its bulk and weight. Cope and drag mounts are sometimes called tubs.

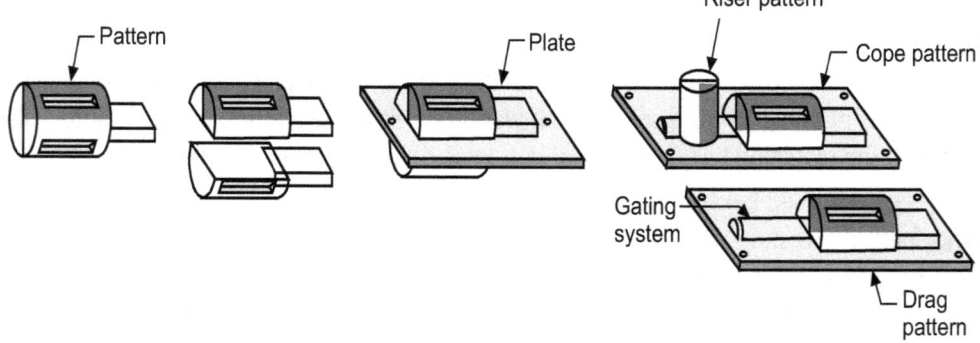

Fig. 1.5 : Types of patterns used in sand casting : (a) solid pattern, (b) split pattern, (c) match-pattern and (d) cope and drag pattern

(L) Follow Board :

A board with a cavity or socket in it which conforms to the form of the pattern and defines the parting surface of the drag. It can be made of wood, plaster or metal. When made of sand, it is called a dry sand match.

The pattern rests in the follow board while making up the drag half of the mould and in doing so, establishes the correct sand parting. The follow board is removed leaving the pattern rammed in the drag up to the parting. The cope then takes the place of the follow board and is rammed in the usual manner.

A simple follow board might consist of a moulding board with a hole in it to allow the pattern to rest firmly on the board while the drag rammed.

Card of Patterns :

When several different loose gated patterns are assembled as a unit to be all moulded in the same flask, this arrangement is called a card of patterns.

(M) Sweep Pattern :

A sweep pattern consists of a board having a profile of the desired mould, which when revolved around a suitable spindle or guide produces that mould. Two are usually required, one to sweep the cope profile and the other the drag profile.

(N) Skeleton Pattern :

This is a frame work of wooden bars which represent the interior and exterior form and the metal thickness of the required casting. This type of pattern is only used for huge castings.

(O) Expendable Pattern :

As in Lost Wax casting the pattern is lost. Expendable patterns for sand casting are Styrofoam which is shaped to the desired form with attached Styrofoam gates, runners and risers. The Styrofoam pattern is moulded with dry clay-free sharp silica sand in a box or steel frame. The pattern is vaporized by the metal poured into the mould, leaving the casting.

(L) Wood Patterns :

Wood patterns used for sand casting are given several coats of Orange Shellac to which a pinch of oxalic acid has been added. This gives them a good waterproof smooth hard surface.

The majority of wood patterns are made of white pine (sugar pine) as it is easily worked and when shellacked properly will not warp under ordinary foundry use. The approximate weight of a casting can be determined by weighing the wood pattern and multiplying by the appropriate factor indicated. Aluminium 8, cast iron 16.7, copper 19.8, brass 19.0, steel 17.0

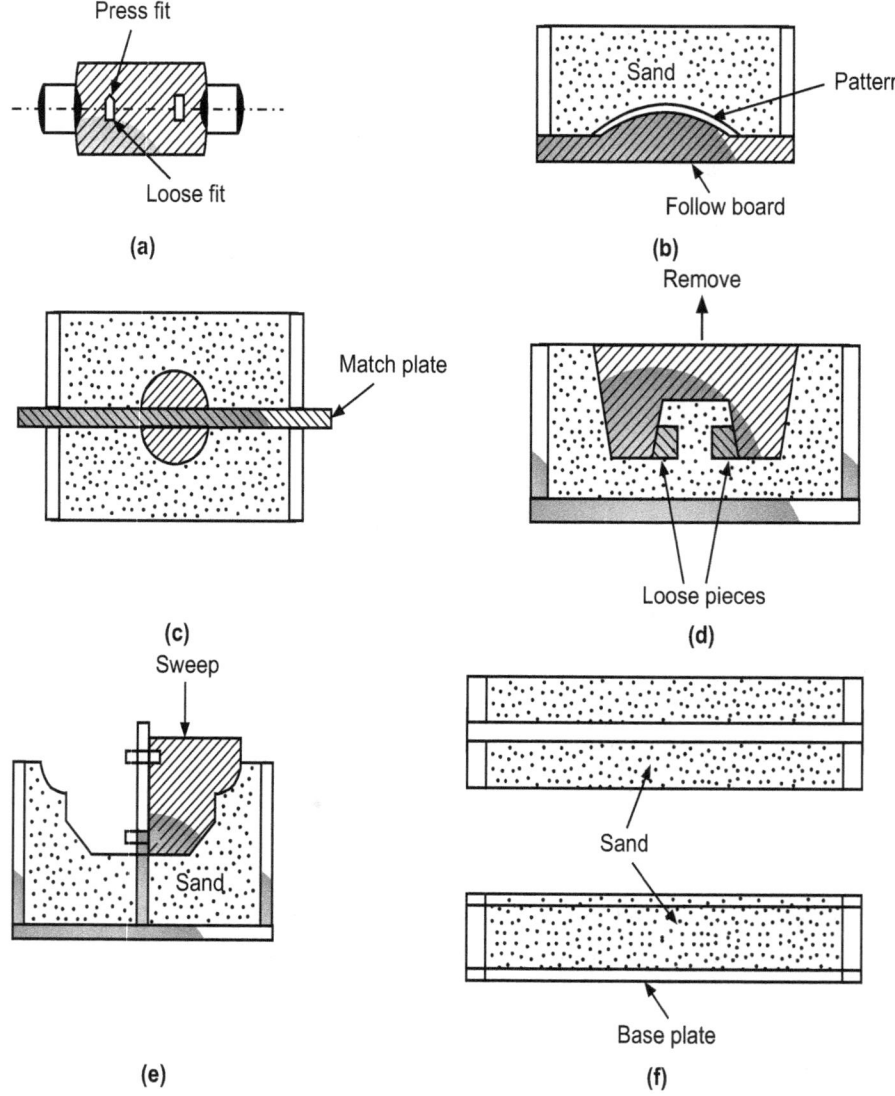

Fig. 1.6 Types of patterns
(a) Split pattern, (b) Follow-board, (c) Match Plate, (d) Loose-piece, (e) Sweep (f) Skeleton pattern

1.4.2 Pattern Materials

The required accuracy, strength and life of a pattern set depend on the pattern material. In the piece and short run production, wood patterns find the most extensive application; in large scale and mass production metal patterns are preferable since they are most durable then wood counterparts, through costlier; in batch production, use is often made of pattern manufactured from plastic, for example, epoxy resin, and also from gypsum and cement.

The following materials used for making pattern:

1. Wood
2. Metal e g. Brass, Cast Iron, Aluminium alloy, White Metal etc
3. Plaster
4. Plastic Compound
5. Wax

- **Wood :**

Wood is the most common material for pattern, the main reasons being ease of availability, ease of shaping, light in weight, low cost, ease to machine and cut into complicated shape, surface preparation is easy as compare to metal. In other end, wood is readily affected by moisture, wears out quickly as a result of sand abrasion, storing problem, strength is low this common drawbacks in wood owing to which sometimes other materials have to be used for pattern making.

- **Metallic Pattern :**

Commonly a metal pattern is itself cast from a wooden pattern called master pattern. When metal patterns are to be cast from master patterns, double shrinkage must be allowed. These are advantageously used when a large number of castings area desired from a pattern or when conditions for wooden pattern are too severe. Metallic pattern do not change their shape when subjected to moist conditions. They are free from warping in storage. They are very much suited to machine moulding because of their accuracy, durability and strength. The main draw backs of metallic pattern are expensive than wood hence not generally suited for small production, less easy to shape and work, tendency to get rusted and excessive weight. The metals uses for making patterns are

Cast Iron	Low cost, It is strong gives a good smooth mould surface with sharp edges, is resistant to the abrasive action of the sand and can easily cast to obtain desired shape.
Brass	It is strong, does not rust, takes a better surface finish than cast iron, is able to withstand the wear of the moulding sand and is easy to join by soldering
Aluminium	It is probably the best all round metal because it melts at a relatively low temperature, it is soft and easy to work, light in weight, and resistant to corrosion, rust and abrasive action of sand. Besides, it also gives sufficient strength and good surface finish.
White Metal	The main characteristic of white metal which is an alloy of antimony, copper and lead are the low melting temperature, ease of pouring, little appreciable shrinkage and immunity from the effects of chill.

- **Plaster Pattern :**

Plaster pattern and core boxes are made of gypsum cement. Gypsum cement has a high compressive strength (up to 30 MPa), and controlled expansion. By means of careful design and use of reinforcement, plaster patterns may be made to have strength up to 115MPa. It can be readily worked with wood working tools. When the plaster is mixed with water, it forms a plastic mass capable of being cast into a mould made earlier by a master pattern or may be swept into desired shape or form by sweep and stickle method. Unlike the metals, gypsum cement expands on solidification and so, by choosing cement of proper expansion coefficient, the shrinkage of casting can be completely offset.

- **Plastic Pattern :**

Plastic (Phenolic thermosetting resins) are now finding their place as a modern pattern material because they do not absorb moisture, are strong and dimensionally stable, resistance to wear, have a very smooth and glossy surface and are light in weight. Due to its glossy surface it can be withdrawn from the mould very easily without damaging mould. Moreover, the plastic material has a very low solid shrinkage. It is manufactured from a combination of carbolic acid and formaldehyde. For preparing plastic pattern, dies or moulds are first prepared in two halves in metal or plaster of Paris. The thermosetting resin is them poured in the required amount into the moulds.

- **Wax Patterns**

These are used in investment casting process. Their use helps in imparting a high degree of surface finish and dimensional accuracy to casting. Wax pattern is prepared by pouring heated wax into the split moulds or a pair of dies while the latter are kept water cooled. The dies after having been cooled down are parted off. Now the wax pattern is taken out and used for moulding. Wax pattern need not be drawn out solid from the mould. After the mould is ready, the wax is poured out by heating the mould and keeping it upside down.

1.4.3 Color Coding

Patterns have also some identifiers such as colours on them, each of which has different meaning that represent different treatments and requirements for the patterns. The colour-coding for patterns in sand casting is as follows

- Red indicates that the surface of the material should be left as it is after casting.
- Black indicates that the surface needs core and shows the position of the sand core.
- Yellow indicates that the surface needs machining.
- Red strips on yellow base indicates that the seats for loose pieces
- Black strips on yellow base indicates stop offs
- Clear or no colour indicates that the parting surface.

1.4.4 Storing of patterns

Patterns are made from various materials like wood metal plastic and wax. Wood patterns changes its shape when the moisture dries out of it, and when it picks up moisture from the damp moulding sand. Due to this problem the wood patterns are sprayed with a thin metallic coating of bismuth, zinc or aluminium of about 0.25 mm thickness. If wood patterns are not stored properly, it may warp badly. For metallic plastic and wax pattern, such type of problem never occurs. Pattern sorting is similar to storing of raw material on shop floor, but precaution should be taken at the time of handling of patterns and separate dry space is required.

QUESTIONS

1. What are the pattern materials? State the application of sweep and Skelton pattern.
2. Define casting. What are the advantages and limitation of casting?
3. Define pattern. What is split pattern?
4. What are the factors you will consider before selecting material for pattern?
5. Explain in detail step involved in casting.
6. What are the advantages and application of casting?
7. Explain different types of pattern any four.
8. What are the color code used for patterns and core boxes
9. What are the common allowances provided on pattern?
10. What are the different types of foundries?
11. What is storing of pattern?

Unit - II
MOULDING AND CASTING PROCESSES

2.1 INTORUDCTION (MOULDING)

The process of forming moulds is called moulding. It is one of the important operations in casting. The degree of mechanization of moulding process, there are hand, machine and automated type of moulding methods available.

After preparing moulds at the mould section and making cores at core room of the foundry, the next important operation is the assembly of moulds for further operations like pouring of molten metal, etc.

Automatic moulding is suitable to high volume production of casting, and machine moulding is best suitable to batch and large lot production and rarely to job production. The fig 2.1 shows the classification of moulding process

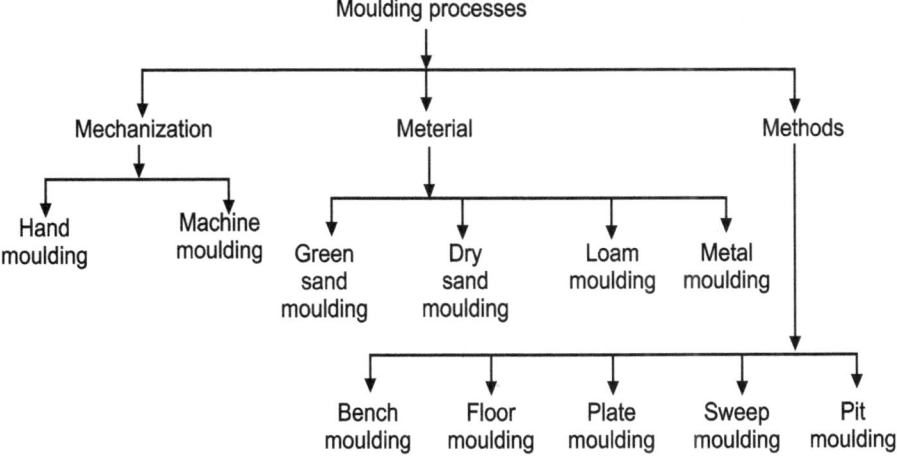

Fig. 2.1 : Classification of moulding processes

2.1.1 Green Sand Moulding

In this type of moulding the mould is in moist state while pouring the metal into it. Here the word green means wet or moist. Green sand moulding is widely used for casting practically all ferrous and non ferrous alloys. It is suitable for small, medium and often large casting.

Advantages	Disadvantages
It is a cheap and least expensive method.	The surface finish of the casting obtained from green sand mould is rough as compare to other methods
Large output can be obtained from a given floor space	The green sand mould lacks permeability and strength, which causes certain defects like blow holes, etc
Green sand moulds are quite strong for a small depths, as the gases escape from them	The green sand moulds being not so strong as other moulds are liable to damaged during handing or pouring
This allows greater freedom in contraction when the castings solidify and cool.	The green sand moulds cannot be stored for long time
Green sand moulds do not require any backing operation or equipment but dry sand cores are to be used for the work	
Money and time involved in drying the moulds are also saved in this moulding process.	

Principal methods of green sand moulding are:

Open-Sand Methods :

It is simplest form of green sand moulding used for simple casting with flat tops e.g. floor plates, grills, moulding boxes, weight etc. In which if the upper surface is rough, it does not matter. The entire mould is made in the foundry floor (moulding box is not necessary) upper surface of mould is opened to air. The pattern is pressed in the sand; pouring basin is made at one end of the mould. The overflow channel prepared at the side of cavity at the exact height from the bottom face for giving desired thickness.

Bedded in Method :

In this method, the pattern is pressed into bed on the foundry floor. Sand should be rammed closed to the pattern, the joint and spreading the parting sand, a cope is placed properly over the pattern. The runners and risers are cut and the cope box is removed. The pattern is withdrawn, the surfaces of drag and cope replaced in its correct position for preparing desire mould.

Turn-Over Method :

One pattern- half is placed with its flat side on a moulding board, a dragged is fitted over the cope. The other patterns half and a cope box is placed in position after assembly of cope and drag with proper ramming, the cope is lifted off and the two pattern halves shaken and withdrawn. Now the cope is replaced on the drag for assembly the mould.

2.1.2 Dry Sand Moulding

The mould is dried before pouring, until the moisture is driven off. The strength erosion resistance and better surface condition achieved with drying of mode. The dry sand mould is strong and easy to handle with minor damaged, can be store for longer time. It resists shrinkage and they are more rigid. The dry sand mould is very accurate rate and defect less and better surface as compared to green sand mould. The disadvantages of dry sand mould are more expensive moulding material, high labour cost, maximum operation space and equipments. The applications are used often for large work like engine cylinders and engine blocks etc. This required more smootheness soundness and accuracy.

2.1.2.1 Skin Dried Moulding

Skin dried moulding is process, when the moisture is dried from the surface layer of the sand to a depth of about 25mm by heater. In this process the advantage of both dry and green sand moulding are achieved. The time require for drying is less than in case of dry sand moulding, the method is less expensive.

2.1.3 Loam Moulding

The loam is the mixture of sand and clay mixed with water to form a thin plastic mixture to the consistency of mud. The loam is applied as plaster to the rough structure of mould. The loam sand mould is prepared with porous brick cemented together with loam mixture. It requires adequate ventilation so as to open out poured in the otherwise compact, closely knit mass, by artificial means. A typical loam sand mixture contain silica sand 22, clay 5, cope 10, moisture 18-20 others 40(by volume). Loam moulding is used for large size castings e.g. large cylinders, round bottom kettles, chemical pan large gears etc.

2.1.4 Metal Moulds

When the impression or the mould is made of metal, it is known as metal mould. Metal moulds are used for the production of large number of identical casting. Die casting, permanent casting and centrifugal casting processes used metal mould.

2.1.5 Bench Moulding

Bench moulding applies to small size casting which are light in weight and easy to handle. The moulds are prepared in moulding boxes place at desire height on a bench. Mould is prepared by worker while standing near the bench. The below Fig. 2.2 shows various methods of bench moulding are two box moulding, three box moulding, plate moulding, stacked moulding, moulding with flask cheek and odd side moulding.

In a two box moulding uses of a moulding box or flask which is in two parts (fig 2.2 (a)). The upper part and the lower part are called cope and drag respectively. The two parts are fitted with a suitable clamping and locating device. Three box moulding used for flanged type of pattern which is difficult to fit in two box moulding (Fig. 2.2 (b)).

Additional middle box called cheek, all three boxes clamped with one another during pouring. The stacked moulding were used for large number of small casting is required. The systematic arrangement of cope and drag gives one flat surface support to one another by stacking (Fig. 2.2 (c)).

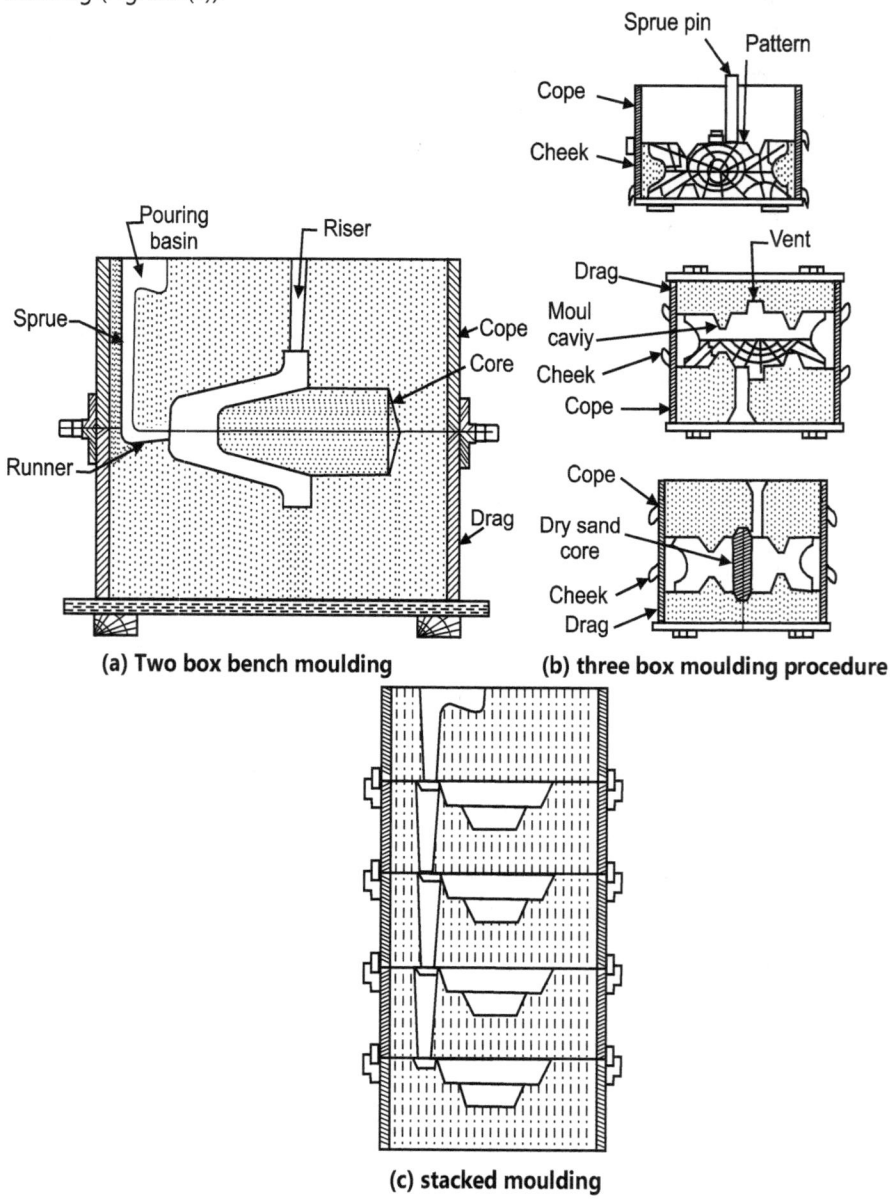

(a) Two box bench moulding

(b) three box moulding procedure

(c) stacked moulding

Fig. 2.2 : Various type of bench moulding

2.1.6 Floor Moulding

It is used for very heavy casting or those having certain depth or area moulded in the sand of the foundry floor in such as the same way as green sand moulding. The floor itself acts as the drag and this is covered with a cope.

2.1.7 Plate Moulding

It is divided into the two halves and the patterns which are usually made of the metal are fastened to each side of a board or plate. One side is moulded in the drag, turned over and cope side is moulded. Then, the two boxes are separated and the board with patterns is removed. The moulded impressions match up on reassembling the two boxes and the mould is ready to be poured.

2.1.8 Pit Moulding

In this process the moulds of large jobs are generally prepared in a pit dug in the foundry floor. This facilitates in lifting the pattern and casting the mould easily. The sand under the pattern is rammed by bedding in because a pit which functions as a drag cannot be rolled over. A coke bed is laid on the bottom of the pit. It is covered with straw and then a layer of sand is rammed and levelled. To provide and outlet for the escape of gases generated, the coke bed is connected with atmosphere by vertical vent pipes in corners of the pit. The inside surfaces of the pit are lined with bricks. To complete the mould, generally one box is required for cutting runners, pouring basin, feeders in it.

2.1.9 Sweep Moulding

It is used for those castings whose shape is that of surface of revolution. Sweep is a plate whose outer profile is made as that of the casting. It is fastened to a holder, which is placed firmly at a centre in the foundry floor. The sand is filled and rammed until the shape and size of the casting is near about formed by the excavation. Now, the sweep is rotated which forms the required moulding. After the sweeping the spindle is removed and the mould is patched at the centre. Finally the gate is cut and the mould is ready for pouring.

2.2 EQUIPMENT FOR MOULDING

Moulding requires many tool and equipment for the preparation of desired casing. Small or medium sized casting is made in flask a box shaped container without top and bottom which confines the sand moulds. Some flask made in three parts, the centre one is called check and upper part called as cope and lower part is called drag. Steel or cast iron flask used because of their rigidity and permanence in production work. A snap flask is a small flask with a hinge on one corner and snap catch on the other. With its use moulds can be made repeatedly using the same flask. A moulding board and a bottom board complete the flask. The moulding board is a smooth board on which the flask and pattern are placed when the moulding started. When the mould is turned over, the function of this board is over. The mould is placed on a similar board called bottom board, which acts as a support for the mould until metal is poured in the mould. Before any metal is poured into a mould, it is necessary that the flask be clamped in some way to prevent the buoyant effect of the molten metal from lifting up the cope. Small moulds are usually held down by flat cast iron weights, placed on the top of the moulds. Larger flasks are usually held together by clams, placed on the side or end either u shaped clamps, held tight by driving wooden wedges under the end, or clamps that can be quickly adjusted to fit the height of the flask. A gagger is small L-shaped metallic accessory used in floor moulds to help support hanging bodies of sand in core. It is used only in large moulds having cross bars. The gagger is first coated with a clay wash and then placed next to one of the cross bars. The lower end should be close to the pattern, and the upper end should extend to the top of mould. The various other tools used are - Showel is used for mixing and tempering moulding sand and for moving the sand from pile to flask.

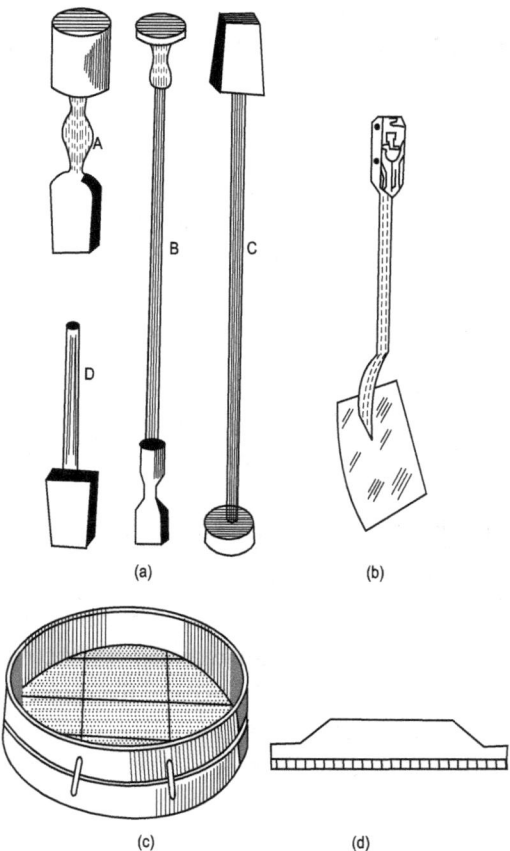

Fig. 2.3 (a) Rammers (b) Riddle (c) Shwel (d) Strike off bar

Riddle or screen is used to remove bits of metal and foreign particles from the moulding sand. The size of the opening in the mesh indicates the size of the riddle. Moulding board and bottom board is a smooth wooden board used for placing flask and pattern while starting moulding. After turning over the mould from the moulding board, the mould is place on a similar board called bottom board, which acts as a support for the mould.

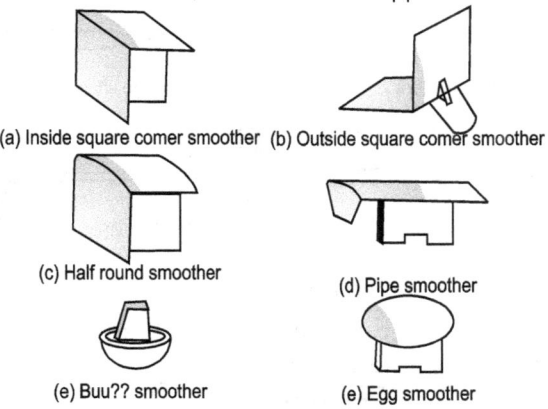

(a) Inside square corner smoother (b) Outside square corner smoother
(c) Half round smoother (d) Pipe smoother
(e) Buu?? smoother (e) Egg smoother

Fig. 2.4 : Types of smoother

Rammers are used to pack the sand evenly in the mould and for ramming into corners. The hand rammer is made of wood and resembles a handless mallet with one end flat and the other a blunt wedge. Trowels are used to shape and smoothen the surface of the mould and for doing minor repairs. These are made of steel and are relatively long and narrow. The end of trowel may be pointed, rounded or blunt.

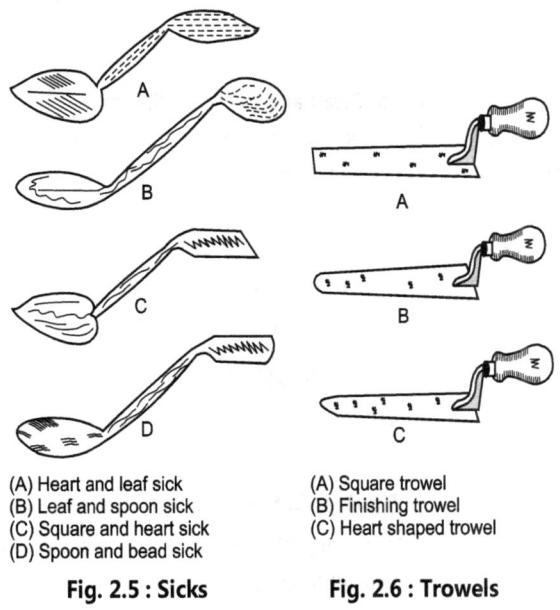

(A) Heart and leaf sick
(B) Leaf and spoon sick
(C) Square and heart sick
(D) Spoon and bead sick

Fig. 2.5 : Sicks

(A) Square trowel
(B) Finishing trowel
(C) Heart shaped trowel

Fig. 2.6 : Trowels

Slicks are spoon shaped trowels used for repairing or slicking (smoothing) a mould surface. They may be leaf shaped but are generally pointed. Lifters are long, narrow tools with hooked ends used for finishing work in tight places, doing repair work, or removing loose sand which has fallen to the bottom of the mould.

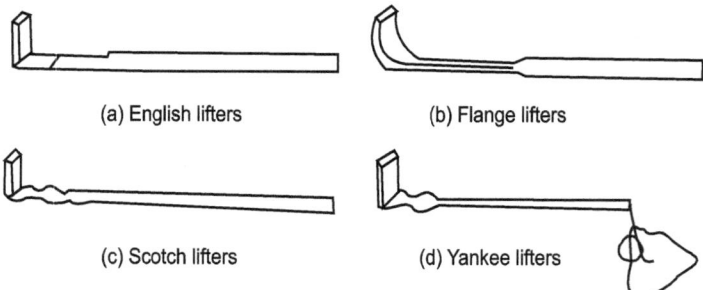

(a) English lifters (b) Flange lifters
(c) Scotch lifters (d) Yankee lifters

Fig. 2.7 : Lifters

Draw spikes are used to remove the pattern from the mould and also for rapping the pattern gently to loosen it from the sand to assure a clean draw.

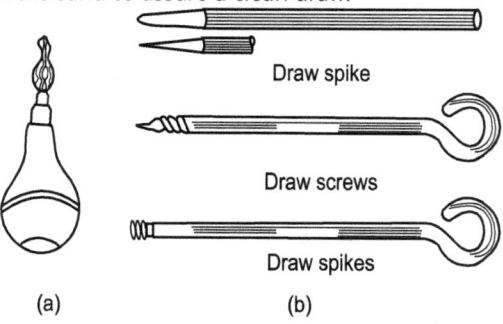

Draw spike

Draw screws

Draw spikes

(a) (b)

Fig. 2.8 : (a) Swab and (b) Draw Spikes

Swab is made of flax or hemp and is used for applying water to the mould around the edge of the pattern. This presents the sand edges from crumbling when the pattern is removed from the mould. Raw hide mallet is used to loosen the pattern in the mould so that it can be withdrawn without damage to the mould. A rawhide mallet will not mar or deface the pattern as a metal mallet would. Gate cutter is a piece of sheet metal used cut the opening that connects the sprue with the mould cavity. This opening is called gate.

Fig. 2.9 : Gate Cutter

Clamps are used to hold the cope and drag of the completed mould together so that the cope may not float or rise when metal is poured into the mould.

2.3 SAND USED IN CASTING

There are various types of sand used in casting. These different types of casting sand have their own advantages and disadvantages. The type of metal required to be cast influences, which additives and what gradation of sand is used. Some of the most common types of casting sand used in hobby foundries are -

1. Green Sand
2. Natural
3. Synthetic
4. Oil Tempered Sand
5. Core Sand
6. Sodium Silicate
7. Baked Binder

2.3.1 Sands

Most sand casting operations use silica sand (SiO_2). Sand is the product of the disintegration of rocks over extremely long periods of time. It is inexpensive and is suitable as mould material because of its resistance to high temperatures. There are two general types of sand : naturally bonded (bank sands) and synthetic (lake sands). Because its composition can be controlled more accurately, synthetic sand is preferred by most foundries. Several factors are important in the selection of sand for moulds. Sand having fine, round grains can be closely packed and forms a smooth mould surface. Good permeability of moulds and cores allows gases and steam evolved during casting to escape easily. The mould should have good collapsibility (the casting shrinks while cooling) to avoid defects in the casting, such as hot tearing and cracking.

Types of Moulding Sand :

1. **Natural Sand :** Contains silica, 5 to 20% of clay as binding material. About 8 to 10% of water is mixed before the sand is used for moulding. It is less refractory than synthetic sand.
2. **Synthetic Sand :** Silica and binders and moisture are the constituents of this sand. This sand is prepared by adding ingradients. This sand has better moulding properties like permeability and refractoriness and suitable for casting of ferrous and non-ferrous metals.
3. **Loam Sand :** Fine sand, refractories, clay, graphite and fibres. Clay content is about 50% or more.
4. **Dry Sand :** When moisture is evaporated from natural sand it is called dry sand.

5. **Facing Sand :** This is freshly prepared fine sand rammed around the pattern and thus is available on face of mould cavity.
6. **Parting Sand :** To avoid sticking of 2 halves of mould flasks and sticking of pattern to mould, this sand is sprinkled in between areas. Dry silica sand and burnt sand, wood floor are used for this purpose.
7. **Backing Sand :** After casting is taken out by destroying mould, the used sand is riddled to remove foreign particles. This sand can be used to prepare moulding sand for next moulds. This is poured at the back of facing sand where it is rammed. This saves cost of replacing entire sand for preparation of new mould.
8. **Core Sand :** Sand has high silica content and is used to make cores.

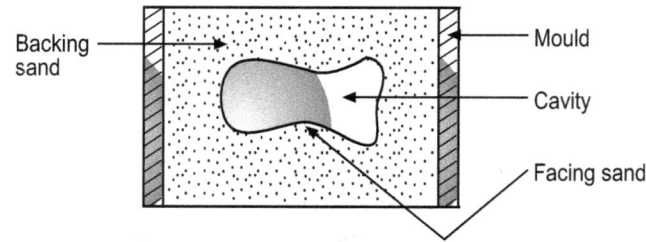

Fig. 2.10 : Moulding sand

Binders in sand : (Additives)

To give strength and cohesiveness in order to retain its shape after ramming, some binders are necessary in sand.

- **Organic Binders :** Dextrin, molasses, linseed oil, cereals, resins like phenol formaldehyde. Organic binders are used in core making.

- **Inorganic Binders :** Clay (Bentonite, kaolonite, fire clay etc.) sodium silicate and porland cement.

Additives :

Different properties are obtained by adding various additives in sand. They are as follows.

- **Coal Dust :** Reacts with oxygen in mould cavity and provides reducing atmosphere and prevents oxidation of metal. It is added in facing sand. It reduces strength and cohesiveness of sand. Sea coal restricts mould wall movement and improves surface finish.

- **Cereals or Cornflower :** Addition of this improves strength and toughness and collapsibility of sand.

- **Wood Flour :** Gives thermal stability and collapsibility to sand.

- **Dextrin and Mollases :** Increase dry strength of sand.

2.3.2 Sand Conditioning (Characteristic Requirements)

The sand used to make moulds must be carefully prepared if it is to provide satisfactory and uniform results. Ordinary silica (SiO_2), zircon, or olivine (forsterite and fayalite) sands are compounded with additives to meet four requirements.

   (1) Refractoriness : The ability to withstand high temperatures.

   (2) Cohesiveness : (Also referred to as bond) : The ability to retain a given shape when packed into a mould.

   (3) Permeability : The ability to permit gases to escape through it.

   (4) Collapsibility : The ability to permit the metal to shrink after it solidifies and ultimately to free the casting by disintegration of the surrounding mould.

Refractoriness is provided by the basic nature of the sand. Cohesiveness, bond or strength is obtained by coating the sand grains with clays, such as bentonite, kaolinite, or illite, that become cohesive when moistened. Collapsibility is sometimes obtained by adding cereals or other organic material, such as cellulose, that burn out when they come in contact with the hot metal. The combustion reduces both the volume and strength of the restraining sand. Permeability is a function of the size of the sand particles, the amount and type of clay or bonding agent, the moisture content, and the compacting pressure.

Good moulding sand always represents a compromise between conflicting factors. The size of the sand particles, the amount of bonding agent (such as clay), the moisture content, and the organic matter are all selected to obtain an acceptable compromise of the four requirements. The composition must be carefully controlled to assure satisfactory and consistent results. (A typical green-sand mixture contains about 88% silica sand, 9% clay, and 3% water). Since moulding material is often reclaimed and recycled, the temperature of the mould during pouring and solidification is also important. If organic materials have been incorporated into the mix to provide collapsibility, a portion will burn during the pour. Some of the mould material may have to be discarded and replaced with new.

It is also important for each grain of the sand to be coated uniformly with the additive agents. This is achieved by putting the ingredients through a muller, a device that kneads, rolls, and stirs the sand. After mixing, the sand is often discharged through a aerator, which fluffs it, so that it does not pack too and hard during handling.

2.3.3 Types of Sand Moulds

Sand moulds are characterized by the types of sand that comprise them and by the methods used to produce them. There are three basic types of sand moulds : green-sand, cold-box, and no-bake moulds. The most common mould material is green moulding sand. The term green refers to that fact that the sand in the mould is moist or damp while the metal is being poured into it. Green moulding sand is a mixture of sand, clay and water. Green-sand moulding is the least expensive method of making moulds. In the skin-dried method, the mould surfaces are dried, either by storing the mould in air or drying it with torches. Skin-dried moulds are generally used for large castings because of their higher strength. Sand moulds are also oven dried (baked) prior to receiving the molten metal. They are stronger than green-sand moulds and impart better dimensional accuracy and surface finish to the casting. However, distortion of the lower collapsibility of the mould, and the production rate is slower because of the drying time required.

In the cold-box mould process, various organic and inorganic binders are blended into the sand to bond the grains chemically for greater strength. These moulds are dimensionally more accurate than green-sand moulds but are more expensive.

In the no-bake mould process, a synthetic liquid resin is mixed with the sand, and the mixture hardens at room temperature. Because bonding of the mould in this and the cold-box process takes place without heat, they are called cold-setting processes.

2.3.4 Sand Testing

Foundry worker has to maintain consistent sand quality to produce high quality castings. Sand specimens must be tested before sand mixture is used for making mould.

Testing of Moulding Sand :

Following tests are performed on moulding sand to check and control properties of sand before it is used for moulding.

(1) Grain Fineness Test :

It is important to have proper grain size. Large castings require larger grains to have porosity for release of gases. The surface finish resulting is coarse. If small castings having better surface finish are required, use of fine sand grains is essential. For testing grain size, AFS number (American Foundrymen's Society) is found out. This is determined by shaking a known amount of clean, dry sand downwards through a set of 11 standard sieves of decreasing mesh size. After shaking for 15 minutes, the amount remaining on each sieve is weighed and the weights are converted into AFS grain number. AFS no. of 200 to 300 indicates high quality first grade sand, i.e. finest sand.

(2) Moisture Content :

If moisture is more, strength of mould will be poor and also more gases will be formed. To check the moisture content a special device that measures the electrical conductivity of small sample of sand that it is compressed between two prongs, is used.

In another simple method weight lost from 50 gram sample after it is heated to 110°C for sufficient time to remove water, is measured.

In direct reading moisture teller, the pressure of acetylene gas is used to know moisture content. In an air tight container sample of sand and calcium carbide are thoroughly mixed.

Calcium carbide reacts with moisture (water) and forms acetylene gas. The pressure of this gas gives direct reading of moisture content.

$CaC_2 + 2 H_2O \rightarrow Ca(OH)_2 + C_2H_2$

(3) Clay Content :

Amount of clay affects binding strength as well as porosity. Clay content is determined by washing a 50 gram sample of sand in water that contains sodium hydroxide to make it alkaline. Many cycles of repeated agitation and washing the sand and water are required to fully remove clay. The remaining sand is dried and weighed to determine amount of clay in original sample. The difference in weights gives the clay content.

(4) Permeability :

This is a measure of how easily gases can pass through the narrow voids between sand grains. If gases are not escaped after hot metal is poured in mould, they remain entrapped in solidified casting and defective castings are produced.

Permeability is tested by means of an apparatus called 'a permeability meter' which carries an arrangement to allow to exit of controlled amount of air through sand sample at a definite pressure difference. The corresponding time taken by air in passing through the same is recorded separately. The permeability number is given by

$$P = \frac{Vh}{p \cdot a \cdot t}$$

where,
- P = permeability number
- V = volume in c.c. of air passing through specimen
- h = height of specimen in cm
- p = air pressure in cm
- a = cross sectional area of specimen in cm^2
- t = time in minutes taken by air to pass

(5) Refractoriness Test :

Sand sample is heated from $1000^\circ C$ and above in steps of say $50^\circ C$ and kept for 3 minutes at each step. Thus temperature when sand fuses is found out.

(6) Compressive Strength of Sand :

This is found out by removing rammed specimen from tube and placing it in a mechanical testing device. A compressive load is applied until specimen breaks. (say about 0.07 to 0.2 MPa).

2.4 CORE AND CORE MAKING

2.4.1 Core

When a casting is to have a cavity or recess in it such as a hole some form of core must be introduced into the mould. Core can be defined as a body of sand, generally prepared separately in a core box, which is used to form a cavity of desired shape and size in a casting.

2.4.2 Core Sand

Core sand is a sand mixture suitable for cores. Core-sand mixture consists of sand grains, binders for green and cured strength, and other additives used for special purposes.

The core sand mixture commonly used comprise sand, 1% core oil, 1% cereal, and 2.5 to 6% water. Core sand is somewhat different from regular moulding sand in that it has a very low clay content and grain size is somewhat larger. Large grain sand assures permeability.

2.4.3 Core Binders

Core sand is mixed with a binder which holds the form of the core while it is being baked in the core oven, and as it is used in the mould. There are four common core binders in core making viz. water soluble binders, oil binders, pitch and resin binders. Linseed oil or fish oil is often used for core oils. Foundry molasses, a by-product of the manufacture of industrial alcohol, is also a good core binder. Fire clay, bentonite, silica flour, iron oxide etc. are some of the inorganic binders. Portland cement, rubber cement, sodium silicate are also used as core binders.

Water :

In a core sand mixture, water content may vary from 2.5 to 7%. Binders and additives work only in presence of moisture. Correct quantity of moisture develops good green strength, edge hardness and good tensile strength.

Special Additives :

Seal coal, pitch, graphite, coke, silica flour, wood flour, celluses, dextrin are also added in core sand as special additives.

2.4.4 Core Characteristics

A core must have,

    (a) Porosity.

    (b) Sufficient strength to support itself.

    (c) Good refractoriness to resist the action of heat until the hot metal has stabilized.

    (d) Smooth surface to ensure a smooth casting.

2.4.5 Types of Cores

There are three main classifications of cores which are commonly used in casting such as, Green sand core, Dry sand core, Chilled core. According to shape and position of the core, the cores are classified as, Horizontal core, vertical core, cover core, kiss core, ram up core and drop core. The detail of various types of cores are as follows :

(1) Horizontal Core :

Core is held in the mould horizontally. The core is often used in the mould prepared with split pattern (Fig. 2.11)

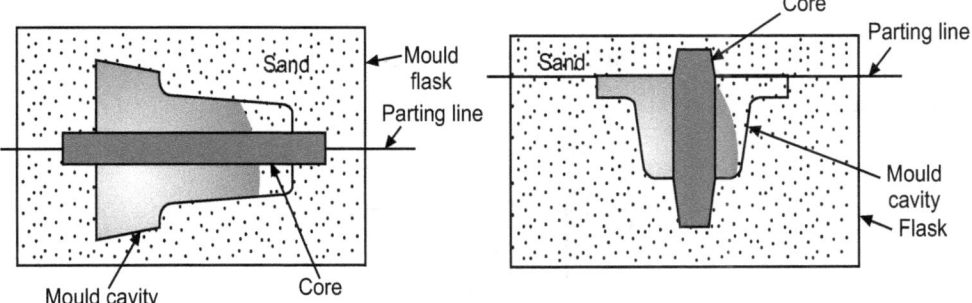

Fig. 2.11 : Horizontal Core   Fig. 2.12 : Vertical Core

(2) Vertical Core :

The core is shown in Fig. 2.12. The upper end of the core requires considerable taper so as not to tear the sand in the cope when the flask is assembled.

(3) Hanging or Cover Core :

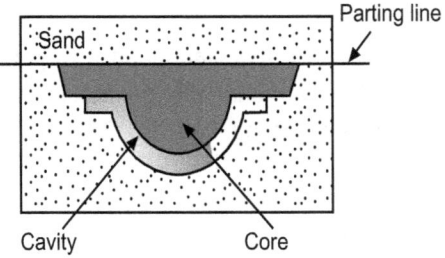

Fig. 2.13 : A Hanging or Cover Core

When a core hangs vertically from the cope without any support on the drag, it is called hanging core. Such core is held in position by means of wires. Refer Fig. 2.13.

(4) Balanced Core :

Core of this type is supported at only one end, the embedded portion has sufficient length. It is used when a blind hole along horizontal axis is required. Refer Fig. 2.14.

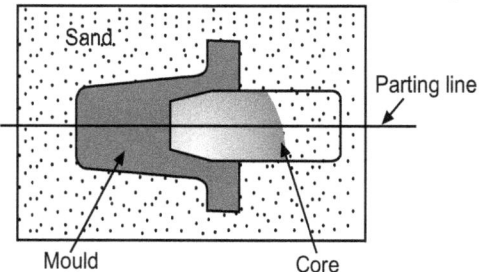

Fig. 2.14 : A Balanced Core

(5) Kiss Core :

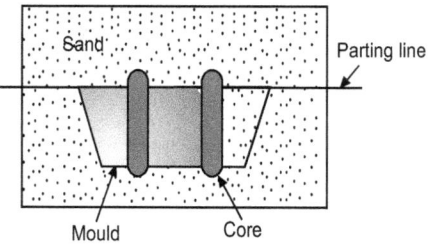

Fig. 2.15 : A Kiss Core

Sometimes a pattern is used which carries no core prints, the core is held between cope and drag simply due to the pressure put by the former. Such core is known as kiss core. (Fig. 2.15).

(6) Ram Up Core :

A ram up core is one which is placed in the sand along with pattern before ramming the mould. This core cannot be placed in the mould after the mould has been rammed. It is used to make internal and external details of casting. Refer Fig. 2.16.

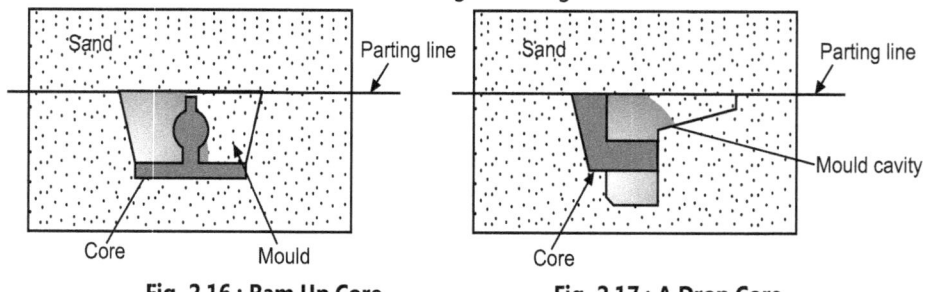

Fig. 2.16 : Ram Up Core   Fig. 2.17 : A Drop Core

(7) Drop Core :

A drop core is required when a hole is not in line with the parting surface and must be formed at a lower level. (Fig. 2.17).

2.4.6 Core Making

Core making basically consists of following steps.

(1) Core sand preparation.

(2) Core making.

(3) Core baking.

(4) Core dressing or finishing.

After preparing sand with the help of roller mills and core sand mixer, core is produced on core making machine or in core boxes.

Core Baking :

After the cores are prepared they are baked in baking furnace where the moisture is removed from the core. The core oven may be batch type oven or continuous type oven. The prepared cores are kept in portable racks and sent into the oven.

Core Dressing :

After baking, cores are given certain finishing operations before they are finally set in the mould. The fins and other sand projections are removed from the sand surface of the cores by rubbing or filing to bring them to correct dimensions and to provide a good surface finish. The cores are also coated with refractory or protective materials to improve their refractoriness. The surfaces may be coated with heat resistant paint.

2.4.7 Core Boxes

For moulding cores a core box may be made into halves held together by dowel pins. A core is moulded by filling sand in the cavity formed by joining the two halves and when it is ready the two halves of the core box are separated so that the core may be taken out easily.

The common types of core boxes are :

(1) Half Core-Box (Fig. 2.18) :

A core is prepared in two halves which are later on cemented together to form the complete core.

(2) Dump Core-Box (Fig. 2.19) :

It is used to prepare complete core in it. Generally rectangular cores are prepared in these boxes. The box is made with open one side and the sand is rammed up level with the edges of this opening.

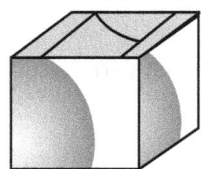
Fig. 2.18 : Half Core-Box

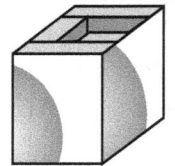
Fig. 2.19 : Dump Corr-Box

(3) Split Core Box (Fig. 2.20) :

This type of core box moulds the entire core; but in order to remove the core after moulding, the box is separated in two or more parts. One end of this box may be closed in some cases. The split core box is held together by a clamp while the core is being rammed from one end. One half of the box has two or more guide pins to hold the part in correct alignment.

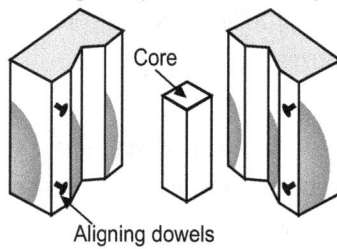
Fig. 2.20 : Split Core Box

(4) Strickle Core Box (Fig. 2.21) :

The strickle core box is often used when a core with an irregular cope is required. In this core box, the desired shape on the cope of the core is produced by striking off the core sand from the top of the core box with a piece of stock cut to correspond to contour of the required core.

This irregularly shaped board is known as "strickle board". The use of strickle board frequently simplifies the construction of core box, which otherwise might require more time to construct.

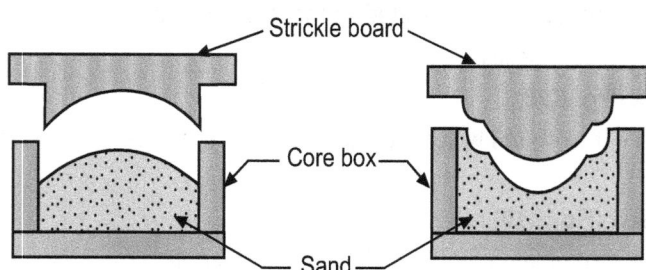
Fig. 2.21 : Strickle Core Box

(5) Loose Piece Core Box (Fig. 2.22):

In some cases, a single box can be constructed to mould both halves of the right-left core with a single core box. It may be desirable to make the core box recess in the form of a cross and use loose pieces of wood (stop-offs) to close the end by the box that is not in use at the time of ramming each of the alternate halves of the core. When second half is to be rammed, the stop-off is shifted to the opposite side of the core box.

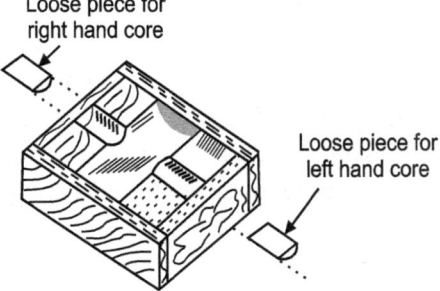

Fig. 2.22 : A Loose Piece Core Box

(6) Right and Left Hand Box (Fig. 2.23):

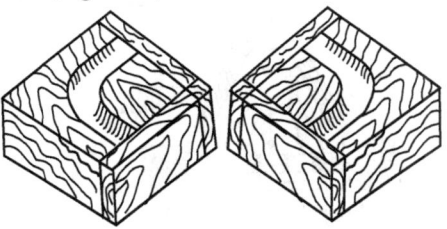

Fig. 2.23 : A Right and Left Core Box

The necessity of constructing two boxes which will form two halves of the core that are not identical requires still another type of core box. In such cases, a right-hand and left-hand core box are used. The core halved thus formed in these boxes are pasted together to form complete core.

2.4.8 Machine Making of Cores

Manual core making is time consuming. A lot of time is required to pack the core boxes and also in drying the cores. For production core making, machine assistance is useful in cutting down the packing time.

Roll Over Jolting Machine :

The core box along with core is placed on a roll over platform. The box is packed with the sand and sand is bonded by the hot plate placed on the top. After the curing time the plate rolls over and inverts the box. The core is then easily removed.

Core Blowing Machine :

In this machine, compressed air is used to transport the core sand to the core box and pack it there under pressure. A properly vented empty core box rests on machine platform. The box is covered by a cover plate with holes. A open topped bin (container) of core sand is lowered on the core box. The top of the bin is connected to a regulated supply of compressed air. On turning on the air supply core, sand gets entrained in the air stream and enters and packs in the core box. The air escapes through the vent holes. A similar machine without the holed cover plate acts as a core shooter and directly packs the core box with sand. A hot core box fixed on the core making machines described above, bonds are sand and dries it as the mould filling or packing process goes on. This modification of course calls for the use of a carefully formulated synthetic resin (bakelite) bonding sand mixture. On these machines, a perfectly sized and bonded core can be produced in 2-3 minutes.

2.4.9 Core Inspection

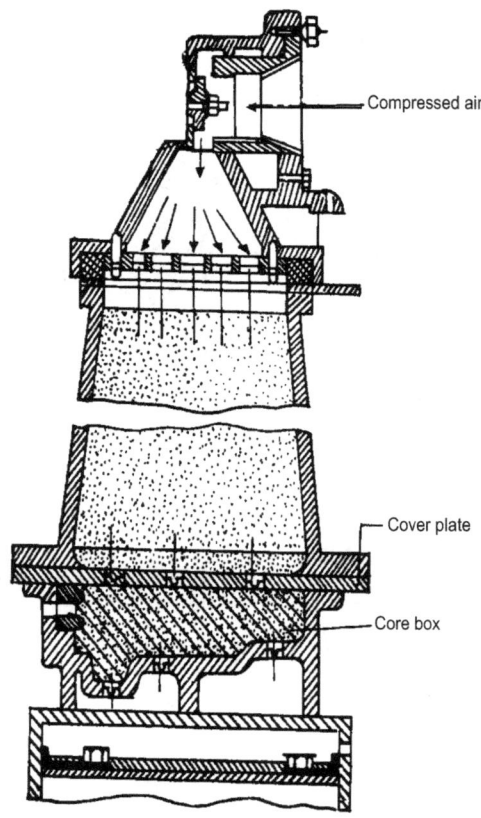

Fig. 2.24 : Core Blowing

The cores made on machines or manually are inspected visually for cracks and deformations. Production cores are inspected for their dimensions by using standard templates. Oversized cores can be sized on a grinder if they have a strong bond.

Sodium Silicate Process (CO_2 process) :

The mould material in this process is a mixture of sand and 1.5 to 6 percent of sodium silicate (water glass) as the binder for sand.

The mixture is rammed around the pattern and is hardened by passing carbon-di-oxide (CO_2) gas through it. This process is used for making cores. Cores made by this process have fewer tendencies to tear.

2.5 MACHINE MOULDING

When number of moulds at fast rates is required the moulds are made by ramming the sand with the help of machines. The techniques used in the machines are described below.

(1) Jolt Machines :

In these machines, sand is placed on top of pattern, and the pattern, flask and sand are then lifted and dropped several times as shown in Fig. 2.25. The kinetic energy of the sand produces optimum packing around the pattern. Jolting machines can be used on the first half of a match plate pattern or on both halves of a cope and drag operation. The construction of another such machine is shown in Fig. 2.25.

Fig. 2.25 shows table mounted in a sleeve. Through table hole compressed air is admitted and it fills the space between table end and sleeve and starts raising the table up. At topmost position when table end clears the hole present is sleeve air escapes through sleeve to atmosphere and hence table drops down on top of sleeve. In the process, sand gets jolt and is compacted on the pattern.

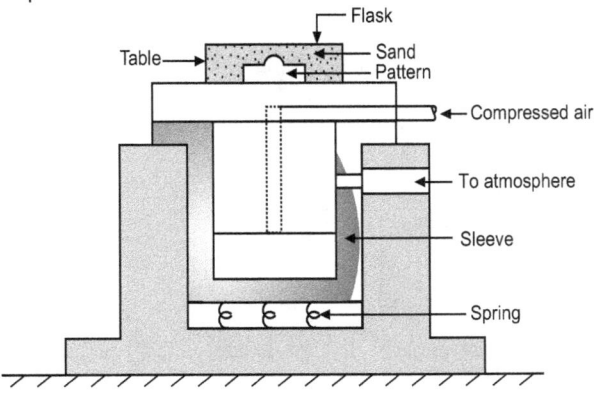

Fig. 2.25 : Jolt machine

(2) Squeeze Machines :

Fig. 2.26 shows stationary squeeze head.

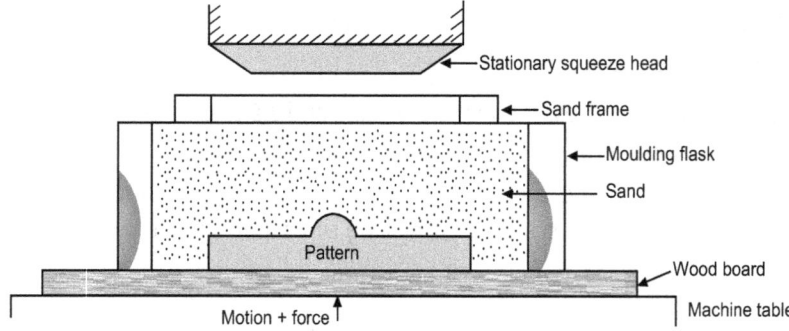

Fig. 2.26 : Squeeze machine

Machine table on which mould, sand and flask pattern are placed, is raised up and squeeze head physically pushes the sand against the pattern. Squeezing provides firm packing near squeeze head but density lowers as you move further into the mould.

(3) Jolt and Squeeze Machines :

A combination of jolting and squeezing is often used to produce more uniform density throughout the mould (Refer Fig. 2.27). Here a match-plate pattern is positioned between the cope and drag sections of a flask, and the assembly is placed upside down on the moulding machine. A parting compound is sprinkled on the pattern, and the top section of the flask is filled with sand. The entire assembly is then jolted a specified number of times to pack the sand around the pattern. A squeeze head is then swung into place and pressure is applied to complete the upper portion of the mould. The flask can be inverted and operations repeated on the cope half, or the cope and drag can be made on separate machines using cope-and-drag patterns. Unless the moulds are very small, the moulding machines usually provide mechanical assistance for inverting the heavy moulds.

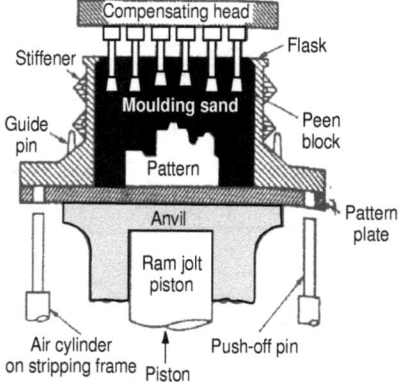

Fig. 2.27 : Jolt & squeeze machine

(4) Sand Slinging Machines :

Sand slingers fill the flask uniformly with sand under a stream of high pressure (Refer Fig. 2.28). They are used to fill large flasks and are typically operated by machine. An impeller in the machine throws sand from its blades or cups at such high speeds that the machine not only places the sand but also rams it appropriately.

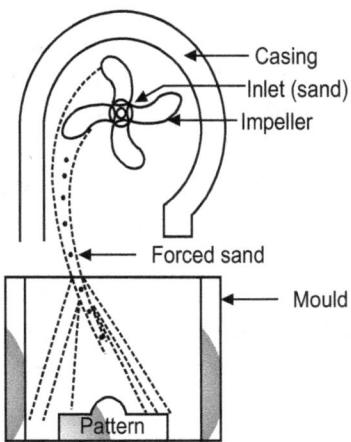

Fig. 2.28 sand slining machine

2.6 DESIGN CONSIDERATION IN CASTING

- Some degree of taper, or draft is recommended to provide to the pattern for its easy removal (Contoured parting lines are not economical)
- Compensate the shrinkage of the solidified molten metal by making patterns of slightly oversize. Parting line is on a flat plane in sand casting is more economical.
- It is recommended to attach the raiser near to the heavier section. The thinnest sections are farthest from the raiser and solidify first and then the solidification proceeds toward the direction of raiser i.e. towards the heavier section
- Uneven cooling due to sharp corners in a casting and lead to formation of hot spots in the final cast structure. Rounding the corner decreases the severity of the hot spot and reduce the stress concentration
- Complex nature in sections should be avoided. When a hole is placed in a highly stressed section, add extra material around the hole as reinforcement.
- Fillets and tapers are preferable to sharp.

- The interior walls and sections are recommended to be 25% thinner than the outside members to reduce the thermal and residual stresses, and metallurgical changes.
- Similar to sand casting, permanent mould castings also require draft for the easy withdrawal of the casting from the mould.

2.7 GATING

A most important condition for the production of sound casting is precision design of the gating system. The main functions of a gating system are to fill steadily the mould and supply metal to the cavity to compensate for shrinkage. An ideal gating system must enable the molten metal to fill completely the mould and furnish means for feeding the metal to the casting during its solidification, insure the desire dimensional accuracy of the casting free of surface defects (sand holes, scabs, slag inclusion and others), produce directional solidification and require a minimum of metal for its element. All the passage ways through which the metal enters the mould cavity is known as 'gating system'. A pouring basin, sprue, runner, strainer, core, gates, etc., are included in 'gating system'. The important provisions of gating system are:

- Metal should be able to flow through the gating system with a minimum of turbulence and aspiration of mould gases so as to prevent sand erosion and gas pick-up. Turbulence is the most important single factor affecting the gating. Excessive turbulence results in the aspiration of air and the formation of dross.
- The metal should be so introduce in the metal cavity that the temperature gradients established on the mould surface and within the metal facilitate directional solidification towards the riser.
- The mould cavity should be completely filled with molten metal in the shortest possible time; the gating system should, therefore, be so designed that the rate of entry of metal in the mould cavity is well regulated.
- The Casting should be produced with minimum of excess metal in gates and risers.
- Loose sand, oxides and slag should be prevented from entering the mould cavity by providing a proper skimming action on the metal as it flows through the gating system.
- Erosion of the mould walls should be avoided.

These requisites can be achieved by controller pouring, use of proper pouring equipment, pouring metal at a specific temperature and by correct design of sprue, runner and gates. Foundries should follow the practice of designing and testing their gating systems on one or more pilot casting and then mounting the gates and runners directly on the pattern equipment before a production run is started. The gating systems should be carefully designed so that the casting produced conforms to the prescribed specification. Improving the design of a gating system can augment the casting yield and reduce rejection. The functions of an ideal gating system are :

1. Perfectly fill the mould cavity,
2. Introduce to the molten metal into the mould with as little turbulence as possible to prevent mould erosion and gas pick up,
3. Establish the best possible temperature gradients in the casting,
4. Introduce proper skimming action on the metal as it flows through the sprue system, and
5. Regulate rate of entry of metal into the mould cavity. In order for gates to function properly, one must control
   1. Type of pouring equipment, such as ladles, runner cups pr pouring basins
   2. Rate of pouring,
   3. Temperature of the metal
   4. Size, number and location of gates leading to the casting,
   5. Size and type of sprue and runner,
   6. Position of the mould during casting and freezing, and

Gates and risers are part of the system to provide molten metal to the part your are casting. First some definitions will make it easier to understand these cast parts.

- **(a) Choke :** A restriction in the gating system that limits the flow rate of the molten metal.
- **(b) Cope :** The top part of the mould.
- **(c) Drag :** The lower part of the mould.
- **(d) Gate :** A short passageway that connects the runner to the mould.
- **(e) Match Plate :** A type of pattern that is used for making a run of the same part, it is possible to make it so that it includes the gates, runners and sprue bases.
- **(f) Pouring Basin :** An enlarged portion at the top of the sprue.
- **(g) Riser :** A vertical passageway which provides a source of hot metal to prevent shrinkage in the casting.
- **(h) Runner :** The passageway the metal flows through to get to the gates from the sprue.
- **(i) Runner Extension :** A short extension of the runner which goes beyond the last gate
- **(j) Sprue :** A vertical passageway through which the molten metal gets to the runner.

The goals for the gating system are :
- To minimize turbulence to avoid trapping gases and breaking up the sand mould.
- To get enough metal into the mould cavity before the metal starts to solidify.
- To avoid shrinkage.

2.7.1 Gating System

Gating system is nothing but the basic design which is needed to construct a smooth and proper filling of the mould cavity of the casting without any discontinuity, voids or solid inclusions. The channel layout is means that the efficiency of the gating system also depend on the number of ingates and location of ingates. It symbolically means that "channel" is the "number" of ingates used and "layout" is the location of ingates.

The location of the ingates is governed by the following criterias :

(a) **Side Ingates :** The ingates at the sides increase the efficiency of the gating system by filling the stream of molten metals through them. It helps to reduce the fettling effort too.

(b) **Thick Ingate Sections :** Using thick ingates helps to reduce the breakage of the ingates during fettling process, since it allows the flow of molten metal with minimal cooling.

(c) **Ingate Path :** Sand casting is accompanied with molten metal, which flows moderately with minimum disturbance and directional change. They should not be placed in a position opposite to the core.

(d) **Ingate Position :** If the free fall of the molten metal at the cavity is low, then the ingate should be placed in that position, because it reduces the oxidation and thus the erosion of the metal.

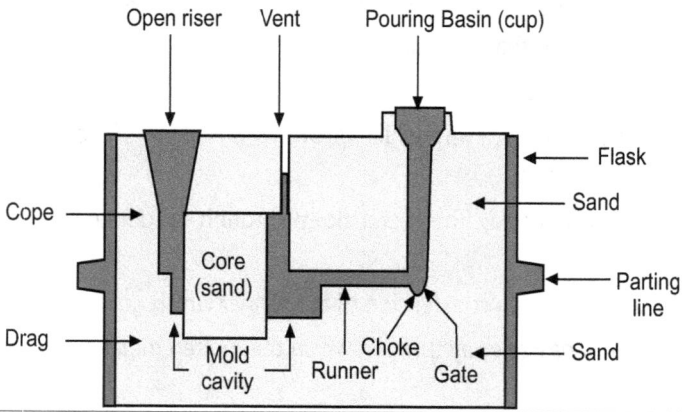

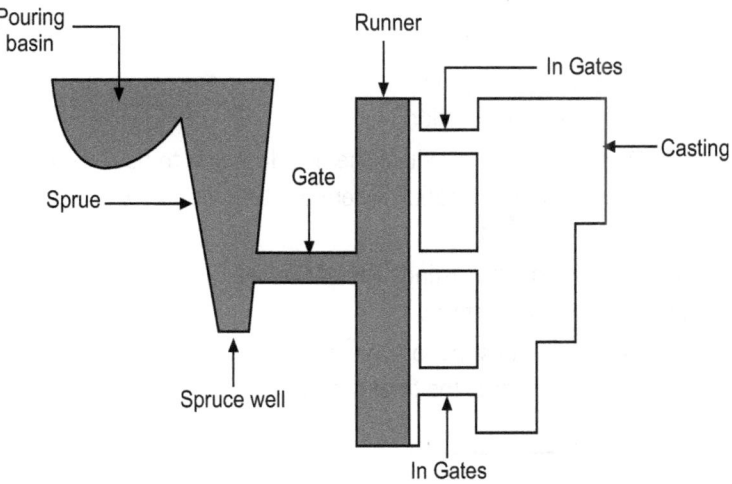

Fig. 2.29 : Basic Gating System

2.7.2 Sprue Design

The design of the pouring basin and sprue can affect turbulence. To get best results can be obtained by keeping the sprue full of molten metal throughout your pour. A sprue tapered to a smaller size at its bottom will create a choke which will help keep the sprue full of molten metal. In case of tapered sprue choke is put in while making the runners, moreover locating it as close to the bottom of the sprue as possible. The choke will also increase the speed of the molten metal, which is undesirable. To overcome this problem, the bottom of the sprue area can be enlarged, called a sprue base. This decreases the speed of the molten metal. There are two basic types of sprue bases, enlargement and well base. The general rules of thumb for enlargement bases are;

- Diameter is roughly 2.5 times the width of the runner.
- Depth is equal to the depth of the runner.

The general rules of thumb for well bases are;

- Depth of a well base is twice that of the runners.
- Cross-sectional area of the base is 5 times the cross-sectional area of the sprue exit (a 1/2 sq. in. sprue exit would mean you need a base with an area of 2.5 sq. in. which would be a 1.5 inch diameter).

The bottom of the sprue base should be flat, not rounded like a bowl. If it is it will cause turbulence in the metal.

2.7.3 Location of the Sprue

The sprue collects the molten metal from the pouring basin to the plane of the runner and ingates. So, even the location of the sprue plays a vital role in the gating system. So let us see the factors, which govern the sprue location.

- **(a) Distance of Flow :** In order to reduce the heat loss and to have maximum yield, the sprue should be placed in a location where the total flow distance within the gating channel is minimum.
- **(b) Concentration of Heat :** In castings the sprue must be away from hot spots, since hot metal flows through the sprue.
- **(c) Sprue Location :** Sprue must be located in such a way that it reduces the size of the bounding box, which encloses the total cast, including the gating channels.

2.8 RUNNER

One of the most important things to remember in your runners and gates is to avoid sharp corners. Any changes in direction or cross sectional area should make use of rounded corners. Also make sure the runners and gates are well rammed and smooth. This will help avoid sand erosion and turbulence.

To ensure that the metal is not flowing too fast in the runners the rule of thumb is that the cross sectional area of the runners should be greater than the area of the choke. The walls of the runners should be as smooth as possible to avoid causing turbulence. The runners should be filled with metal before the gates are, one way to ensure this happens is to put the runners in the drag and the gates in the cope. If you need to have a choke in the runner to restrict flow it should be at least 6" from the first gate.

The cross-sectional area of the runners should decrease as the gates come off them to keep the same gating ratio. A good gating ration for aluminum is 1:4:4. The 1 is for the cross-sectional area of the choke. The first 4 is the total cross-sectional area of the runners (measured after the choke but before the first gate) and the final 4 is total cross sectional area of the gates. For example, say you have a tapered sprue with an exit area of 0.5 sq. in., two runners with 2 gates off of each runner. The total runner area should be 2 sq. in so each runner would be 1 sq. in. The total gate area should be 2 sq. in., there are 4 gates so each gate would have an area of 0.5 sq. in. The gate calculation only works this way if there are an equal number of gates on each runner. If that is not the case divide the area of the runner by the number of gates on that runner to get the area of each gate.

The area of the runners should be reduced just after a gate by an amount equal to the area of that gate. This will insure that each gate in the system will have the same flow of metal, even if it's farther from the sprue. The first bit of metal poured is most likely to be contaminated by air and sand entrapment. To prevent this metal from going into the mould cavity you use a runner extension. That first bit of metal will flow to the end of this dead end and be trapped there, where it can't harm the piece you're trying to cast. The runner extension will have the same area as that of the last gate on that runner.

2.9 RISERS

Risers are important to ensure a flow of molten metal to the part being cast as it is starting to solidify. Without a riser heavier parts of the casting will have shrinkage defects, either on the surface or internally.

As molten metal solidifies it shrinks. If it does not have a source of more molten metal to feed it as it shrinks you will get defects in your casting. A riser's purpose is to provide that extra molten metal. Basically a riser is a vertical portion of the gating system, similar to a straight sprue, that stores the molten metal until it is needed by the casting. This means the metal in the riser must stay liquid longer than the metal in the part being cast.

A riser may be required for every hot spot in your cast part. In other words, the part of the casting that solidifies last, usually are with a larger volume of metal. The risers can either be attached to the top or the side of a part. They may also be blind risers. A blind riser is completely contained in the mould, not exposed to the air. Since it's not open to the air this type of riser cools slower and thus will stay liquid longer. It's important that no matter where it's located the gate that connects the riser to the casting is not too small and as short as possible or else the gate will solidify too soon and prevent the metal in the riser from reaching the casting, try and keep the length to 1/2 the diameter of the riser.

Risers may be upstream from the casting in the runner/gate system. In this case the metal must flow through the riser prior to reaching the casting and after the pour is completed the metal in the riser will be hotter than the metal in the casting. They may also be placed downstream, after the casting. This means the metal flows through the casting to get to the riser so the metal in the riser will be cooler than the metal in the casting. This could cause the metal in the casting to feed the riser as it cools, definitely not desired.

You want the metal in the riser to solidify last, after the part being cast. Since the more surface area something has the faster it cools you want to minimize the surface area of the riser for a given volume. Because of this the optimum shape for a riser would be a sphere, however that is not an easy shape to mould. The next best alternative is a cylinder, which is easy to make.

Ideally the cylinders height should be some where between 1/2 and 1 1/2 times the diameter. If possible the bottom, and top if it's a blind riser, should be spherical, or bowl shaped. This will also help the metal stay molten longer.

2.9.1 Feeder

A feeder is a reservoir built into a metal casting mould to prevent cavities due to shrinkage. Most metals are less dense as a liquid than as a solid so castings shrink upon cooling, which can leave a void at the last point to solidify. Risers prevent this by providing molten metal to the casting as it solidifies, so that the cavity forms in the riser and not the casting. Risers are not effective on materials that have a large freezing range, because directional solidification is not possible. They are also not needed for casting processes that utilized pressure to fill the mould cavity. The activity of planning of how a casting will be gated and risered is called foundry methoding or foundry engineering.

Fig 2.30 : A bronze casting showing the sprue and risers

Risers are only be effective if three conditions are met: the riser cools after the casting, the riser has enough material compensate for the casting shrinkage, and the casting directionally solidifies towards the riser.

In order for the riser to cool after the casting the riser must cool more slowly than the casting. Chvorinov's rule briefly states that the slowest cooling time is achieved with the greatest volume and the least surface area; geometrically speaking, this is a sphere. So, ideally, a riser should be a sphere, but this isn't a very practical shape to insert into a mould, so a cylinder is used instead. The height to diameter ratio of the cylinder varies depending on the material, location of the riser, size of the flask, etc.

The shrinkage must be calculated for the casting to confirm that there is enough material in the riser to compensate for the shrinkage. If it appears there is not enough material then the size of the riser must be increased. This requirement is more important for plate-like shapes, while the first requirement is more important for chunky shapes.

Finally, the casting must be designed to produce directional solidification, which sweeps from the extremities of the mould cavity toward the riser(s). In this way, the riser can feed molten metal continuously to part of the casting that is solidifying. One part of achieving this end is by placing the riser near the thickest and largest part of the casting, as that part of the casting will naturally want to solidify last. If this type of solidification is not possible, multiple risers that feed various sections of the casting or chills may be necessary.

2.9.2 Types of Risers

Risers are categorized based on three criteria : location, if it is open to the atmosphere, and how it is filled. If the riser is located on the casting then it is known as a top riser, but if it is located next to the casting it is known as a **side riser**.

Top risers are advantageous because they take up less space in the flask than a side riser, plus they have a shorter feeding distance.

If the riser is open to the atmosphere it is known as an **open riser**, but if the riser is completely contained in the mould it is known as a **blind riser**. A blind riser is usually bigger than an open riser because the blind riser loses more heat to mould through the top of the riser.

Finally, if the riser receives material from the gating system and fills after the mould cavity it is known as a **live riser** or **hot riser**.

If the riser fills with material that has already flowed through the mould cavity it is known as a **dead riser** or **cold riser**. Live risers are usually smaller than dead risers. Note that top risers are almost always dead risers and risers in the gating system are almost always live risers.

Note that the connection of the riser to the moulding cavity can be an issue for side risers. On one hand the connection should be as small as possible to make separation as easy as possible, but, on the other, the connection must be big enough for it to not solidify before the riser.

The connection is usually made short to take advantage of the heat of both the riser and the moulding cavity, which will keep it hot throughout the process. These are risering aids that can be implemented to slow the cooling of a riser or decrease its size. One is using an insulating sleeve and top around the riser. Another is placing a heater around only the riser.

The efficiency, or yield, of a casting is defined as the weight of the casting divided by the weight of the total amount of metal poured. Risers can add a lot to the total weight being poured, so it is important to optimize their size and shape. Because risers exist only to ensure the integrity of the casting, they are removed after the part has cooled, and their metal is re-melted to be used again.

As a result, riser size, number, and placement should be carefully planned to reduce waste while filling all the shrinkage in the casting. One way to calculate the minimum size of a riser is to use Chvorinov's rule by setting the solidification time for the riser to be longer than that of the casting. Any time can be chosen but 25% longer is usually a safe choice.

2.9.3 Gating System Design

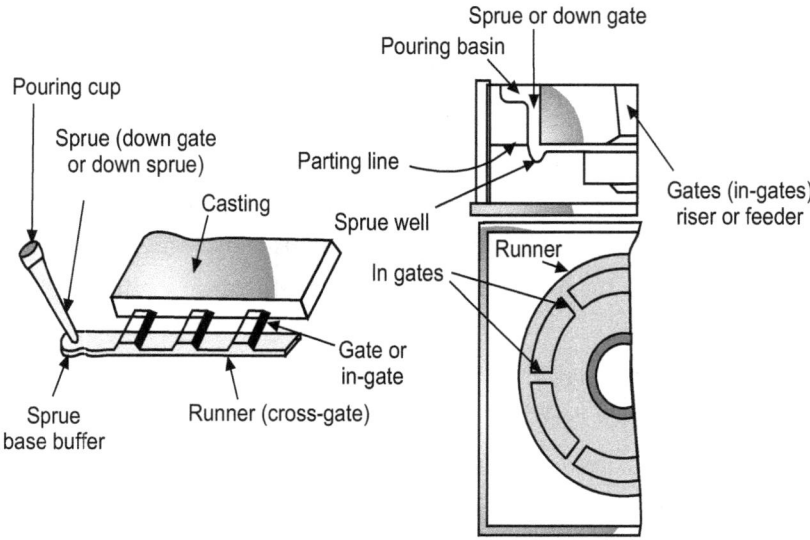

Fig. 2.31

The gating systems refer to all those elements which are connected with the flow of molten metal from the ladle to the mould cavity. The elements of gating systems are

- Pouring Basin
- Sprue
- Sprue Base Well
- Runner
- Runner Extension
- Ingate

Any gating system designed should aim at providing a defect free casting. This can be achieved by considering following requirements.

- The mould should be completely filled in the smallest possible time without having to raise neither metal temperature nor use of higher metal heads.
- The metal should flow smoothly into the mould without any turbulence. A turbulence metal flow tends to form dross in the mould.
- Unwanted materials such as slag, dross and other mould materials should not be allowed to enter the mould cavity.
- The metal entry into the mould cavity should be properly controlled in such a way that aspiration of the atmospheric air is prevented.

- A proper thermal gradient should be maintained so that the casting is cooled without any shrinkage cavities or distortions.
- Metal flow should be maintained in such a way that no gating or mould erosion takes place.
- The gating system should ensure that enough molten metal reaches the mould cavity.
- It should be economical and easy to implement and remove after casting solidification.
- The casting yield should be maximized.

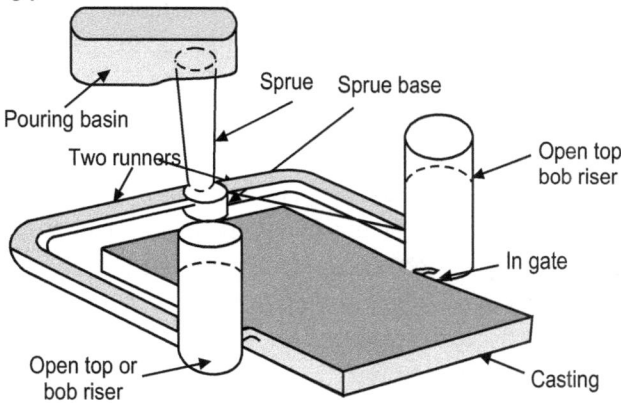

Fig. 2.32 : Components of gating system

The liquid metal that runs through the various channels in the mould obeys the Bernoulli's theorem which states that the total energy head remains constant at any section. Ignoring frictional losses, we have

$$h = \frac{P}{rg} + \frac{v^2}{2g} = \text{constant}$$

Where h = Potential Head, m
P = Static Pressure, Pa
v = Liquid Velocity, m / s
ρ*g = w = Specific weight of liquid, N / m^2
g = Acceleration due to gravity, m / s^2

Though quantitatively Bernoulli's theorem may not be applied, it helps to understand qualitatively, the metal flow in the sand mould. As the metal enters the pouring basin, it has the highest potential energy with no kinetic or pressure energies. But as the metal moves through the gating system, a loss of energy occurs because of the friction between the molten metal and the mould walls. Heat is continuously lost through the mould material though it is not represented in the Bernoulli's equation.

Another law of fluid mechanics, which is useful in understanding the gating system behaviour, is the law of continuity which says that the volume of metal flowing at any section in the mould is constant. The same in equation form is

$$Q = A_1V_1 = A_2V_2$$

Where Q = Rate of flow, m³/sec.

A = Area of cross section, m²

V = Velocity of metal flow, m/s

2.9.4 Pouring Time

The main objective for the gating system design is to fill the mould in the smallest time. The time for complete filling of a mould is called pouring time. Too long a pouring time requires a higher pouring temperature and too less a pouring time means turbulent flow in the mould which makes the casting defect prone.

The pouring time depends on the casting materials, complexity of the casting, section thickness and casting size. Steels lose heat very fast, so required less pouring time while for non-ferrous materials longer pouring time is beneficial because they lose heat slowly and tend to form dross if metal is pour too quickly. Ratio of surface area to volume of casting is important in addition to the mass of the casting. Also gating mass is considered when its mass is comparable to the mass of the casting.

For Gray cast Iron upto 450 kg.

$$\text{Pouring time, } t = K \left\{1.41 + \frac{T}{14.59}\right\} \sqrt{W} \text{ seconds.}$$

Where, K = Fluidity of iron inches/40

T = Average section thickness, mm

W = Mass of the casting kg.

For Gray cast Iron weight grater than 450 kg.

$$\text{Pouring time, } t = K \left\{1.236 + \frac{T}{16.65}\right\} \sqrt[3]{W} \text{ seconds.}$$

Typical pouring times for cast Iron are :

Casting mass	Proving time in seconds
20 Kg	6 to 10
100 kg	15 to 30

Steel casting

$$\text{Pouring time } t = (2.4335 - 0.3953 \log W) \sqrt{W}$$

Shell moulded ductile iron (vertical pouring)

Pouring time $t = K_1 \sqrt{W}$ sections.

Where $k_1 = 2.080$ for tinner sections

$\quad\quad\quad = 2.670$ for section 10 to 25 mm thick.

$\quad\quad\quad = 2.970$ for heavier sections

Copper alloy cortings.

Pouring time $t = K_2 \sqrt{W}$ sections.

Where K_2 constant whose value is given as

for top getting system 1.30

Bottom getting system 1.80

Brass getting system 1.90

Tin branze 2.80

2.9.5 Choke Area

After calculation of pouring time, it is required to establish the main control area which meters the metal flow into the mould cavity so that the mould is completely filled within the calculated pouring time. The controlling area is the choke area. The choke area happens to be at the bottom of the sprue and hence the first element to be designed in the gating system is the sprue size and its proportions. The main advantage in having sprue bottom as the choke area is that proper flow characteristics are established early in the mould. The choke area can be calculated using Bernoulli's equation as

$$A = \frac{W}{dtc\sqrt{29H}}$$

Where A = choke area in mm2

$\quad\quad\quad W$ = casting mass kg

$\quad\quad\quad t$ = pouring time – S

$\quad\quad\quad d$ = mass density of molten metal in kg/mm3

$\quad\quad\quad g$ = acceleration due to gravity mm/s2

$\quad\quad\quad H$ = Effective metal head (Spur Height) mm.

$\quad\quad\quad c$ = efficiency factor, which is function of gating system.

For Top gate

$$H = h$$

Bottom gate $\quad\quad H = h - \frac{c}{2}$? $H = h - \frac{p \times p}{2c}$

Where h = Height of the sprue

$\quad\quad\quad p$ = Height of mould cavity in cope

$\quad\quad\quad c$ = Total height of the mould cavity

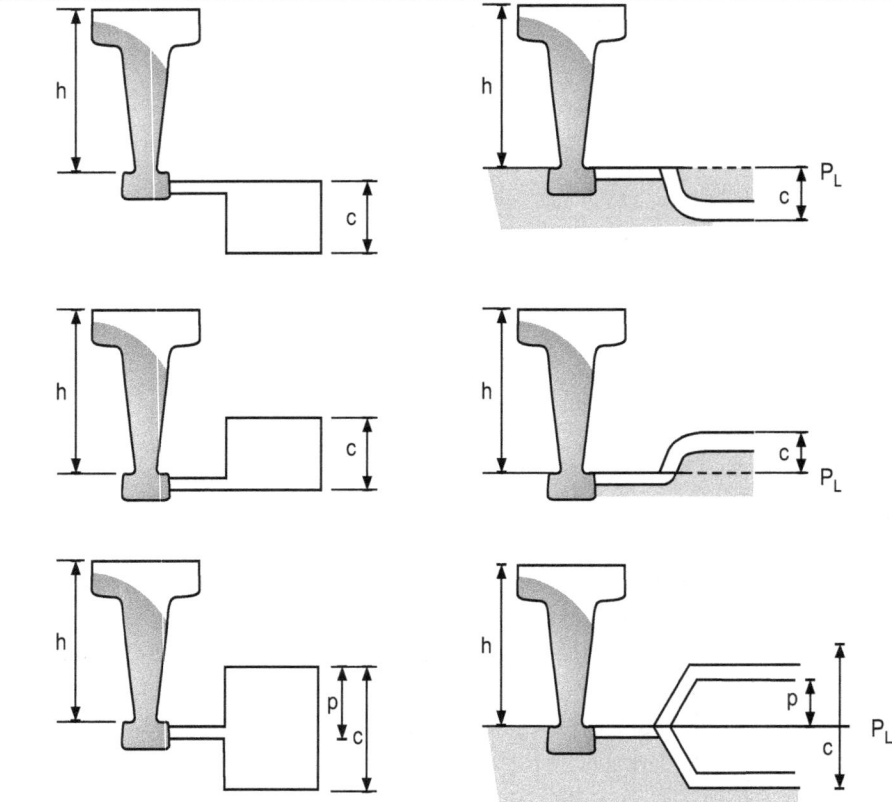

Fig. 2.33 : Effective spure height

The efficiency coefficient of the gating system depends on the various sections that are normally used in a gating system. The elements of a gating system should be circular in cross section since they have lower surface area to volume ratio which would reduce heat loss and have less friction. Moreover, streamlining the various gating elements would greatly increase volumetric efficiency of the gating system and allow for smaller size gates and runners which would increase the casting yield. Whenever a runner changes direction or joins with another runner or gate, there is some loss in the metal head, all of which when taken properly into consideration would give the overall efficiency of the gating system.

2.9.6 Sprue

The sprues should be tapered down to take into account the gain in velocity of the metal as it flows down reducing the air aspiration. The exact tapering can be obtained by equation of continuity. Denoting the top and the choke sections of the sprue by the subscripts t and c respectively, we get

$$A_t \cdot V_t = A_c V_c$$

$$A_t = A_c \cdot \frac{V_c}{V_t}$$

Since the velocities are proportional to the square of the potential heads, the Benoullij equation.

$$A_t = A_c \cdot \sqrt{\frac{h_c}{h_t}}$$

The square root suggested that profile of spure should be parabolic if exactly done as per above equation. But making parabolic spure is inconvenient in practice and therefore taper is preferable.

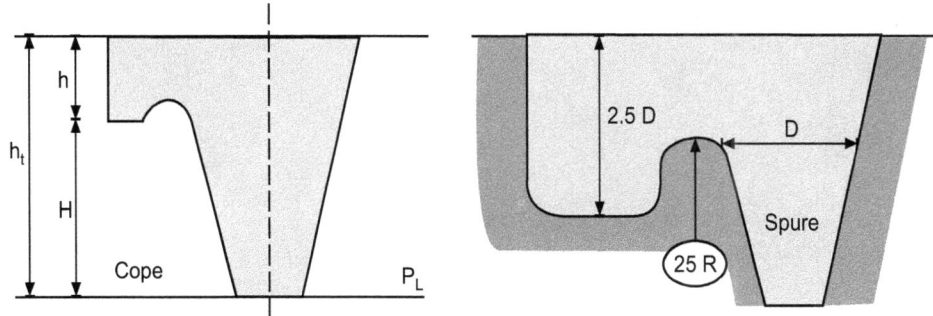

Fig. 2.34 : Spure and pouring basin height and area

Theoretical ratios of spure top and chore areas based on pouring basin depth.

2.9.7 Pouring Basin

The main function of a pouring basin is to reduce the momentum of the liquid flowing into the mould by settling first into it. In order that the metal enters into the sprue without any turbulence it is necessary that the pouring basin be deep enough, also the entrance into the sprue be a smooth radius of at least 25 mm.

The pouring basin depth of 2.5 times the sprue entrance diameter is enough for smooth metal flow and to prevent vortex formation. In order that vortex is not formed during pouring, it is necessary that the pouring basin be kept full and constant conditions of flow are established. This can be achieved by using a delay screen or a strainer core.

A delay screen is a small piece of perforated thin tin sheet placed in the pouring basin at the top of the down sprue. This screen usually melts because of the heat from the metal and in the process delays the entrance of metal into the sprue thus filling the pouring basin fully. This ensures a constant flow of metal as also exclude slag and dirt since only metal from below is allowed to go into the sprue.

A similar effect is also achieved by a strainer core which is a ceramic coated screen with many holes. The strainer restricts the flow of metal into the sprue and thus helps in quick filling of the pouring basin.

Pouring basins are most desirable for alloys which form troublesome oxide skins (aluminum, aluminum bronze, etc.)

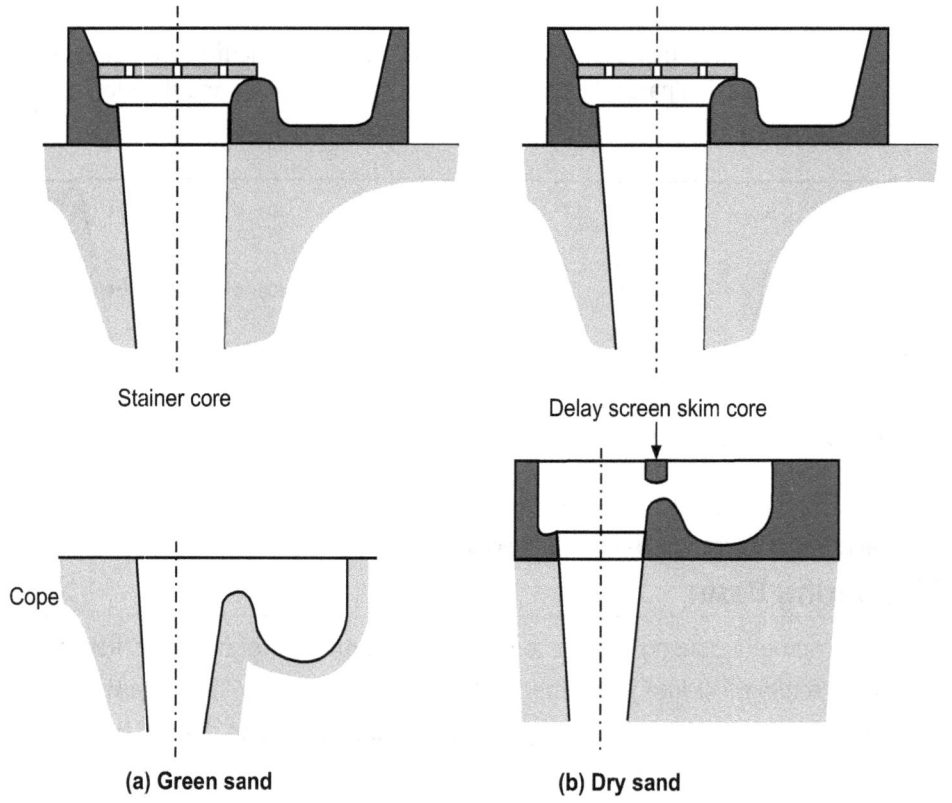

Fig. 2.35: Pouring Basin

2.9.8 Sprue Base Well

The provision of a sprue base well at the bottom of the sprue helps in reducing the velocity of the incoming metal and also the mould erosion.

A general guide line could be that the sprue base well area should be five times that of the sprue choke area and the well depth should be approximately equal to that the runner.

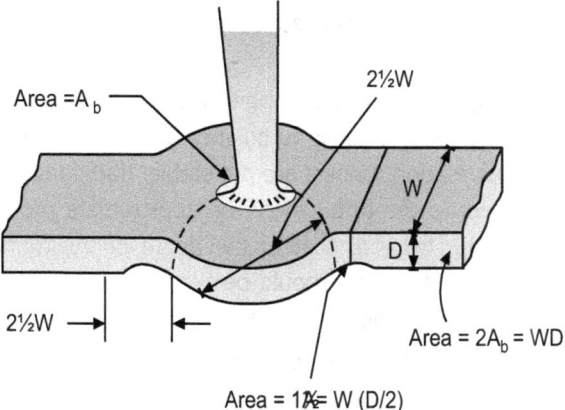

Fig. 2.36 sprue well

2.9.9 Gating Ratios

It refers to the proportion of the cross sectional areas between the sprue, runner and ingates and is generally denoted as sprue area: runner area: ingate area. Depending on the choke area there can be two types of gating systems:

- Non-pressurised
- Pressurised

A non –pressurised gating system having choke at the sprue base, has total runner area and ingate area higher than the sprue area. In this system there is no pressure existing in the metal flow system and thus it helps to reduce turbulence. This is particularly useful for casting drossy alloys such as aluminum alloy sand magnesium alloys. When metal is to enter the mould cavity through multiple ingates, the cross section of the runner should accordingly be reduced at each of a runner break-up to allow for equal distribution of metal through all ingates. A typical gating ratio is 1:4:4.

The disadvantages of unpressurised gating are:

- The gating system needs to be carefully designed to see that all parts flow full. Otherwise some elements of the gating system may flow partially allowing for the air aspiration. Tapered sprues are invariably used with unpressurised system. The runners are maintained in drag while the gates are kept in cope to ensure that runners are full.
- Casting yield gets reduced because of large metal involved in the runners and gates. In the case of pressurised gating system normally the ingates area is the smallest, thus maintaining a back pressure throughout and generally flows full and thereby, can minimize the air aspiration even when a straight sprue is used. It provided higher casting yield since the volume of metal used up in the runners and gates is reduced. Because of turbulence and associated dross formation, this type of gating system is not used for

light alloys but can be advantageously used for ferrous castings. A typical gating ratio is 1:2:1.

While designing the runner system, care should be taken to reduce sharp corners or sudden change of sections since they tend to cause turbulence and gas entrapment. Though from heat loss factor circular cross section runners are preferable, traditionally trapezoidal runner sections are employed to reduce the turbulence. The approximate proportions are from a square to rectangle with width twice as that of the depth of the runner. When multiple ingates are used, the runner cross section should be suitably restricted at the separation of each runner in the interest of uniform flow through all sections.

It is a general practice to cut runner in the cope and the ingate in the drag to help in the trapping of the slag. Sometimes it is good to have half of the runner in the cope side and rest in the drag.

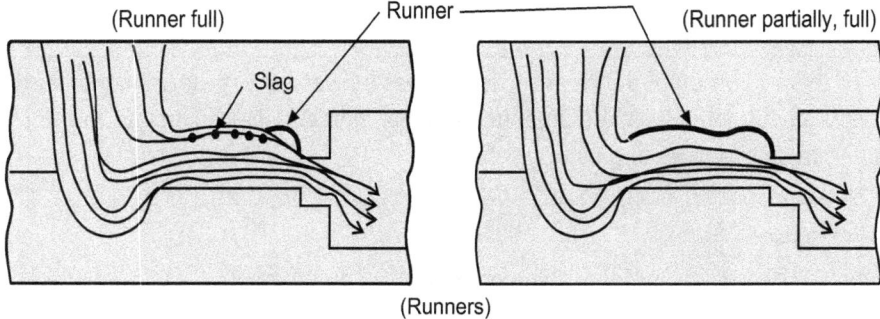

Fig. 2.37 runners conditions

But for aluminum alloy castings, it is recommended that the runners be placed in the drag and the ingates in the cope so that dross (3.99 g/cm) which is heavier compared to aluminum (2.70 g/cm) is restricted. Also the entry into runners from sprue base well should be made as smooth as possible in such castings, otherwise the direction of flow would tend to be turbulent and leads to drossing when any change abruptly occurs in the cross sectional area.

2.9.10 Ingate

The ingate can be considered as a weir with no reduction in cross section of the stream at the gate. Then the rate of flow of molten metal through the gates depends on the free height of the metal in the runner and the gate area & the velocity with which metal is flowing in the runner. The free height, h can be calculated as

$$h = 1.6 \sqrt[3]{\frac{Q \times Q}{g \times b \times b}} + \frac{v \times v}{2g} \text{ mm}$$

Q = Metal flow rate mm³/sec.
b = Sute width mm
v = Metal velocity in runner mm/sec.
g = Acceleration due to gravity mm/s²

Having obtained the head of metal, the height of the gate h, is given by

$$H_1 = h - 5 \text{ mm}$$

Gates higher than this will not fill completely and those lower than this will increase the velocities of the stream entering into. The ingates are generally made wider compared to depth, up to a ratio of 4. This facilitates in the severing of the gates from the casting after solidification.

It may sometimes preferable to reduce the actual connection between the ingate and the casting by means of a neck-down so that the removal of it is simplified. The following points should be kept in mind while choosing the positioning of the ingate

Ingate should not be located near a protruding part of the mould to avoid the striking of vertical mould walls by molten metal stream.

- Ingates should be preferably be placed along the longitudinal axis of the mould wall.
- It should not be placed near a core print or a chill.
- Ingate cross sectional area should preferably be smaller than the smallest thickness of the casting so that the ingates solidify first and isolate the casting from the gating system. This would reduce the possibility of air aspiration through gating system in case of metal shrinkage.
- It is possible that the farthest gate from the sprue is likely to flow more metal than others, particularly in the case of unpressurised system. To make for more uniform flow through all the gates, the runner area should be reduced progressively after each ingate, such that restriction on the metal flow would be provided.

Slag Trap Systems :

In order to obtain sound casting quality, it is essential that the slag and other impurities be removed from the molten metal fully before it enters the mould cavity. Apart from the use of pouring basins and strainer cores the following methods are also used.

Runner Extension :

Normally the metal which moves first into the gating system is likely to contain slag and dross which should not be allowed to get into the mould cavity. This could be achieved by extending the runner beyond the ingates so that the momentum of the metal will carry it past the gates and to a blind alley called runner extension. A runner extension having a minimum of twice the runner width is desirable.

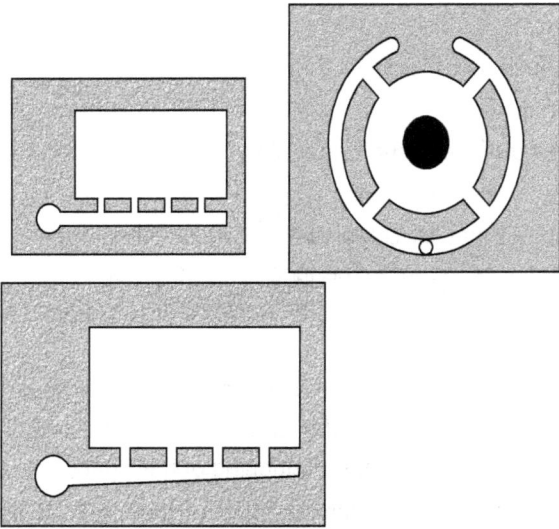

Fig. 2.38 : Multiple ingates

Whirl Gate :

Another method employed successfully to trap the slag from entering steel casting is a whirl gate. This utilizes the principle of centrifugal action to throw the dense metal to the periphery and retain the lighter slag at the centre. In order to achieve this action, it is necessary that entry area should be at least 1.5 times the exit area so that the metal is built up at the centre quickly. Also the metal should revolve 270° before reaching the exit gate so as to gain enough time for separating the impurities.

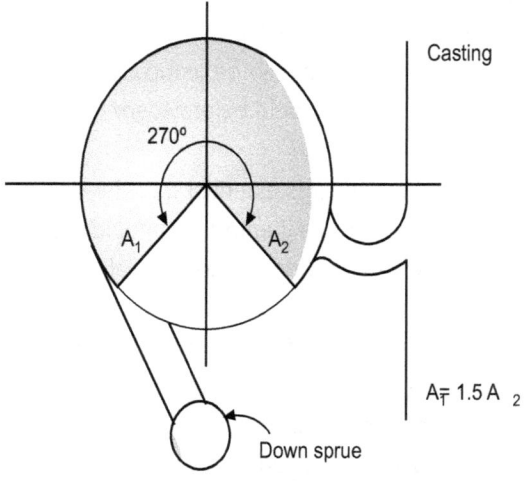

Fig. 2.39 : Whirl gate

2.9.11 Design of Riser

The function of a riser (also called reservoir, feeders, or headers) is to feed the casting during solidification so that no shrinkage cavities are formed. The requirement of risers depends to a great extent upon the type of metal poured and the complexity of the casting. Let us consider the mould of a cube which is filled with liquid metal. As time progresses, the metal starts losing heat through all sides and as a result starts freezing from all sides equally trapping the liquid metal inside. But further solidification and subsequent volumetric shrinkage and the metal contraction due to change in temperature causes formation of a void. The solidification when complete, finally results in the shrinkage cavity as shown in the figure. The reason for the formation of the void in the cube casting is that the liquid metal in the centre which solidifies in the end is not fed during the solidification; hence the liquid shrinkage ends up as a void. Such isolated spots which remain hot till the end are called hot spots

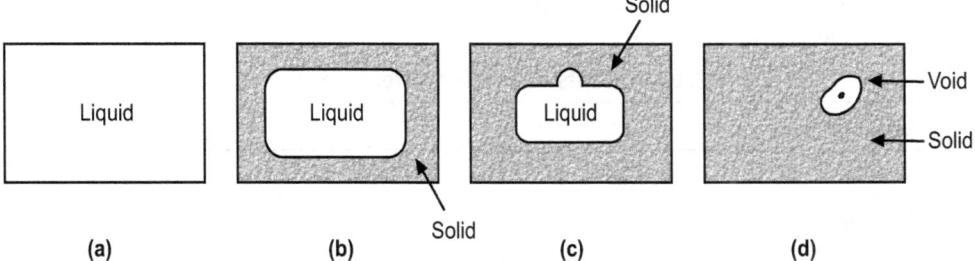

Fig. 2.40 : Hot Spots Functions of Risers

- Provide extra metal to compensate for the volumetric shrinkage
- Allow mould gases to escape
- Provide extra metal pressure on the solidifying metal to reproduce mould details more exactly.
- To compensate mould expansion during pouring of hot liquid metal because of soft mould.

It is the task of casting designer to reduce all hot spots so that no shrinkage cavities occurred. Since solidification of the casting occurs by loosing heat from the surfaces and the amount of the heat is given by the volume of the casting, the cooling characteristics of a casting can be represented by the surface area to the volume ratio. Since the riser is almost similar to the casting in its solidification behavior, the riser characteristics can also be specified by the ratio of its surface area to volume. If this ratio of casting is higher, then it is expected to cool faster. According to Chvorinov, solidification time can be calculated as

$$t_s = K \left(\frac{V}{S_A} \right)^2$$

Where

    ts = solidification time, s
    V = volume of the casting,
    SA = surface area
    K = mould constant which depends on pouring temperature, casting & mould thermal Characteristics

The freezing ratio, X of a mould is defined as the ratio of cooling characteristics of casting to that of the riser

$$X = \frac{SA\ casting\ /\ V\ casting}{SA\ riser\ /\ V\ riser}$$

CAINE's Method

$X = \{a / Y-b\} + c$

Where Y = riser volume / casting volume a, b, c are constants whose values for different materials are given here

Table 2.1 Constants values for different materials

Material	a	b	c
Steel	0.10	0.03	1.00
Aluminium	0.10	0.06	1.08
CI, Brass	0.-4	0.017	1.00
Gra C1	0.33	0.030	1.00
Al-bronze	0.24	0.017	1.00
Sl-bronze	0.24	0.017	1.00

Design Requirements of Risers :

1. **Riser Size:** For a sound casting riser must be last to freeze. The ratio of (volume / surface area) ^{2} of the riser must be greater than that of the casting. However, when this condition does not meet, the metal in the riser can be kept in liquid state by heating it externally or using exothermic materials in the risers.
2. **Riser Placement:** the spacing of risers in the casting must be considered by effectively calculating the feeding distance of the risers.
3. **Riser Shape:** cylindrical risers are recommended for most of the castings as spherical risers, although considers as best, are difficult to cast. To increase volume/surface area ratio the bottom of the riser can be shaped as hemisphere.

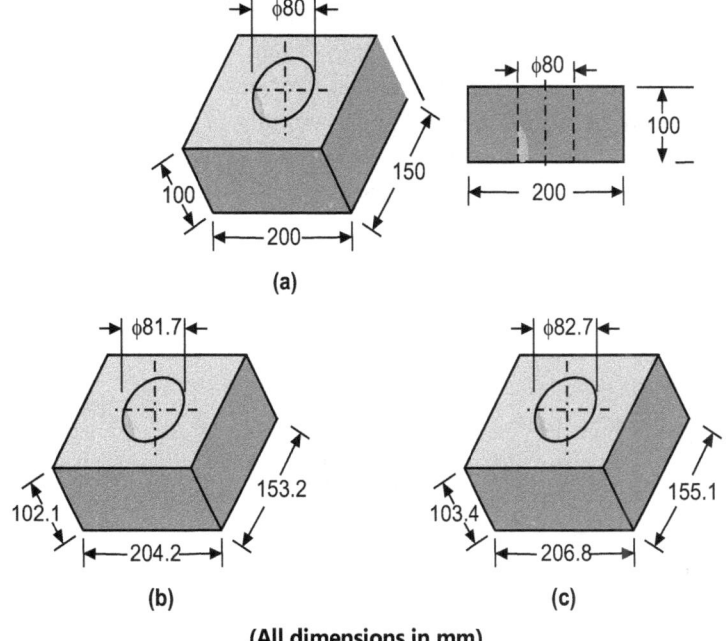

(All dimensions in mm)

Fig. 2.41 : Provision of allowances for patterns in sand castings

2.10 SOLIDIFICATION OF CASTINGS

After molten metal is poured into a mould, a series of events takes place during the solidification of the casting and its cooling to ambient temperature. These events greatly influence the size, shape, uniformity, and chemical composition of the grains formed throughout the casting, which in turn influences its overall properties. The significant factors affecting these events are the type of metal, thermal properties of both the metal and the mould, the geometric relationship between volume and surface area of the casting, and shape of the mould.

Nucleation and Grain Growth :

When the free energy of a parent phase is reduced by means of temperature or pressure then there is a driving force leading to crystallization. At the melting point, the thermal fluctuations result in the formation of tiny particles (containing only a few atoms) of the product phase within the parent volume. Such a tiny particle has an interface that separates it from the parent matrix. It grows by transfer of atoms across its interface. The process of formation of the first stable tiny particle is called nucleation. And the process of increase in the sizes of these particles is called grain growth .The grain size in the product phase depends on the relative rates of nucleation and grain growth. Each nucleating particle becomes a grain in the final product. So a high nucleation rate means a larger number of grains. Also, when this is combined with a low growth rate, more time is available for further nucleation to take place in the parent phase that lies between slowly growing particles. A combination of high nucleation rate with low growth rate yields a fine grain size. On the other hand, a low nucleation rate combined with a high growth rate yields a coarse grain size. The temperature of maximum rate of nucleation is lower than that of maximum growth rate. An increase in cooling rate lowers the effective transformation temperature and results in the combination of high nucleation rate and a relatively slow growth rate and yields a fine grain size.

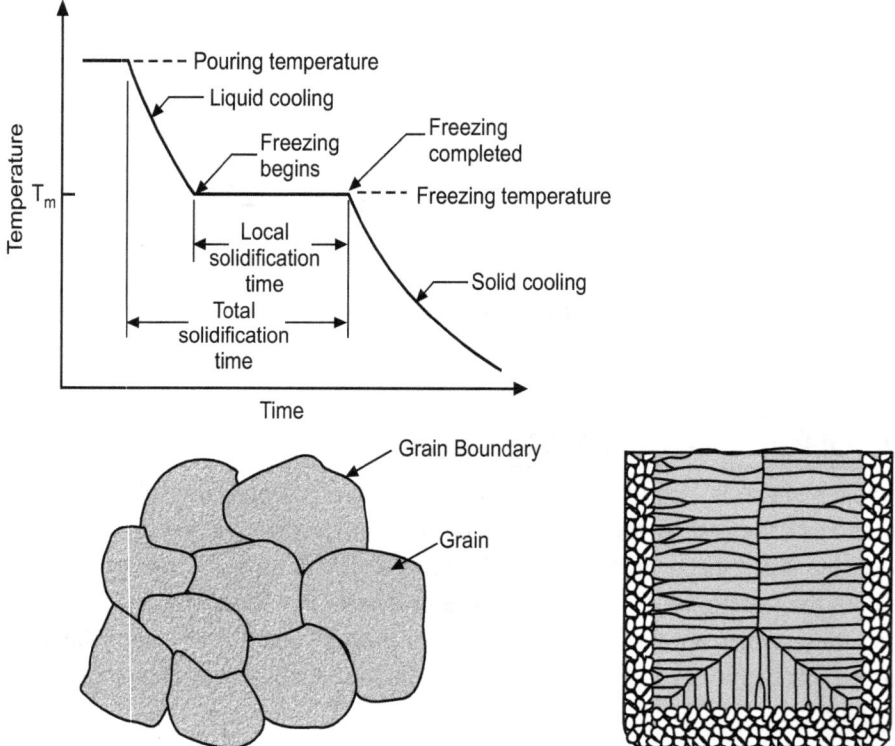

Fig. 2.42 : Nucleation and Grain Growth

Because a pure metal or eutectic alloy has a clearly defined melting or freezing point, it solidifies at a constant temperature. After the temperature of the molten metal drops to its freezing point, its temperature remains constant while the latent heat of fusion is given off. The solidification front (solid-liquid interface) moves through the molten metal solidifying from the mould walls in toward the centre. Once solidification has taken place at any point, cooling resumes. The above Figure of Cooling curve for metal solidified metal, called casting, is taken out of the mould and is allowed to cool to ambient temperature. At the mould walls, which are at ambient temperature, the metal cools rapidly. Rapid cooling produces a solidified skin or shell. The grains grow in a direction opposite to that of the heat transfer through the mould. Those grains that have favorable orientation will grow preferentially and are called columnar grains.

As the driving force of the heat transfer is reduced away from the mould walls, the grains become equiaxed and coarse. Those grains that have substantially different orientations are blocked from further growth. This grain development is called homogeneous nucleation, meaning that grains grow upon themselves, starting from the mould wall.

2.11 CONTROL OF SOLIDIFICATION FOR OBTAINING SOUND CASTINGS

The solidification which starts from the mould wall toward the centre line of the cavity is called Lateral or Progressive Solidification. The longitudinal or Directional Solidification occurs at right angles to lateral solidification at the centre line and is shown in the Fig. 2.43. The casting shown is a simple bar or plate and the metal is a pure metal, or a skin forming alloy. Fig. 2.43 Solidification of a plate In order to obtain a sound casting with no shrinkage void along the centerline, two requirements must be satisfied as follows:

1. The longitudinal solidification must be progressive toward the riser from the point, or points, most distant from the riser.
2. The temperature gradient, in addition to being properly directed, must be sufficiently steep so that liquid metal can pass through the wedge-shaped channel to compensate for shrinkage as it occurs at the centerline.

If the temperature gradient is not sufficiently steep, the included angle of the wedge-shaped channel will be too small and proper passage of feed metal is not possible. If there were no temperature gradient, the lateral solidification at all points would reach the centerline at the same time.

The result in either case is a lack of metal at the centerline, which causes an elongated narrow void known as centerline shrinkage. In other casting sections, voids of various shapes are caused by the shrinkage of skin forming type of alloy.

Solidification of Alloys :

Solidification in alloys begins when the temperature drops below the liquidus temperature and is complete when it reaches the solidus temperature. Within this temperature range, the alloy is in a mushy or pasty state with columnar dendrites. The mushy zone is described in terms of a temperature difference, known as the freezing range, as follows: Freezing Range = TL – TS.

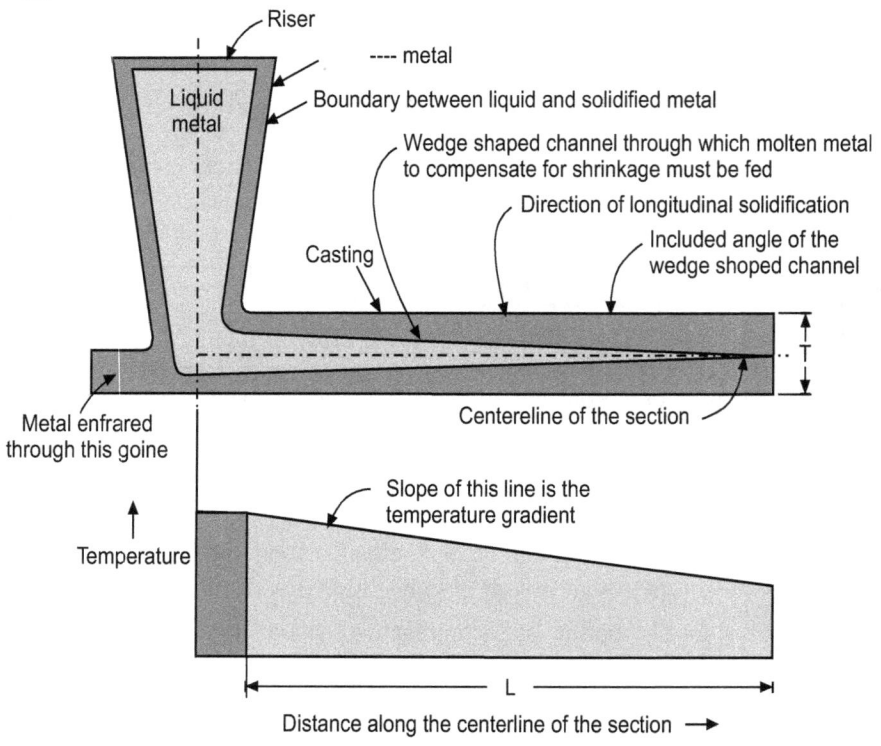

Fig. 2.43 Control of solidification

The control of solidification of alloys which solidify throughout a temperature range is more complicated. It has been determined that steeper temperature gradients with these alloys produce sounder castings. Let us consider the entire casting and riser consist of mushy alloy for a period of time. During the early stage, the mushy alloy is quite fluid, and there is no problem. Then the solid dendrites gradually become thicker, surrounded by only a small amount of liquid metal. At this stage, whole sections may move to accomplish what is known as mass feeding.

Later near the end of solidification, the mushy alloy becomes rigid, so it will be no longer move as a body. Some liquid metal still surrounds some dendrites, but since it is practically impossible to supply feed metal through the narrow passageways, small voids in the form of porosity are formed. This is known as shrinkage porosity or micro shrinkage and it is dispersed throughout Fig. 2.44 : Solidification of alloy the metal in which the temperature gradient is not sufficiently steep.

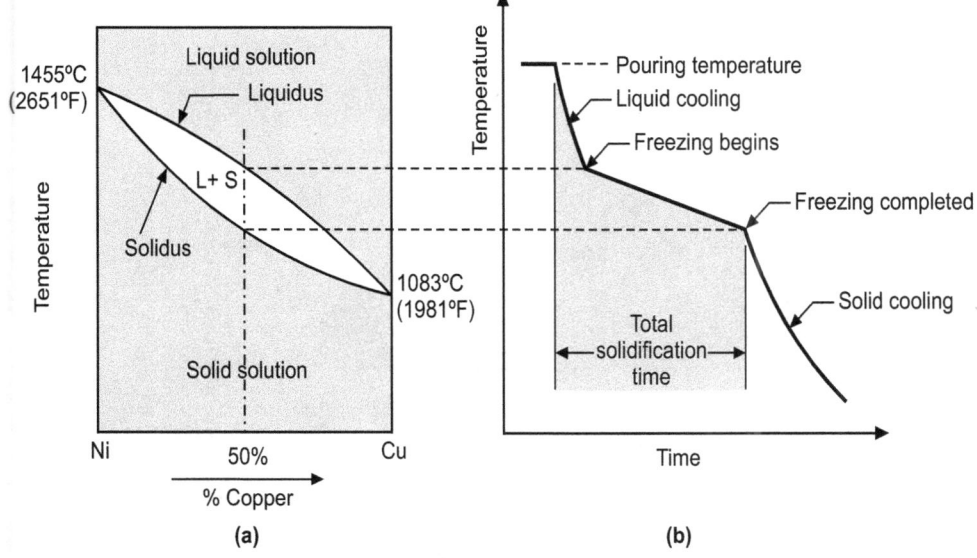

Fig. 2.44 : Solidification of alloy

Riser Feeding or Centerline Feeding Distance For steel castings, a riser as shown in figure will promote proper solidification if the distance L is no greater than 4.5 times the minimum thickness T. This maximum distance for L is known as the feeding distance for the riser. An effective metal chill located at the end most distant from the riser has been found to add about 50 mm to the riser feeding distance.

Centerline Feeding Resistance :

Fig 2.45 : Freezing pattern

The freezing patterns of a chilled and an ordinary mould are shown in Fig. 1.46 (a). The solidification starts at the centre line of the mould before the solidification is completed even at the mould Face. In the chilled mould, on the other hand, due to rapid heat extraction, a narrow liquid zone quickly sweeps across the molten metal. The difficulty of feeding a given alloy in a mould is expressed by a quantity, called centre line feeding resistance (CFR).

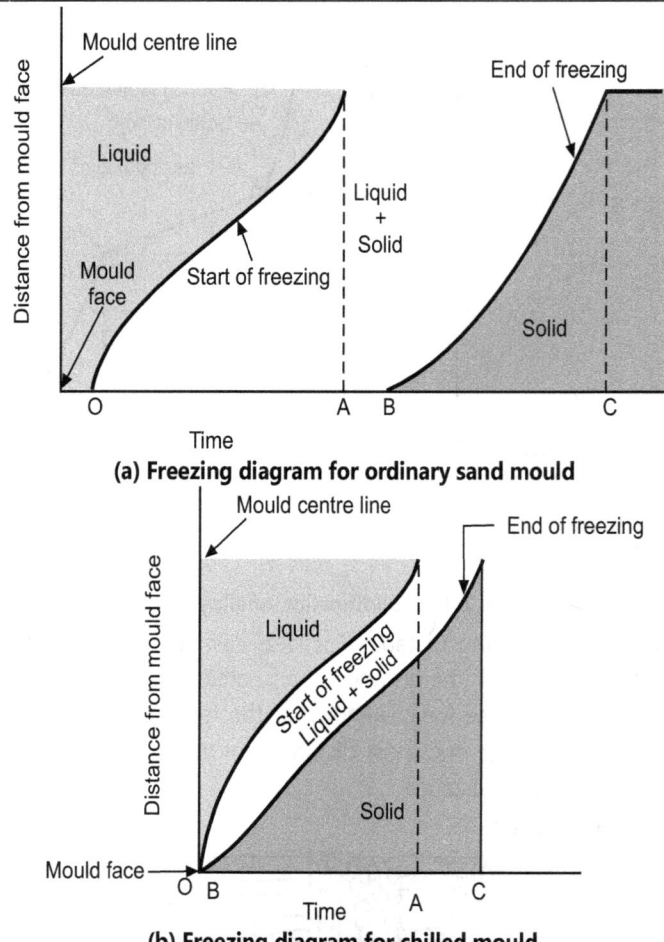

Fig. 2.46 freezing pattern for various mould

Normally, feeding is considered to be difficult if CFR > 70 %.

2.11.1 Chills

These are provided in the mould so as to increase the heat extraction capability of the sand mould. A chill normally provides a steeper temperature gradient so that directional solidification as required in a casting is obtained. These are metallic objects having a higher heat absorbing capability than the sand mould. The chills can be of two types: external and internal. The external chills are placed adjoining the mould cavity at any required position. Providing a chill at the edge may not normally have the desired effect as the temperature gradient is steeper at the end of the casting since heat is removed from all sides. However, if it is placed between two risers it would have maximum effect. The chills when placed in the mould should be clean and dry, otherwise gas inclusions be left in the castings. Also, after placing the chills in the mould, they should not be kept for long since moisture may condense on the chills causing blow holes in the casting. The internal chills are placed inside the mould cavity where an external chill cannot be provided. The material of chill should approximately resemble the composition of the pouring metal for proper fusing. Cleanliness of the internal chills is far more important because they are surrounded on all sides by the molten metal.

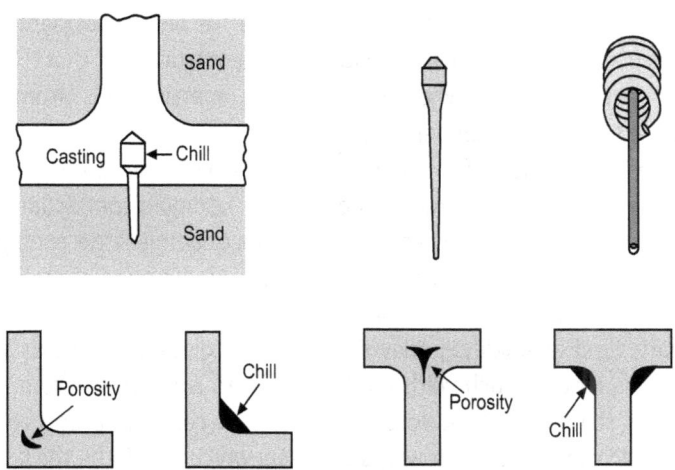

Fig. 2.47 : Types of chills

2.11.2 Chaplets

Chaplets are metallic support often kept inside the mould cavity to support the cores. These are of the same composition as that of the pouring metal so that the molten metal would provide enough heat to completely melt them and thus fuse with it during solidification.

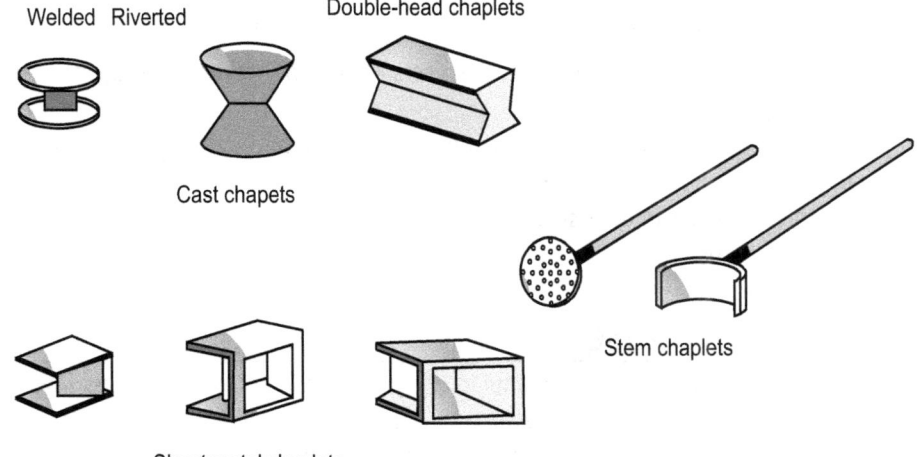

Fig. 2.48 : Types of chaplets

2.12 DIRECTIONAL SOLIDIFICATION

The molten metal in the mould as it cools down, solidifiers and contacts in volume. This metal contraction takes place in three stages: liquid, solidification and solid.
- Liquid contraction occurs when the molten metal's cools from the temperature at which it is poured to the temperature at which solidification just commences.
- Solidification contraction: occurs during the time the change of state from liquid to solid takes place, i. e. When the metal loses its latent heat.
- Solid contraction: occurs when the solidified metals cools from the freezing temperature to the room temperature.

Out of above three contractions for rising purpose, the last one is compensated by the contraction allowance of the pattern maker. The first one, i.e. liquid contractions are generally negligible. But the second one, i.e. the solidification contraction is large enough and should be considered during designing and positioning of risers. All the parts of casting do not cool at the same rate due to varying section, varying rate of heat loss to adjoining mould walls etc. So, some parts tend to solidify quickly than others. It gives rise to voids and cavities in certain regions of the casting. Such voids are filled up with liquid metal from the portion of the casting which is still liquid. Thus, solidification should continue progressively from the thinnest sections which solidifies first towards the risers which should be the last solidify. The casting will be sound, without voids or internal shrinkage, if the solidification occurs in the above fashion; this process is known as directional solidification, which is aimed at for producing sound casting. It may not always be easy to achieve directional solidification in actual casting practice due to the factors like method of casting used, the shape and design of the cast etc. In a general, the following ways are adapted for a controlling directional solidification:
- The gating system should be designed at positioned properly.
- Chills in the moulds may be used the risers should be designed and positioned properly.
- The thickness of certain sections of the casting may be increased by the use of padding.
- Exothermic materials in the risers or in the facing sand around certain portions of the casting may be used.

2.13 CASTING PROCESSES

Casting is the most important and old manufacturing process. The casting process involves pouring of liquid metal in to a mould cavity and allowing it to solidify to obtain the final casting. The flow of molten metal into the mould cavity depends on following factors minimum section thickness of the part, corners in parts, non-uniform cross-section of the cast. The fig 2.48 shows the classification of casting processes.

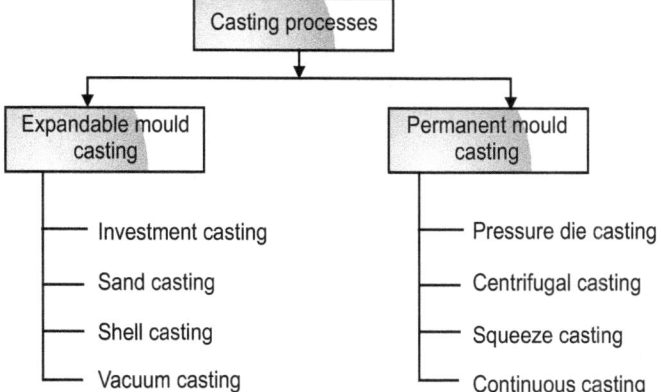

Fig 2.49 : Classification of casting processes

2.13.1 Expendable Mould Casting

The expendable mould casting types are sand, plastic, shell, plaster, and investment (lost-wax technique) moulds. All these methods use temporary, non-reusable moulds. After the molten metal in the mould cavity solidifies, the mould is broken to take out the solidified cast. This process is suitable for very complex shaped parts and materials with high melting point temperature. However, the rate of production is often limited by the time to make mould rather than the casting itself. Following are a few examples of expendable mould casting processes.

2.13.1.1 Investment Casting

Investment casting is also known as lost-wax casting since the pattern is made of wax as a material. The wax patterns are first dipped into slurry of refractory material. Then heated so that the wax melts away keeping a refractory mould. The mould is then further cured to achieve proper strength. Very high melting temperature material can be cast in investment casting process because of the refractory mould. Figure 2.50 shows steps in investment casting process.

The molten metal is poured into the mould and is taken out after solidification by breaking the mould. Very high dimensional accuracy and surface finish can be achieved in investment casting process.

However, the tooling cast is usually high and hence, investment casting process is primarily used for large size batch production or for specific requirements of complex shape or casting of very high melting temperature material.

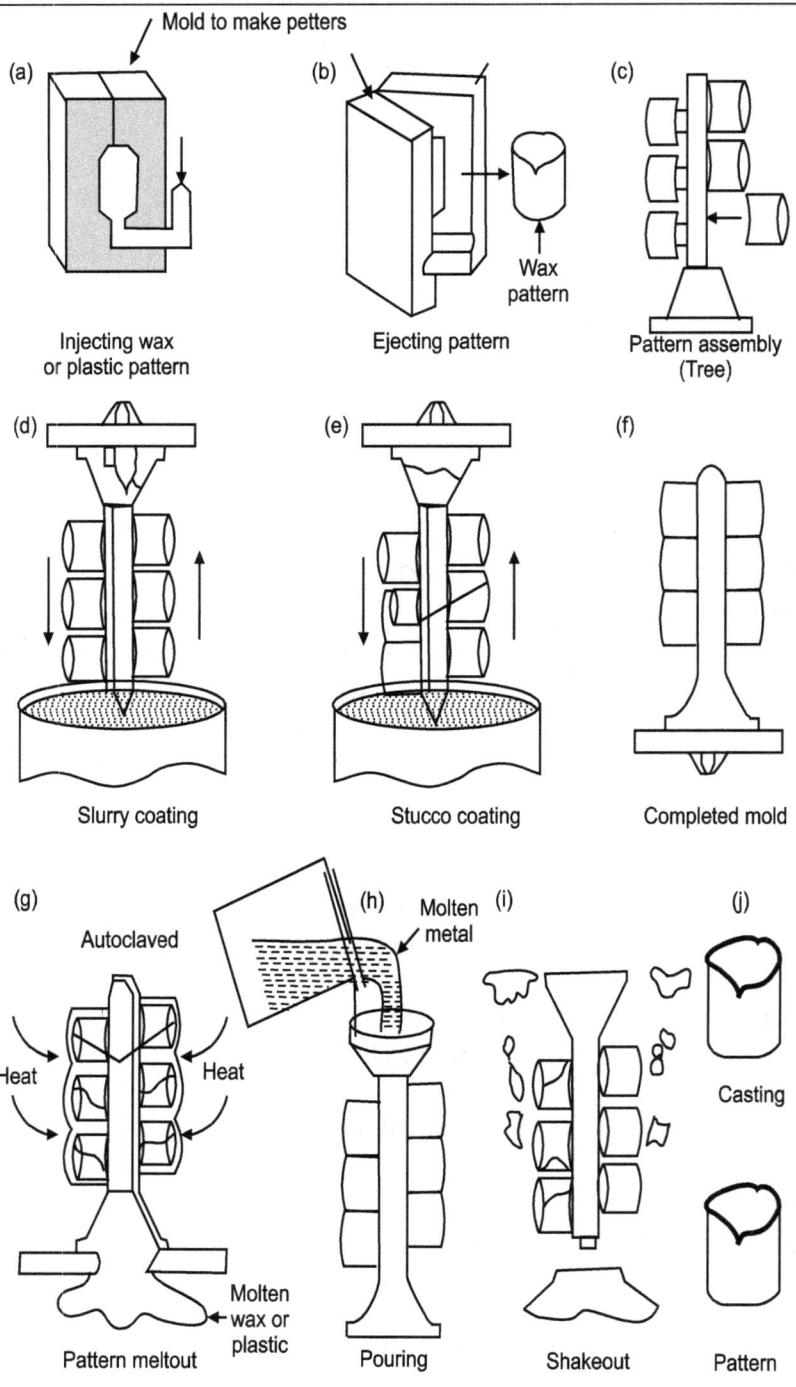

Fig 2.50 : Steps in Investment casting process

2.13.1.2 Sand Casting

Sand casting is widely used for because of the simplicity in working of the process. The sand casting process involves basic steps such as place a wooden or metallic pattern in sand to create a mould, fit in the pattern and sand in a gating system, remove the pattern, fill the mould cavity with molten metal, and allow the metal to cool, and break the sand mould and remove the casting. It is usually economical for small batch size production. The quality of the sand casting depends on the quality and uniformity of green sand material that is used for making the mould. Fig. 2.51 shows a two-part sand mould, also referred to as a cope-and-drag sand mould. The molten metal is poured through the pouring cup and it fills the mould cavity after passing through downsprue, runner and gate. The core refers to loose pieces which are placed inside the mould cavity to create internal holes or open section. The riser serves as a reservoir of excess molten metal that facilitates additional filling of mould cavity to compensate for volumetric shrinkage during solidification. Sand castings process provides several advantages. It can be employed for all types of metal. The tooling cost is low and can be used to cast very complex shapes. However sand castings offer poor dimensional accuracy and surface finish as compare to other casting processes.

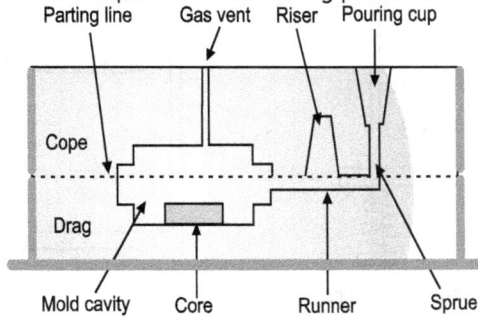

Fig. 2.51 : Sand Casting Process

2.13.1.3 Shell Moulding

Shell moulding is near about same as sand casting. In this process grey cast iron and aluminium pattern materials are widely used. The pattern is heated to 2500°C to 2600°C and the sand resin mixture is poured over pattern. The heated pattern melts the resin creating bonds between the sand grains. After a dwell period the pattern and sand inverted and extra sand is cleaned off. The mould cavity is now formed by a hardened shell of sand. The mould is then heated in an oven for further curing. The shell thus formed constitutes one half of the mould. Two such halves are placed over one another to make the complete mould. The sands used in shell moulding process are usually finer than the same used in sand casting. This process is ideal for complex shaped medium sized parts. Figure 2.52 represents the steps of shell mould casting. This method can be employed for making an integrate shapes, thin and sharp corners small projection which are not possible in green sand mould. Machining operation reduced due to more dimensional accuracy in produced component.

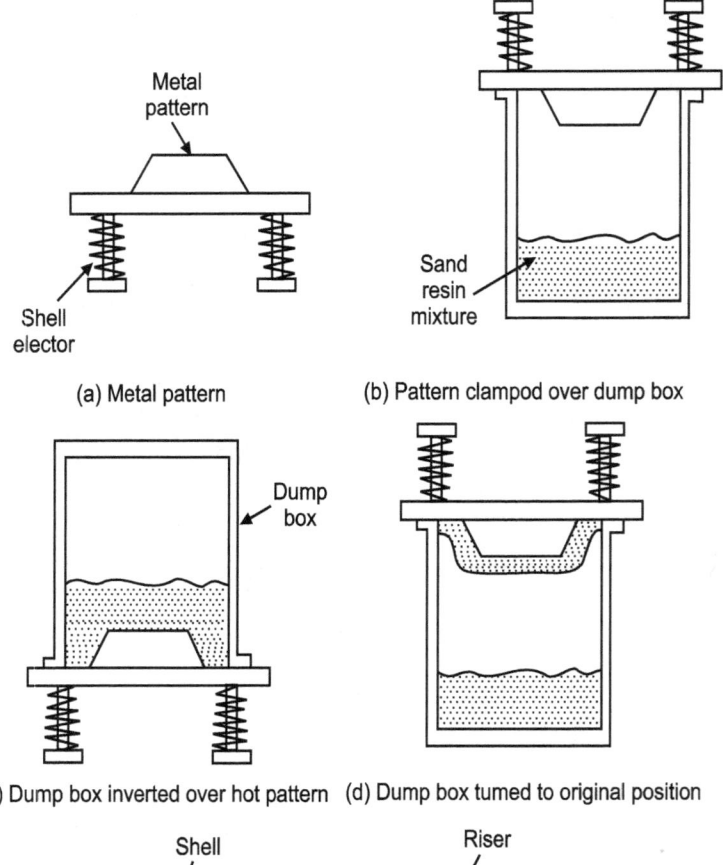

(a) Metal pattern   (b) Pattern clampod over dump box

(c) Dump box inverted over hot pattern   (d) Dump box turned to original position

(e) Shell stripped from the pattern   (f) Shell assembly

Fig. 2.52 : Shell mould casting

2.13.1.4 Vacuum Casting

The Fig. 2.53 shows typical vacuum casting process. In this process, a mixture of fine sand and urethane is moulded over metal dies and cured with amino vapor. The molted metal is drawn into the mould cavity through a gating system from the bottom of the mould. The pressure inside the mould is usually one-third of the atmospheric pressure. Because the mould cavity is filled under vacuum, the vacuum casting process is very suitable for thin walled, complex shapes with uniform properties.

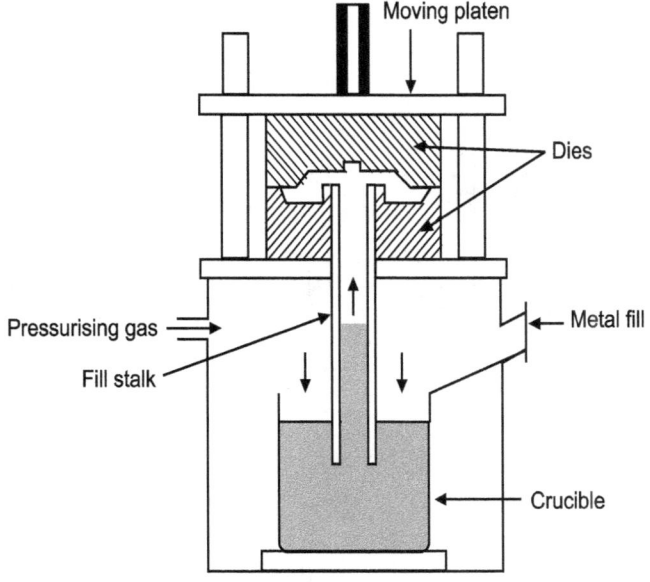

Fig. 2.53 : Vacuum Casting

2.13.2 Permanent Mould Casting Processes

The permanent mould casting processes broadly include pressure die casting, centrifugal casting, squeeze casting and continuous casting. Permanent mould casting processes involve the use of metallic dies that are permanent in nature and can be used repeatedly. The metal moulds are also called dies and provide superior surface finish and close tolerance than typical sand moulds.

2.13.2.1 Pressures Die Casting

The fig 2.54 shows the hot-chamber and the cold-chamber die casting processes The pressure die casting process is the most common for aluminium , Zinc and magnesium castings (low melting point). The liquid metal is injected into the mould under high pressure and allowed to solidify at the high pressure. The solidified cast is then taken out of the mould or the die which is ready for the next cast. Pressure die casting is suitable for large batch size production. Two types of pressure die casting are generally common in the industry high pressure die casting and low pressure die casting. Very high production rates can be achieved in pressure die casting process with close dimensional control of the casting. However, the process is not suitable for casting of high melting temperature materials as the die material has to withstand the melting (or superheated) temperature of the casting.

Pressure die castings also contain porosity due to the entrapped air. Furthermore, the dies in the pressure die casting process are usually very costly. In the hot-chamber die casting process, the furnace to melt material is part of the die itself and hence, this process is suitable primarily for low-melting point temperature materials such as aluminium, magnesium etc.

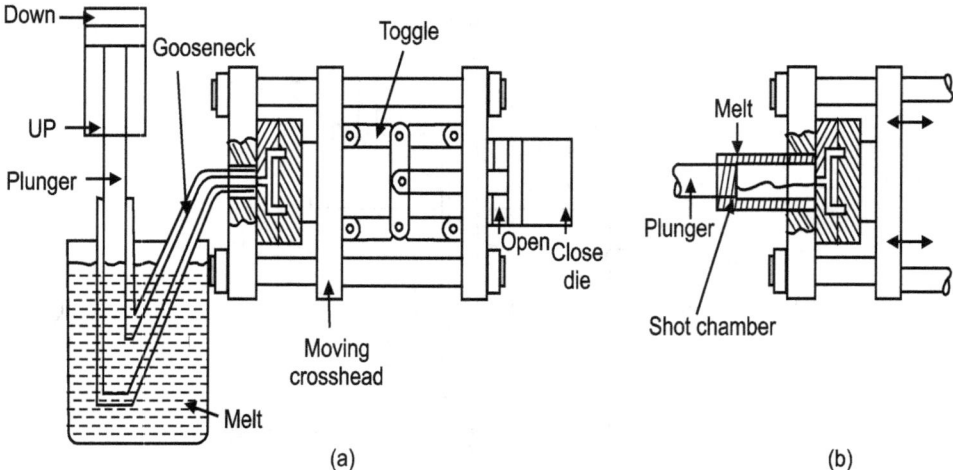

Fig. 2.54 : Die castings (a) hot-chamber and (b) cold-chamber die casting processes

2.13.2.2 Centrifugal Casting

In centrifugal casting process, the molten metal poured at the center of a rotating mould or die. Because of the centrifugal force, the lighter impurities are crowded towards the center of the case.

For producing a hollow part, the axis of rotation is placed at the center of the desired casting. The speed of rotation is maintained high so as to produce a centripetal acceleration of the order of 60g to 75g.

The centrifuge action segregates the less dense non-metallic inclusions near to the center of rotation that can be removed by machining a thin layer.

No cores are therefore required in casting of hollow parts although solid parts can also be cast by this process. The centrifugal casting is very suitable for axisymmetric parts. Very high strength of the casting can be obtained.

Since the molten metal is fed by the centrifugal action, the need for complex metal feeding system is eliminated. Both horizontal and vertical centrifugal castings are widely used in the industry. Fig 2.54 schematically shows a set-up for horizontal centrifugal casting process.

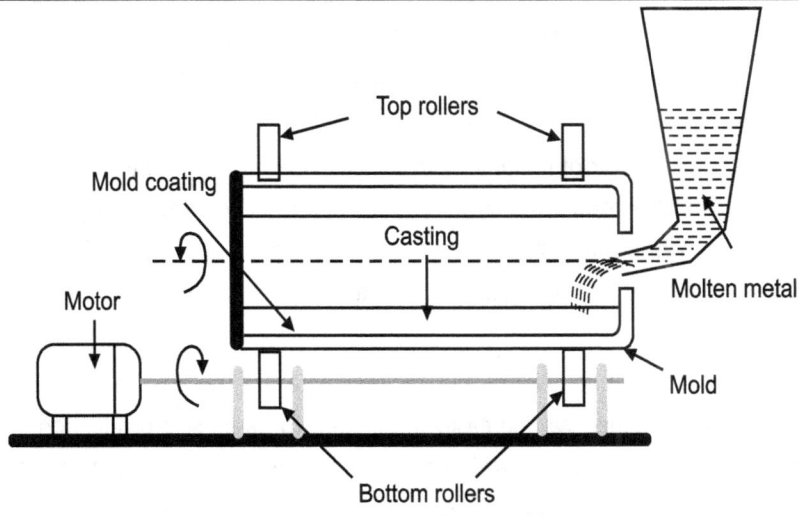

Fig. 2.55 : Centrifugal Casting

2.13.2.3 Squeeze Casting

Molten metal is poured into a metallic mould or die cavity with one-half of the die squeezing the molten metal to fill in the intended cavity under pressure as shown in Fig. 2.56. Fiber reinforced casting with SiC or Al2O3 fibers mixed in metal matrix have been successfully squeeze cast and commercially used to produce automobile pistons. However, squeeze casting is limited only to shallow part or part with smaller dimensions.

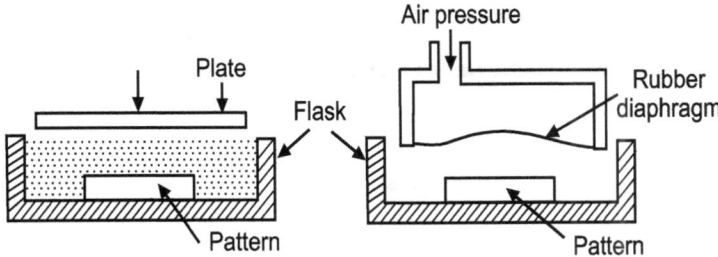

Fig. 2.56 : Squeeze Casting

2.13.2.4 Continuous Casting

The continuous casting is different from the other casting processes in the fact that there is no enclosed mould cavity used during process. Fig. 2.57 schematically shows a set-up for continuous casting process.

Continuous casting process is widely used in the steel industry. Molten steel coming out from the furnace is accumulated in a ladle. After undergoing requisite ladle treatments, such as alloying and degassing, and arriving at the correct temperature, the ladle is transported to the top of the continuous casting set-up. From the ladle, the hot metal is transferred via a refractory shroud (pipe) to a holding bath called a tundish.

The tundish allows a reservoir of metal to feed the casting machine. Metal is then allowed to pass through a open base copper mould. The mould is water-cooled to solidify the hot metal directly in contact with it and removed from the other side of the mould. The continuous casting process is used for casting metal directly into billets or other similar shapes that can be used for rolling.

The process involves continuously pouring molten metal into a externally chilled copper mould or die walls and hence, can be easily automated for large size production. Since the molten metal solidifies from the die wall and in a soft state as it comes out of the die wall such that the same can be directly guided into the rolling mill or can be sheared into a selected size of billets.

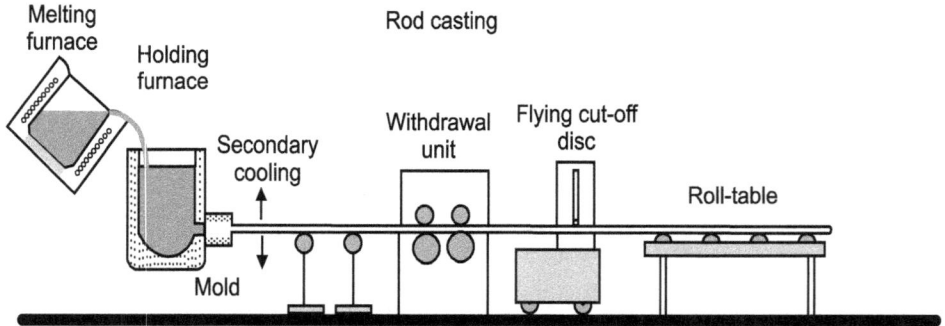

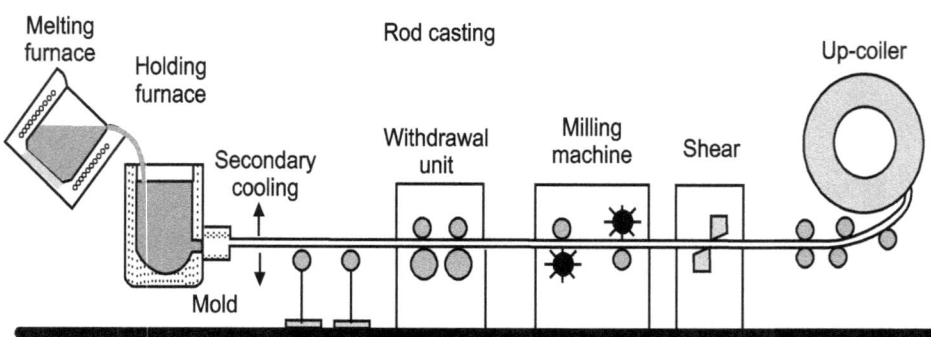

Fig. 2.57 : Continuous Casting Process

QUESTIONS

1. What is the special sand used in foundries?
2. State the properties of good moulding sand.
3. What are the different types of moulding sand?
4. State the classification of moulding methods
5. Draw a neat sketches of moulding equipments and mention their uses
6. What are the moulding sand ingredients
7. Explain sand preparation in detail
8. What are the different types of sand tests
9. What is gate? What is a gating system?
10. Distinguish between hand moulding and machine moulding
11. What are chaplets
12. Define permeability number
13. Mention the difference between green sand mould and dry sand mould.
14. State the disadvantages of casting process.
15. What is die casting
16. Explain any two solidification control devices.
17. What is core
18. What are the different type of core making machine
19. Explain in detail design consideration in casting
20. What is the need for providing chills in casting
21. State importance of directional solidification in casting
22. What is riser?
23. What are important elements in riser system

24. Explain in detail pressure die casting
25. Explain the working of centrifugal casting and state its application
26. What is shell moulding
27. What is the working of principle of continuous casting
28. What is the working of principle of squeeze casting
29. What is the working of principle of permanent mould casting,

Unit - III

MELTING AND POURING

3.1 CASTING FURNACES

There are several types of casting furnaces which include Electric Arc furnaces, Blast furnaces, Cornwall Iron Furnace, etc. The electric arc furnace can be described as a furnace heating charged materials by the way of an electric arc. The Blast Furnace can be referred to as a kind of metallurgical furnace, through which the process of smelting takes place.

Blast Furnaces produce metals, normally iron. These furnaces trace their origin to China (around 500 BC). Electric Arc furnaces exist in all the sizes-right, from the smallest one having a capacity of around 1 ton to the largest one having a capacity of 400 tons. The former one is used in foundries to produce cast iron products, whereas the latter one is used for secondary steel making.

3.1.1 Types of Casting Furnaces

In Metal Casting, the type of furnace you have at your foundry, or workshop determines a lot of the work you can or cannot do. Many metal casters enjoy making their own furnaces and have done so quite successfully. The plans for home made furnaces are eagerly shared among the enthusiasts so finding blueprints and instructions should not be difficult. But before you rush off to find the blueprints you may want to take time to learn about the types of casting furnaces available to help determine which one will suit your needs. This is not saying that you should only have one furnace at any given time, but this way you will know what project will work best for which furnace.

(1) Cupola Furnace :

Cupola furnaces are among the most popular with backyard foundries. Many casters construct their own cupola which proves to be cost effective and highly efficient if done properly. Since cupola furnaces can achieve high melting temperatures they are primarily used for the melting of iron and bronze, though aluminum can also be melted when attention is paid to keeping the temperature low. The primary fuel sources for cupola furnaces are coke using limestone for flux.

With most small home foundries, the cupola furnaces are preferred over that of other furnaces for its high melting rates and for how easily the construction of such a furnace can be. For many years, the cupola was the primary method of melting used in iron foundries. The cupola furnace has several unique characteristics which are responsible for its widespread use as a melting unit for cast iron.

The cupola is one of the only methods of melting which is continuous in its operation:
- High melt rates
- Relatively low operating costs
- Ease of operation

In more recent times, the use of the cupola has declined in favour of electric induction melting, which offers more precise control of melt chemistry and temperature, and much lower levels of emissions.

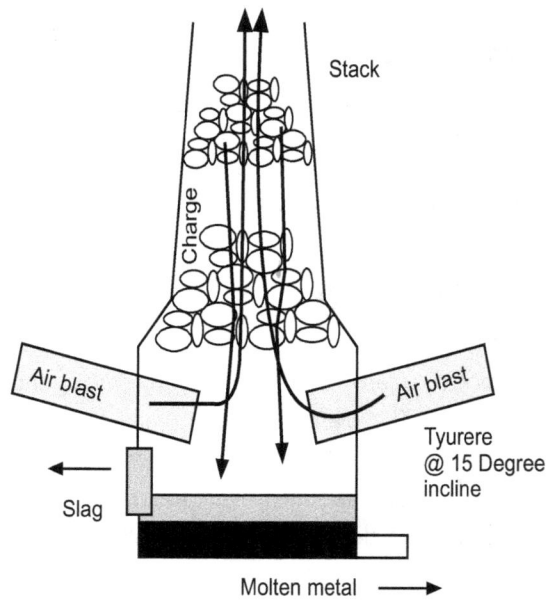

Fig. 3.1 : Basic cupola

The construction of a conventional cupola consists of a vertical steel shell which is lined with a refractory brick. The charge is introduced into the furnace body by means of an opening approximately half way up the vertical shaft. The charge consists of alternate layers of the metal to be melted, coke fuel and limestone flux. The fuel is burnt in air which is introduced through tuyeres positioned above the hearth. The hot gases generated in the lower part of the shaft ascend and preheat the descending charge.

Most cupolas are of the drop bottom type with hinged doors under the hearth, which allows the bottom to drop away at the end of melting to aid cleaning and repaires. At the bottom front is a tap-hole for the molten iron at the rear, positioned above the tap-hole is a slag-hole. The top of the stack is capped with a spark/fume arrester hood.

Typical internal diameters of cupolas are 450 mm to 2000 mm diameter which can be operated on different fuel to metal ratios, giving melt rates of approximately 1 to 30 tonnes per hour. The constructional details and working of cupola furnace are given below:

- A typical cupola melting furnace (See Fig. 3.2) consists of a water-cooled vertical cylinder which is lined with refractory material. The process is as follows :
- The charge, consisting of metal, alloying ingredients, limestone, and coal coke for fuel and carbonisation (8-16% of the metal charge), is fed in alternating layers through an opening in the cylinder.
- Air enters the bottom through tuyeres extending a short distance into the interior of the cylinder. The air inflow often contains enhanced oxygen levels.
- Coke is consumed. The hot exhaust gases rise up through the charge, preheating it. This increases the energy efficiency of the furnace. The charge drops and is melted.

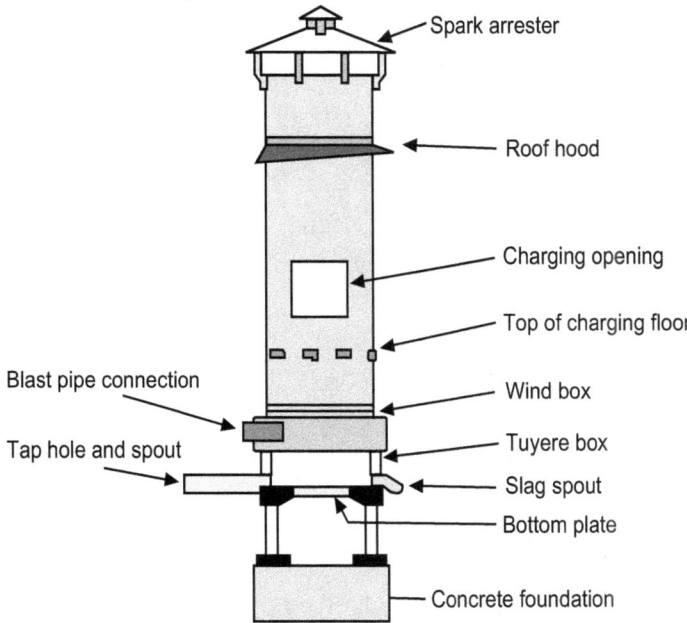

Fig. 3.2: Cupola Furnace

- Although air is fed into the furnace, the environment is a reducing one. Burning of coke under reducing conditions raises the carbon content of the metal charge to the casting specifications.
- As the material is consumed, additional charges can be added to the furnace.
- A continuous flow of iron emerges from the bottom of the furnace.
- Depending on the size of the furnace, the flow rate can be as high as 100 tonnes per hour. As the metal melts, it is refined to some extent, which removes contaminants. This makes this process more suitable than electric furnaces for dirty charges.
- A hole higher than the tap allows slag to be drawn off.

- The exhaust gases emerge from the top of the cupola. Emission control technology is used to treat the emissions to meet environmental standards.
- Hinged doors at the bottom allow the furnace to be emptied when not in use.

Advantages of Cupola Furnace

- The cupola furnace has received a lot of negative publicity in recent years. However, the system does have a number of inherent advantages over electric furnaces :
- It is simple and economical to operate.
- A cupola is capable of accepting a wide range of materials without reducing melt quality. Dirty, oily scrap can be melted as well as a wide range of steel and iron. They therefore play an important role in the metal recycling industry.
- Cupolas can refine the metal charge, removing impurities out of the slag.
- From a life-cycle perspective, cupolas are more efficient and less harmful to the environment than electric furnaces. This is because they derive energy directly from coke rather than from electricity that first has to be generated.
- The continuous rather than batch process suits the demands of a repetition foundry.
- Cupolas can be used to reuse foundry by-products and to destroy other pollutants such as VOC from the core-making area.

(2) Reverberatory Furnace :

The Reverberatory Furnaces are commonly found in industrial plants but there have been quite a number of home grown foundries that have used this furnace type with much success. The basic idea of a Reverberatory Furnace is to use the heat reflecting off a surface, usually brick, to heat the metal, which is aluminium in most cases. This way, the metal does not come into contact with the fuel or the flame. This process is also used in Puddling Furnaces. The name Reverberatory and Puddling are often used interchangeably. By placing the metal in a shallow depression and then directing an intense flame over that depression and to the wall, the heat rebounds to melt the metal. Many casters will adjust the length of the flame since a longer path will mean that the heat will be more intense.

There are many designs for the reverberatory furnace, all of which will include exhaust ports and the rear of the furnace must be able to withstand the intense heat and be able to bounce it back into the chamber.

Bronze, aluminium, tin, and many other ores can be melted in a reverberatory furnace all depending on the construction of the actual furnace and the heat of the flame. This type of furnace has been around since at least the Middle Ages and was used primarily for bronze work. To the right is my interpretation of a Dry-Hearth Sloping Reverb Furnace. Reverbs are typically found in High production Aluminium foundries. They can be fired either with Gas, Oil, Electricity or a combination of the three.

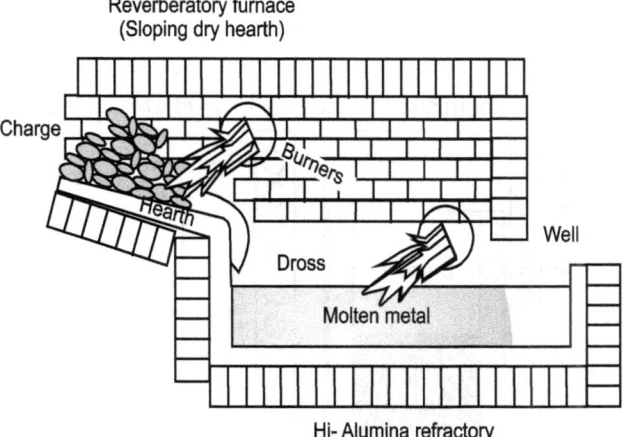

Fig. 3.3 : Reverberatory furnace (Sloping Dry Hearth)

Advantages are High capacity, continuous runs, with issues resulting from gas pick-up and excessive dross formation due to the exposed flame on the charge. There are number of various orientations and styles of reverbs.

(3) Electric Arc :

Electric Arc furnaces are normally used in Industrial foundries. Most hobby casters do not use these furnaces due to cost, space issues, and a general inconvenience. There are two forms of the electric arc furnace, the direct and indirect. The direct arc has three electrodes which are used to heat metal by way of the arc. This creates an incredible amount of heat and so water jackets and other cooling devices will be needed for operation. The indirect arc just uses one electrode and works in much the same way as the direct arc furnace.

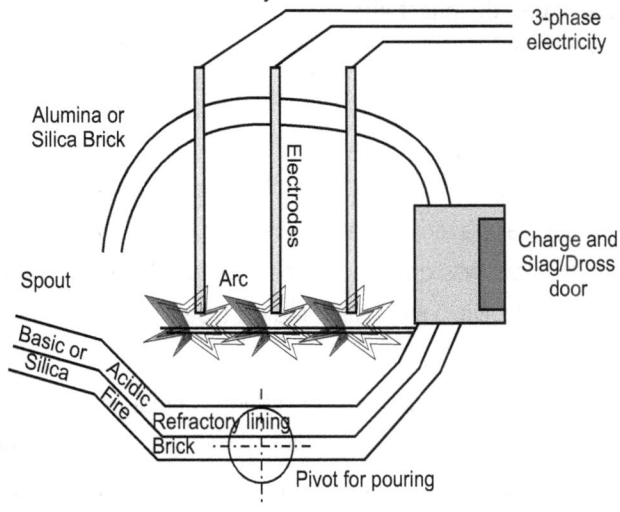

Fig. 3.4 : Arc furnace

(4) Electric Induction :

Electric Induction furnaces are becoming all the more popular with large industrial size foundries that enjoy the clean burning and efficiency of an electrical furnace.

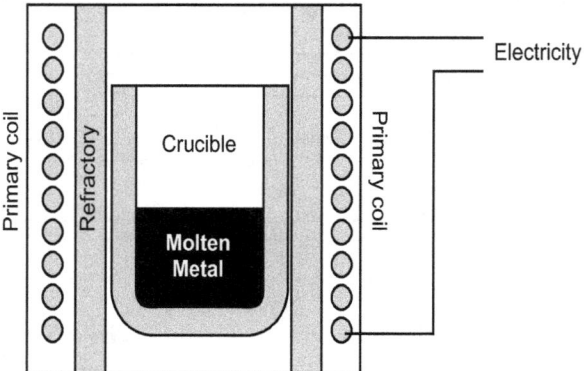

Fig. 3.5: Coreless induction furnace

Copper coils surround the crucible with the metal inside which can reach extremely high temperature suitable for melting most metals.

(5) Rotary Furnace :

The Rotary style furnaces are hailed for their ease of use being fully or at the very least partially automatic. These furnaces tend to be harder to construct though there are resources and companies online that sell rotary furnace.

The different furnace types do affect the quality of the work being produced, so it is important to keep that in mind as you cast. With a little trial and error, you should find the perfect furnace to fit your needs so you can start building one of your very own.

(6) Crucible Furnace :

The earliest forms of clay vessel for holding molten metal's were similar to the crucible currently used. This vessel was placed in a pit dug into the ground; wood was packed around the crucible and ignited. Draft was provided by bellows or chimney to burn the wood and melt the metal in the crucible. Fig. 3.6 is a standard pit type furnace; several crucibles can be placed in a single pit.

Today coke, oil, or gas can be used as fuel. For different metal like ferrous metal and cast iron, required coke fire units with varying melting time period. No expensive chimney is needed for draft, and crucible handling is easier and safer as compared to other furnaces. The fig 3.6 shows different type of crucible furnaces used in foundry.

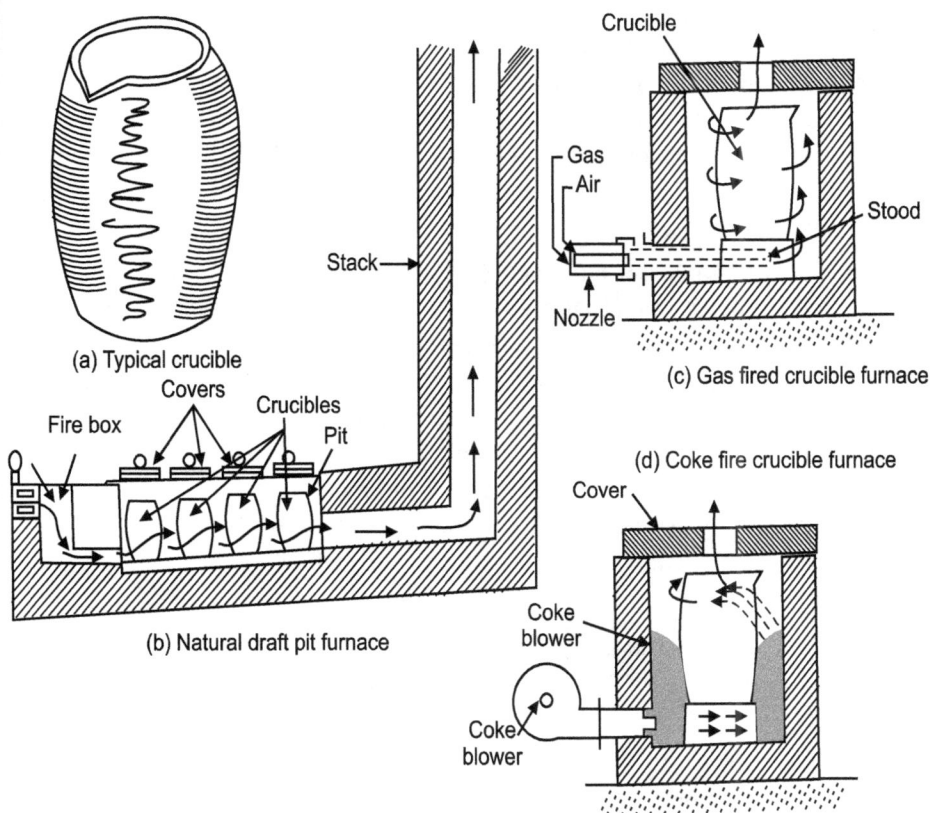

Fig. 3.6 : Crucible Furnaces

3.2 METALLURGICAL CONTROL IN FURNACE

The quality of the casting depends on mechanical properties of the metal cavity for that the important aspect is metallurgical control. The charging materials used in furnaces are metal, alloying elements, and various other materials such as flux and slag formation constituents. Fluxes perform various functions for different materials, like a barrier to oxidation for aluminum alloys, lining material in induction furnace. The surface of the molten metal against atmospheric reaction and contamination protection, and to refine the melt, the metal must be insulated against heat loss. A slag formation is take place when insulation is provided be covering the surface or mixing the melt with compounds. A small amount of molten metal is tapped and analyzed, if addition or inoculation is required then made before pouring the metal into the molds. To obtain desired composition in cavity, pure alloying elements are added to the charge.

3.3 AUTOMATED POURING SYSTEM

Recently most of the manufacturing industrial approaches the automated system for the production for better quality, faster production rate, less waste and better working condition. Automated pouring system is one of the important sections for casting industries. Automated pouring system work as an interface between mould making and melting. The system maintain exact pouring time into the mould, idle time of the machine never affect the molten metal condition.

Induction is the most economical and suitable method for the molten metal preparation. The induction pouring furnaces, using controlled stopper to pour the molten metal direct into the mould onto intermediate casting ladles, are used for this purpose and these posses the various characteristics. Keep the temperature and chemical composition of the molten metal constant during holding and poring eliminate slag inclusions from the poured molten metal add inoculates and alloying materials at the right time and in exactly measured quantities adjust the pouring rate to the intake capacity of the mould measure the weight of the poured metal exactly and adjust pouring to the mould transport (see Fig. 3.7).

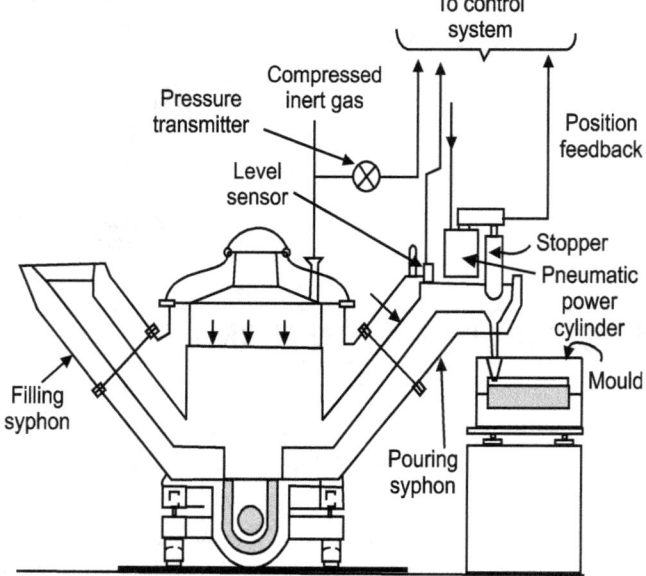

Fig. 3.7 : Automated Pouring System

The pouring furnace consist of a cylindrical shell with refractory lining, pressure sealed cover flanged channel inductor, stopper and a pressure control system. Filling and pouring is through siphon shaped ducts whose bottom ends are located at the base of the furnace, to ensure virtually slag free pouring.

Pressurized gas forces the molten metal into the furnaces pouring nozzle through a stopper. The pressurized gas also keeps the level of the molten metal in the nozzle constant irrespective of varying quantity of metal in the furnace. The rate of metal pouring is controlled by the movement of stopper.

3.4 CASTING DEFECTS

At the time of manufacturing of the components, various defects get developed. Materials, part design and processes techniques such type of factor are responsible for the defects. Some defects affect the aesthetic aspect of the component and some affect the metallurgical aspect of the mould cavity. The International Committee of Foundry Technical Association (ICFTA) has developed a standardized nomenclature for casting defects. The following are the major defects, occur in castings:

Sr. No.	Defect	Diagram
1	**Misrun :** A mis-run defect occurs due to failure of metal to fill the entire mould cavity. A mis-run results when the metal is under low temperature to flow to the extremities of the mold cavity before freezing. Thin sections are subject to this defect and should be avoided in casting design. The mis-run and cold shut defects are caused either by a lower fluidity of the mold or when the section thickness of the casting is very small. Fluidity can be improved by changing the composition of the metal and by increasing the pouring temperature of the metal.	Misrun
2	**Porosity :** This defect developed because of gas formation and absorption by metal at the time of pouring. In some cases the liquid metal solidifies and shrinks between dendrites branches. Metal may dissolve some gas or air from the mould or core faces. The defect cause leaking casings and reduce pressure tightness.	

(Contd.)

3	**Shift :** The mold shift defect occurs when cope and drag or molding boxes have not been properly aligned. It is easy to identify in casting. If the defect reaches the allowable limit, it cannot rectify and then rework is required. Flask. Core and pattern some time creates this defect because of misalignment. Using locating pin for pattern, prints and chaplets for proper alignment of core prevent the shift defect in casting.	
4	**Metal Penetration :** This defect caused when sand has too high permeability. When molten metal enters into the gaps between sand grains, the result is a rough casting surface. This occurs because the sand is coarse or no mold wash was applied on the surface of the mold. The coarser the sand grains more the metal penetration.	
5	**Shrinkage Cavity :** Uncontrolled and haphazard solidification caused void inn depression in casting. To compensate for this, proper feeding of liquid metal is required. For this reason risers are placed at the appropriate places in the mold. Sprues may be too thin, too long or not attached in the proper location, causing shrinkage cavities. It is recommended to use thick sprues to avoid shrinkage cavities.	Shrinkage cavity
6	**Coldshut :** The imperfect fusion of two streams of metal meeting in the mold cavity, do not fuse together properly thus forming a discontinuity in the casting. When the molten metal is poured into the mold cavity through more-than-one gate, multiple liquid fronts will have to flow together and become one solid. If the flowing metal fronts are too cool, they may not flow together, but will leave a seam in the part. Such a seam is called a cold shut, and can be prevented by assuring sufficient superheat in the poured metal and thick enough walls.	Cold shut Core

(Contd.)

7	**Cut and Washes :** These appear as rough spots and areas of excess metal, and are caused by erosion of molding sand by the flowing metal. This is caused by the molding sand not having enough strength and the molten metal flowing at high velocity. The former can be taken care of by the proper choice of molding sand and the latter can be overcome by the proper design of the gating system.	Gate / Wash
8	**Scab:** This defect occurs when a portion of the face of a mould lifts or breaks down and the recess thus made is filled by metal. When the metal is poured into the cavity, gas may be disengaged with such violence as to break up the sand which is then washed away and the resulting cavity filled with metal. The reasons can be: - to fine sand, low permeability of sand, high moisture content of sand and uneven moulds ramming.	Scab
9	**Inclusions :** Particles of slag, refractory materials, sand or deoxidation products are trapped in the casting during pouring solidification. The provision of choke in the gating system and the pouring basin at the top of the mold can prevent this defect.	Dross / Nonmetallic inclusion
10	**Swell :** An enlargement of the mould cavity by pressure resulting in localized casting. Under the influence of metallostatic forces, the mold wall may move back causing a swell in the dimension of the casting. A proper ramming of the mold will correct this defect.	Swett
11	**Dirt :** It is generally in the form of foreign particles and sand embedded on the surface of the casting. It causes for crushing of the mould due to mishandling, sand wash when the metal is poured because of low strength and soft ramming, insufficient fluxing of molten metal, due to its incomplete separation from molten metal.	Dirt

3.5 INSPECTION OF CASTING

The analysis of quality and identification of defect in castings are originator of different methods of inspection. External defect normally indentified by visual inspection and for internal defects nondestructive testing methods are employed. Unexpected or defective castings are rework by remelted and reprocessing operations. The type of defect and their cause investigations are important because of the economic factor of product manufacturing.

3.5.1 Non Destructive Tests

It includes various types of inspection methods for defect in castings. Some methods are very important for internal defect analysis without braking or deformation of part or cavity. The different types of nondestructive tests are as follows:

(1) Visual Inspection :

The surface defects that can be detected provide a means for discovering errors in the pattern equipment or in the molding and casting process. Visual inspection may prove inadequate only in the detection of sub surface or internal defects.

(2) Magnetic Particle Inspection :

Magnetic practical test is used to reveal the location of cracks that extend to the surface of iron or steel castings, which are magnetic nature. The casting is first magnetized and then iron particles are sprinkled all over the path of the magnetic field. The particles align themselves in the direction of the lines of force. A discontinuity in the casting causes the lines of the force to bypass the discontinuity and to concentrate around the extremities of the defect.

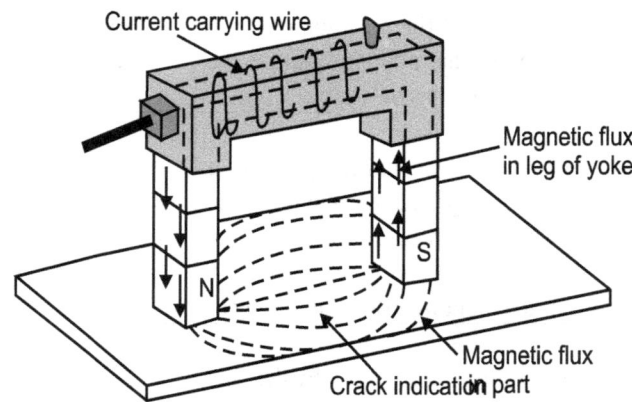

Fig. 3.8 : Magnetic Practical Inspection

(3) Fluorescent Dye-Penetration Test :

Fluorescent dye penetration method is very simple and applied for all cast metals. It entails applying a thin penetration oil-base dye to the surface of the casting and allowing it to stand for some time so that the oil passes into the cracks by means of capillary action. The oil is then thoroughly wiped and cleaned from the surface. To detect the defects, the casting is pained with a coat of whitewash or powdered with talc and then viewed under ultraviolet light. The oil being fluorescent in nature, can be easily detect under this light, and thus the defects are easily revealed.

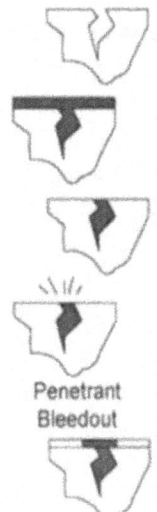

1. Preclean and dry test specimen surface
2. Penetrant application
3. Removal of excess surface penetrant
4. Drying
5. Developer application
6. Inspection
7. Postclean

Fig 3.9 : Fluorescent dye-penetration test

(4) X-Ray Radiography :

Internal defect such as flaw detection test are performed in the casting where the defects are not visible. These tests detecting as well as locating the casting defects present in the interior of the casting. Radiography is one of the important flaw detection test for casting. The radiation used in radiography testing is a higher energy (shorter wavelength) version of the electromagnetic waves that we see as visible light. The radiation can come from an X-ray generator or a radioactive source.

(5) Sulphur Print Test :

Detection of sulphur in casting is done by this method. This method is dutiable for ferrous metal, because sulphur may exist in iron or steel in one of two forms; either as iron sulphide or manganese sulphide. The distribution of sulphur inclusions can easily examined by this test.

(6) Dimensional Inspection :

Quality of the casting is analyzed by dimension of the component. Dimensional inspection is one of the important inspections for casting. When precision casting is required, we make some samples for inspection the tolerance, shape size and also measure the profile of the cast. This dimensional inspection of casting may be conducted by various methods such as standard measuring instruments to check the size of the cast, contour gauges for the checking of profile, curves and shapes, coordinate measuring and Marking Machine, Special fixtures.

(7) Ultrasonic Testing :

This method is used for detecting an internal void in casting is based on the principle of reflection of high frequency sound waves. This method of testing more advantages over other methods is that the defect, even if in the interior, is not only detected and located accurately, but its dimension can also be quickly measured without in any damaging or destroying the casting. If the surface under test contains some defect, the high frequency sound waves when emitted through the section of the casting, will be reflected from the surface of defect and return in a shorter period of time.

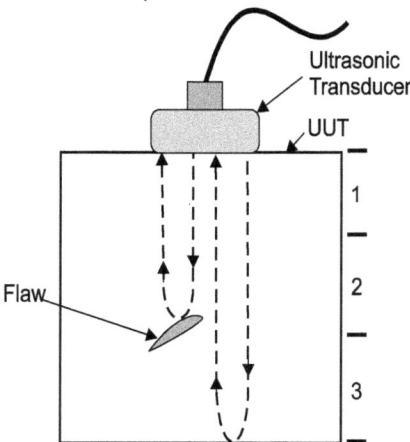

Fig. 3.10 : Ultrasonic Inspection

(8) Macroscopic Examination :

The macroscopic inspection is widely used as a routine control test in steel production because it affords a convenient and effective means of determining internal defects in the metal. Macro etching may make known one of the following conditions such as crystalline heterogeneity, depending on solidification, Chemical heterogeneity, depending on the impurities present or localized segregation and Mechanical heterogeneity, depending on strain introduced on the metal.

(9) Microscopic Examination :

Microscopic examination can enable the study of the microstructure of the metal alloy, elucidating its composition, the type and nature of any treatment given to it, and its mechanical properties. In the case of cast metals, particularly steels, cast iron, malleable iron, and SG iron, microstructure examination is essential for assessing metallurgical structure and composition. Composition analysis can also be done using microscopic inspection. Distribution of phase can be observed by metallographic sample preparation of cast product. Grain size and distribution, grain boundary area can be observed by this procedure. Distribution of nonmetallic inclusion can also be found from this process of inspection.

(10) Chill Test :

Chill test offers a convenient means for an approximate evaluation of the graphitizing tendency of the iron produced and forms an important and quick shop floor test for ascertaining whether this iron will be of the class desired. In chill test, accelerated cooling rate is introduced to induce the formation of a chilled specimen of appropriate dimension. It is then broken by striking with a hammer in such a manner that the fracture is straight and midway of its length. The depth of chill obtained on the test piece is affected by the carbon and silicon present and it can therefore be related to the carbon equivalent, whose value in turn determines the grade of iron.

3.6 MACHINES AND INSTRUMENTS FOR IDENIFICATION OF DEFECTS

A variety of specialized equipment used for analytical, diagnostic and research purposes in casting industry. These equipments are essential and useful in various section and fields of metal casting. The equipments are manufactured using a comprehensive range of quality materials and are of high precision for accurate analysis of tests. These equipments encompass a complete range of tools used by scientists and researchers and include tools like furnaces, thermocouples, testing machines, ovens, pyrometers, analytical equipment, and more. These instruments are made from heat resistant, chemical resistant and expansion resistant materials for conducting various tests and analysis. The various type of equipment used in casting industry are as follows:

- Hydrogen Porosity Tester
- Radiographic Equipment
- Sand Testing Equipment
- Spectrographic Equipment
- Stress Analysis Equipment Abrasive Discs
- Carbon Determinators
- Chemical Analysis Instruments
- Core Hardness Testers
- Gas Analysis Equipment
- Hardness Testing Equipment
- Surface Measuring Equipment
- Temperature Indicating Materials

- Temperature Recording & Control Devices
- Tensile Testing Machines
- Thermocouple Sheaths
- Analytical Equipment Thermocouples

3.7 FOUNDRY LAYOUTS AND MECHANIZATION

Foundry layout discussed in chapter 1 in section (1.2). Foundry deals with the melting of metals and the pouring of molten metal into moulds which castings are obtained. It is a basic industry let us consider its importance in the world of today, which depends extensively upon metal and metal products. These products would be non extent if it were not for the foundry as we cannot metal in usable form from the earth.

The modern home appliances depend largely on foundry products.
- Grey iron casting appear in the form of bath tubs, sink, wash basin, pipe furnaces, cooking utensils etc
- Brass and bronze castings are found in the form of hardware, faucets, parts of washing machines, and other household mechanical equipment.
- Aluminium and magnesium castings appear in the form of cooking utensils and parts of refrigerators, food mixers and vacuum cleaners.
- Our modern land, sea and air transportation systems depend upon castings for their operation. An average automobile has 300 kg or more of cast metal parts in its construction.

Modern communication and lighting systems would be impossible without castings. Modern civilization would not be so far advantages as it is today if it were not for the foundry and its products. The foundry industry is a progressive one, always looking ahead and as it improves so will civilization. An average person visualizes a foundry as a dark, dirty place dotted with mounds of sand, coal, ashes, and metal field with smoke, an enclosure where workers swear and breathe noxious fumes produced during the casting process. This picture is true to a fair extent of many foundries even today. There is thus a vital need for modernization in this particular filed of industry measures that lead to increased production, improved quality and reduction in production costs, measures that aims to improve working conditions in the shop with an eye to ensuring a safe, healthy, and happy life for the worker deserves enthusiastic support. The areas in which such measures are possible may be broadly classified under two heads modernization of production and equipment and modernization of working conditions.

→ **Mechanization :**

Mechanization implies the utilization of machinery to accomplish the work previously done by hand. Mechanized foundries range between simple roller track systems to very complex and partially automatic installations. Mechanized foundries deal with large quantities and

seek for every small economy to reduce the final cost. Foundry mechanization could become possible because of the following two developments.
- Machines were designed and fabricated foe sand mixing, moulding and core making.
- These machines were integrated with the material handling equipments so that continuous processing could be accomplished in the foundries.

In a mechanized foundry castings are knocked out of the moulds on a vibratory grid at knock out station. Sand passes down into a hopper through the grid and the castings vibrate off into the cooling trays. The sand on a conveyor passes through the reconditioning chamber and mixing plant and is then delivered by an overhead belt conveyor into hoppers situated above the moulding machines. After the moulds and cores have been assembled, again on a conveyor, they are carried to casting station.

3.8 AUTOMATION IN CASTING PROCESSES

A wide range of equipment and systems are available for automate common tasks, such as mold handling, mold pouring, casting finishing, casting inspection, and more. By automating routine tasks and systems within the foundry, various benefits can be achieved. Automation helps in improving the production and casting output. Robotic systems can be used to execute hazardous jobs such as pouring and handling mould, and thus help in removing personnel from these jobs. The feedback about the errors given by automated systems help in reducing the errors if they do occur. Automation along with new systems and sub-systems for different foundry tasks, automation controls are also available for existing systems. Technological advancements have enabled the engineers to develop centralized control panels that can be used to operate various pieces of equipment from one location. Through the use of a common control package, a single operator can monitor and control all system parameters. Once again, number of personnel can be reduced to a minimum. Types of Foundry Automation Equipment some of the common foundry automation equipments are:
- Automated casting cleaning stations
- Automated casting inspection stations
- Automated casting pouring stations
- Automated foam coating stations
- Automated shell coating stations
- Removals & pick off systems
- Foam coating stations
- Core production lines
- Robot cells
- Handling systems
- Casting cleaning stations
- Casting inspection stations

These different types of foundry automation equipment offer the benefits of reducing the number of personnel required to perform a specific job. While reducing the number of personnel to perform different tasks, automation also helps in maintaining the production and quality of output. Use of automation systems in foundries has proved to be highly economical than other means. The main benefit of using automation systems in foundries lies in their flexibility - their ability to undertake a variety of other tasks and functions. It is a capital asset, which can be readily reconfigured to respond to changing needs and provide a practical way of automating an array of activities. Cooling the casting by spraying or dipping it, spraying the dies with a lubricant, placing the part into a trimming press - these are just a few of the many added advantages, which can be performed using automation systems. Some of the important advantages of office automation equipment are -

- Automated processes are precisely repeatable, ensuring consistency and improved productivity melt after melt.
- Automated foundries increase productivity, reduce scrap castings, reduce operating costs and improve worker safety.
- Reducing the number of personnel required to perform a specific task.
- Determining the likely causes of production problems and problems.
- Steady improvement in manufacturing yield.
- Realizing higher yield faster gives competitive advantage to foundries.
- Streamlining of production processes and operations.

QUESTIONS

1. What are the different types of furnaces used for casting ?
2. Write a short notes on pit furnace.
3. What are the types of crucible furnace ?
4. What are the different cupola zones?
5. State the importance of metallurgical control in furnace.
6. Explain in detail automatic pouring system.
7. How mechanization important in foundries ?
8. State different type of casting defects.
9. Explain automatic casting system.
10. How does the electric arc furnace melt the metal?
11. Describe the operation of a cupola furnace for melting cast iron.
12. What is the principle of induction furnace ?
13. Explain the various non destructive inspection methods.

Unit - IV
FORMING PROCESSES

4.1 INTRODUCTION

For producing various items required by human being, items like simple pins to automobile; different manufacturing techniques are used. They are casting, powder metallurgy, forging, rolling, machining and welding and many more. Hot and cold working processes fall in the category of metal forming processes. In forming processes, metal is shaped by applying suitable stresses like compression, tension, shear or combined stresses to cause plastic deformation of material.

No material is removed and hence wasted. Material is only displaced and deformed. Various processes such as forging, extrusion, rolling, sheet metal working like deep drawing, bending, ironing, spinning, thread rolling, rotary swaging, wire drawing, etc. fall under this category. Modern forming processes such as explosive forming, electromagnetic forming, hydrostatic forming, etc. also fall under this category.

Forming means changing shape of existing solid body i.e. workpiece. Workpiece before forming may have shape of plate, sheet, bar, rod, wire or tube of various cross-sections.

For example:

- A wire coat hanger is made by forming a straight piece of wire by bending and twisting it into shape of hanger.
- A body of car is made by forming metal sheets in dies, starting with flat sheets.
- Initial material for a typical translucent advertising signboard is a flat piece of plastic. It is formed by heating and then forced under vacuum of air pressure into a mould.

All above examples are of forming processes.

4.1.1 Classification of Forming Processes

Forming processes are classified as follows:

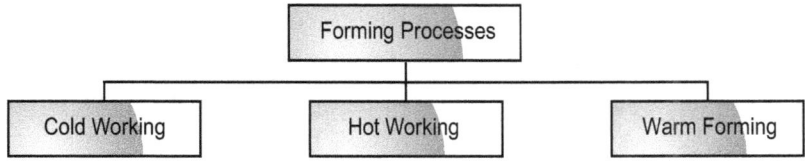

This classification is done referring to recrystallisation temperature of metals being formed.

4.2 HOT WORKING

Hot working is the process of plastically deforming a metal or an alloy under such conditions of temperature and strain rate that 'recovery and recrystallisation occur during or immediately after deformation. To achieve this temperature of deformation is usually higher than [0.6 × melting point of material on absolute scale (i.e. °K)]. Thus hot working is plastic deformation of metals above their recrystallisation temperature.

Note:

Recrystallisation temperature for different materials varies greatly. When Tin is worked at room temperature it is hot working process. Steel requires temperature of 2000 °F for tungsten to fall in hot working; it must be worked at about 4000 °F temperatures.

Thus term 'hot working' usually suggests working at elevated temperature, but may not be always so. In general, increase in temperature brings about a decrease in strength, an increase in ductility and decrease in rate of strain hardening. All these effects help easy deformation of metal being worked.

Effects of Hot Working :

Refer Fig. 4.1. It can be seen that when forces are applied the grains elongate (as seen in microstructure) in the direction of the applied load. Nuclei of new grains are formed due to high temperature. These nuclei grow with time. Ultimately a fine grained equiaxed recrystallised structure is obtained.

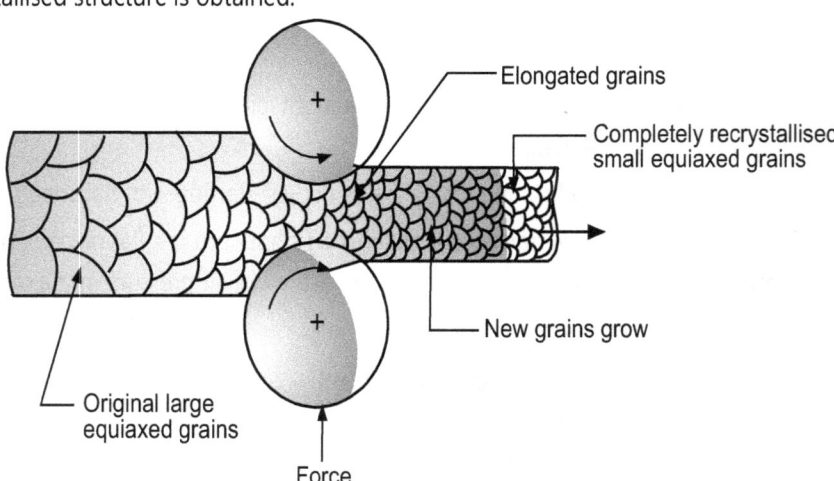

Fig. 4.1 : Microstructure changes in hot working

Process of Recovery, Recrystallisation and Grain Growth in hot working of Metal:

If a highly cold worked metal is heated to successively higher temperature several structural changes takes place in it along with changes in mechanical properties. A cold worked metal highly strained and deformed. As this metal is heated there is no structural change, only the internal stresses are reduced. This temperature internal is called as 'recovery'.

The temperature at which all the strained, distorted grains are completely replaced by new crystals is called as the "**Recrystallisation Temperature**".

On heating to temperature above T_{RC} the small grains grow in size and stabilize at some size. This temperature is called as 'grain growth region'.

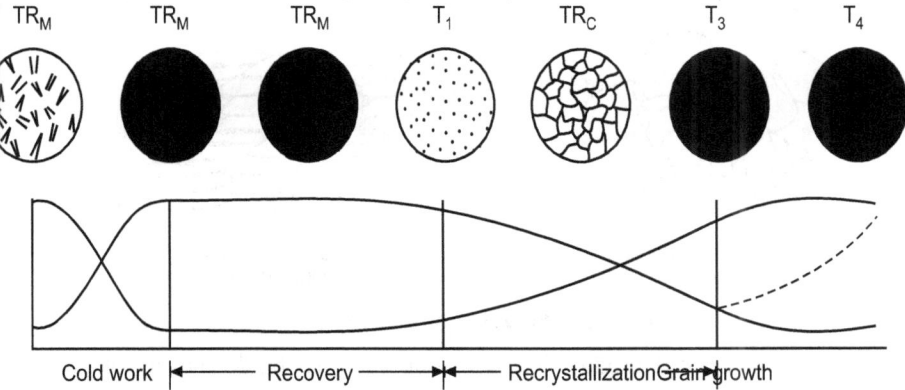

Fig. 4.2 : Grain growth in hot working

Advantages:

- Low tonnage equipments are sufficient, since force required is less.
- High ductility at high temperatures, so numbers of stages required for forming are reduced.
- No work hardening occurs.
- Stress relieving is not necessary.
- Reduced chemical inhomogeneties.
- Blow holes and porosities are eliminated.

Limitations:

- Heating facilities are required.
- Reactive metals pose lot of problems, sometimes inert atmosphere is needed.
- Due to scaling and oxidation there is a heavy metal loss.
- Poor dimensional tolerance and surface finish.
- Thin sheets cannot be produced.
- Automation is difficult.
- Surface decarbonation in steels reduces strength and hardness on surface.
- Non-uniform properties over cross-section. Normalizing may be needed.

4.3 COLD WORKING PROCESS

Cold working is plastic deformation of metals below the recrystallisation temperature. The process is usually performed at room temperature. Fig. 4.3 shows micro structural changes that occur during cold working.

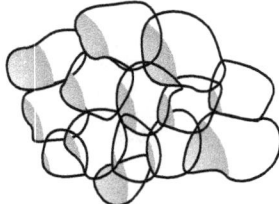
Before cold working
equiaxed polygonal grains

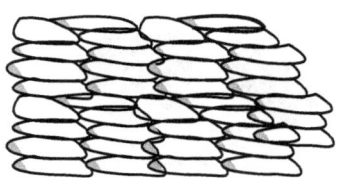
After cold working
elongated grains

Fig. 4.3 : Micro structural changes

The strength of cold worked product increases due to strain hardening. If cold working exceeds certain limits, metal fractures. Hence annealing is required before further processing. Superior finish can be obtained by cold working.

Advantages:

- Since deformation occurs at low temperatures, no scaling and oxidation occurs, hence less wastage of material.
- The surface finish obtained is excellent.
- Very high dimensional tolerances can be achieved. In many case, subsequent machining is not required.
- Automation is possible because of low temperature.
- Thin gauge sheets can be produced.
- Work hardening occurs. The strength of finish product can be controlled within limits.

Disadvantages:

- Large forces are required for deformation, so high capacity costly machines are needed.
- Formability of materials is low at lower temperatures. Hence, intermediate annealing is necessary. This increases cost.
- Severe stresses are introduced in metal. Stress relieving is needed.
- Specially designed tooling's are necessary.

4.4 WARM FORMING

Deformation produced at temperatures intermediate to hot and cold forming is known as warm forming. Advantages of warm forming are:
- Reduced loads on tooling and equipment.
- Increased material ductility.
- Less strain hardening, hence less number of intermediate annealing.
- Various metals can be worked and also of different geometries can be formed.
- Lower temperatures of warm working produce less scaling and decarburization.
- Better dimensional precision and smooth surfaces.
- Finish machining is reduced and less scrap.

Thus warm working combines advantages of cold and hot working.

Cold forming is preferred method for fabricating small components, but large parts (upto about 8 kg) and steels with more than 0.35% carbon and or high alloy content can also be warm worked.

The following part describes rolling of flat and shaped products, forging of discrete parts, extrusion of long pieces with various cross-sections, drawing of rod, wire and tube. These processes are called bulk deformation processes. The workpieces and products have high ratios of volume to surface area or volume to thickness.

4.5 FORGING

Forging is a process of reducing a metal billet between two dies to obtain part of predetermined shape and size by application of compressive stresses.

While rolling produces plates, sheets, etc., forging operation produces discrete parts. e.g. landing gear of air-craft, jet engine shafts, bolts, rivets, connecting rods, gears, shafts of turbine, crank shafts of automobiles are variety of parts made by forging process.

Good strength and toughness is obtained since metal flow and grain structure can be controlled. Forging is done at room temperature (cold forging) or at high temperature (hot forging). There are three types of forging:
- Open die forging
- Closed die forging
- Impression die forging

4.5.1 Open Die Forging

A solid workpiece is placed between two flat dies and reduced in height by compressing it. The dies used are flat i.e. they do not contain negative impression of component (See Fig. 4.4). The same dies are used for producing wide variety of components.

- **Press Forging :** Open die forging performed in a press.
- **Hammer Forging :** Open die forging performed in a hammer.
- **Hand Forging :** Done by hand on an anvil. Light parts are produced by hand forging while medium to heavy forging in small batches are produced in hammers and presses.

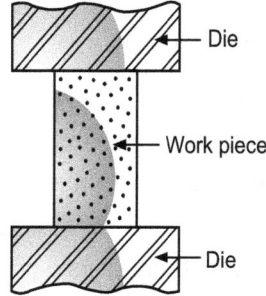

Fig. 4.4: Open die forging

In forging, while material is deformed uniformly, in actual operation barrel shape may get developed on the parts (See Fig. 4.5). This is due to frictional forces at the die workpiece interfaces that oppose the outward flow of materials at these interfaces. Barreling can be minimized by using effective lubricant. The operations involved in open die forging include upsetting, drawing out, fullering or spreading, piercing, expanding, bending, etc. Most open die forgings generally weight 15 - 500 kg, forging as large as 300 tons have been made. Small parts are usually smith forged in pneumatic power forging hammers, large parts in air and steam hammers. A very large parts produced in hydraulic presses.

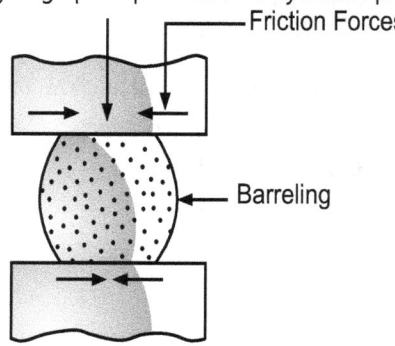

Fig. 4.5 : Forging operation

4.5.1.1 Open Die Forging Operations

In forging, final shape of product cannot be achieved in a single pass, but a number of operations have to be performed to achieve final shape.

• Upsetting :

Also known as heading. This is a process of increasing the cross-sectional area of work at the expense of its length by means of end pressure. In Fig. 4.6, part is heated and held on anvil or swage block and the other end is hammered. The shape and position of upset depends on type of blows given to work piece and location of heating.

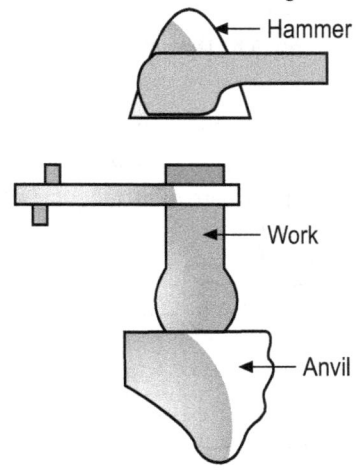

Fig. 4.6: Upsetting

• Heading :

Heading (See Fig. 4.7) is essentially an upsetting operation, performing at the end of a round rod, or wire in order to produce a large cross-section. Heads of screws, bolts, rivets, nails and other fasteners are produced by this method. The process is carried out on automated 'headers' and machines produce hundreds of pieces per minute.

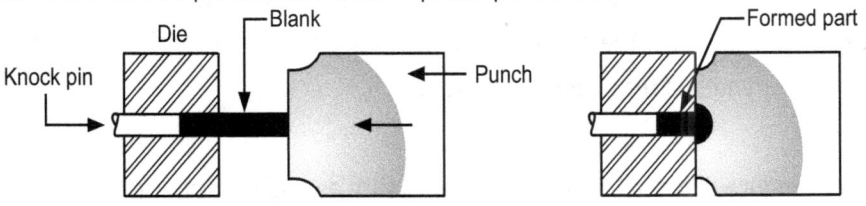

Fig. 4.7 : Heading

• Drawing Out :

This is also known as drawing down. In this operation, length of the part is increased. The cross-sectional area is reduced. A pair of fullers is used for drawing down. See Fig. 4.8.

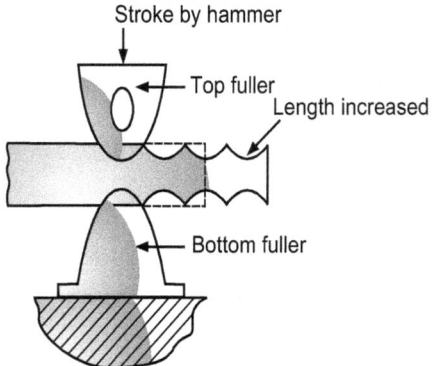

Fig. 4.8 : Drawing out

- **Fullering :**

It is similar to setting down operation. In this, cross section of workpiece is reduced and length is increased. This is local drawing down operation carried by a set of hammer. This method is also used for smoothing off a square of rectangular article(See Fig. 4.9).

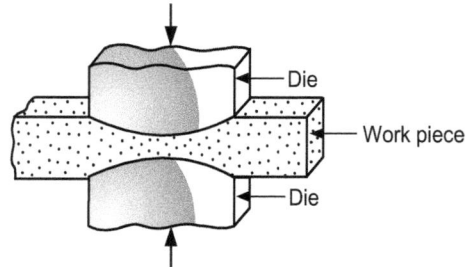

Fig. 4.9 : Fullering : Material is distributed away from area

- **Piercing :**

Piercing is a process of indenting. Here, the workpiece is not broken through. Only the surface of workpiece is punched in order to produce a cavity or an impression. The workpiece may be confined in a die cavity or it may be open. Piercing may be followed by punching to produce a hole in the part. The piercing force depends on cross-sectional area of punch, tip geometry, the strength of the material and friction.

- **Bending :**

In order to produce different types of bent shapes such an angles, ovals, circles, etc. bending process is used. The bents may be either sharp cornered or gradual. Bending is performed by hammering the metal over the edge of the anvil or over the edge or holes of the swage block(See Fig. 4.10).

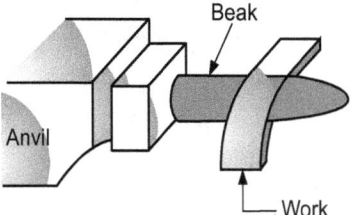

Fig. 4.10 : Bending

• **Cutting :**

Cutting of metal is performed with the help of chisel. Long piece of metal is cut into small pieces. Metal is heated to suitable temperature and then, hammer blows are directed on the chisel head (See Fig. 4.11).

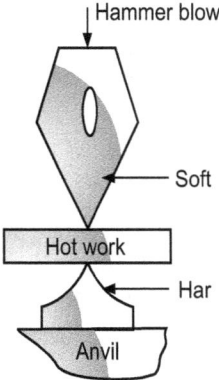

Fig. 4.11: Cutting

4.5.1.2 Forging Force

In open die forging operation, the forging force F, to be applied on a solid cylindrical component can be determined from the relation.

$$F = \sigma_f \cdot \frac{\pi}{4} d^2 \left(1 + \frac{\mu d}{3h}\right)$$

$$\sigma_f = K e^n$$

$$S_f = \left(1 + \frac{\mu d}{3h}\right)$$

Where σ_f is the flow stress of the material ($\sigma_f = K e^n$), μ is the coefficient of friction, and d and h are the diameter and height of the work piece, respectively. Forging shape factor S_f, to consider the effect of friction and d/h ratio.

$$\sigma_f = \left(1 + \frac{\mu d}{3h}\right)$$

Because of very high cost of toolings and machines, precision forging is preferred over conventional forging only where volume of production is extremely large.

SOLVED EXAMPLES

Example 4.1 :

Using open-die forging operation, a solid cylindrical piece of 304 stainless steel having 100 mm diameter x 72 mm height is reduced in the height to 60 mm at room temperature. Assuming the coefficient of friction as 0.22 and the flow stress for this material at the required true strain as 1000 MPa, calculate the forging force at the end of stroke.

Solution : Initial diameter = 100 mm Initial height = 72 mm Final height = 60 mm. If final diameter is d, $(100)^2 \times 72 = d^2 \times 60$ i.e. d =110 mm

$$F = (1000) \cdot \frac{\pi}{4} (110)^2 \left(1 + \frac{0.22(110)}{3 \times 60}\right)$$

$$= 107.7 \text{ kN}$$

Example 4.2 :

A solid cylinder metal pieces of initial diameter 50 mm and height 40 mm is forged by using open-die forging.

The work material has flow curve defined by K = 250 MPa and n = 0.12. if coefficient of friction is 0.15 and forging force at the end is 490 kN. Find the final height of the workpiece. Take shape factor as 1.05.

Solution: Initial diameter = 50 mm; Initial height = 40 mm; K = 250 MPa, n = 0.12; Coefficient of friction = 0.15; Forging force = 490 kN; Shape factor = 1.05

Forging force is given by,

$$F = \sigma_f A S_f = \sigma_f \cdot \frac{\pi}{4} d^2 S_f$$

$$490 \times 10^3 = \sigma_f \cdot \frac{\pi}{4} (50)^2 (1.05)$$

$$\sigma_f = 237.83 \text{ MPa}$$

Flow stress for the material is

$$\sigma_f = K e^n$$
$$237.83 = 250 (e)^{0.12}$$
$$e = 0.65$$

Strain devolve in material is

$$e = \ln\left(\frac{h_o}{h}\right)$$

$$0.65 = \ln\left(\frac{40}{h}\right)$$

$$h = 23.39 \text{ mm}$$

4.5.2 Closed Die Forging

In this process, dies with negative contour of the component to be produced are used (See Fig. 4.12). The heated material is forced into the dies to produce required shape of the component. In true closed die forging (fleshless forging), flash does not form. The work piece completely fills the die cavity.

Accurate control of volume of material and proper die design are essential to obtain correct product. Undersized blank may not fill the cavity fully and produce small size component while oversized blank may cause excessive pressure on dies.

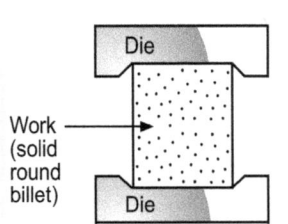 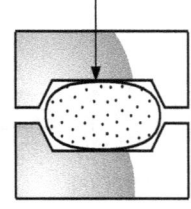 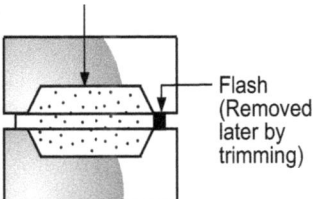

Fig. 4.12 : Closed die forging

Forging Force :

Formula

$$F = K Y_f A$$

Where, K = 3 to 11

Y_f = the flow stress of the material at the forging temperature and

A = the projected area of forging

In hot forging operations, forging force ranges from 550 MPa to 1000 MPa.

4.5.3 Impression Die Forging

The workpiece acquires the shape of the die cavities (impressions) when it is forged (See Fig. 4.12). During forging, some of the material flows outside the die cavities and forms a flash.

The thin flash cools rapidly and applies high pressure to the material in the die cavity. This helps in filling of the die cavity. The starting material (blank) is an extruded or drawn bar or component made by powder metallurgy or casting processes.

The blank is then placed on the lower die. The top die is fastened to the ram of a steam drop hammer. The upper die begins to descend and the blank's shape gradually changes. Following Fig. 4.13 illustrates stages in forging in a connecting rod for an I.C. engine.

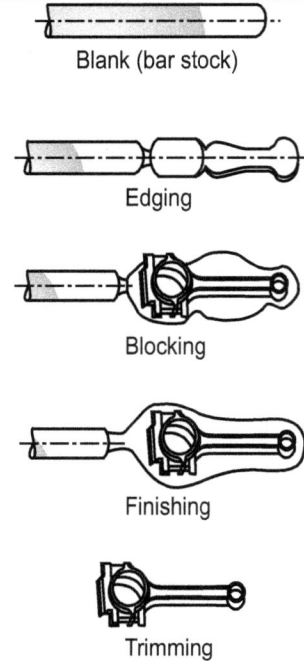

Fig. 4.13 : Connecting rod manufacturing steps in impression die forging

4.5.4 Die Materials and Lubrication

- **Die Materials :**

Common die materials are tool and die steels containing chromium, nickel, molybdenum and vanadium. These dies have strength and toughness at high temperatures, mechanical and thermal shock resistance and wear resistance.

Dies are made from die blocks. Die blocks are forged from casting and are machined and finished to the desired shape and surface finished. The dies should be preheated to temperatures of about 150 - 250° C to reduce failure.

- **Lubrication :**

For hot forging, graphite, molybdenum-disulphide and glass are used as lubricants. For cold forging, mineral oils and soaps are used. In hot forging, lubricant is applied to the dies, while in cold forging, it is applied to the workpiece.

- Use of lubricant has following advantages:
- Reduce friction and wear of dies.
- Reduce forces required for forging.
- Improve flow of metal in die cavities.
- Serve as parting agent to prevent the forging from sticking to the dies.

4.5.5 Forgeability

This is defined as the capability of material to undergo deformation without cracking. Aluminium alloys are hot forged at 400 - 550°C and has highest forgeability while tungsten alloys are hot forged at 1200 - 1300°C and has lowest forgeability.

4.5.6 Defects in Forging

- **Barreling :**

When hot work comes in contact with the dies there will be a decrease in the temperature of the surface coming in contact with dies.

After applying forging load, central portion will have lower flow stresses, it will move faster than the material near the edges. This result in non cylindrical large component called barreling [see Fig. 4.14 (a)].

- **Development of Laps :**

If there is insufficient material that fills the dies, the web, may buckle during forging and develop laps (See Fig. 4.14(b)).

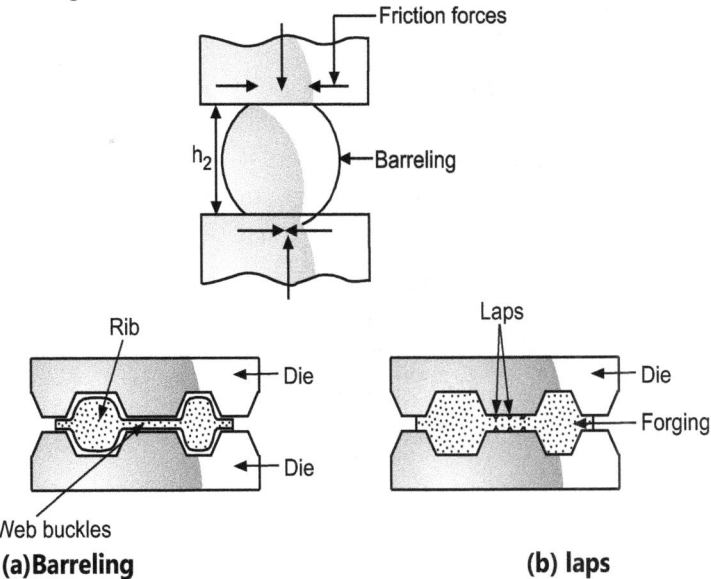

(a) Barreling (b) laps

Fig. 4.14 forging defect

- **Internal Cracks :**

If web is thick, the extra material flows past the already forced portion of forging and develops internal cracks. Defects may also develop from non-uniform deformation of the material in the die cavity, temperature variations throughout the workpiece during forging and microstructural changes caused by phase transformations (See Fig. 4.15).

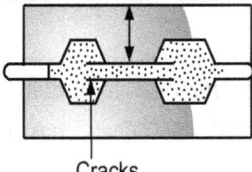

Fig. 4.15 internal cracks

4.5.7 Forging Machines

Forging machines are classified as presses and hammers.

- **Presses (Press Forging) :** It included following types for forging :

(1) Hydraulic Press :

These operate at constant speed. If load exceeds its capacity press stops. Hydraulic press forging takes longer time. So heated dies are used otherwise workpiece may cool rapidly. Hydraulic presses consist of frame with two or four columns, piston, cylinders, rams and hydraulic pumps driven by electrical motors. Press capacities are upto 125 MN for open die forging and 670 MN for closed die forging.

(2) Mechanical Presses :

These presses are either crank or eccentric type. The speed varies from maximum at centre of stroke to zero at the bottom of stroke. In construction they have a large flywheel powered by electric motor. This generates required energy. Fig. 4.16 shows different elements of mechanical press with eccentric drive. Press capacities are 4.7 MN to 107 MN. These presses have high production rates, easier to automate and require less skill.

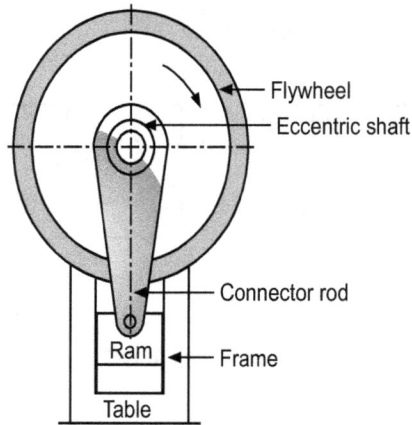

Fig. 4.16: Mechanical press

- **Hammers :**

Hammers operate at high speeds. So cooling of forging is minimized. Hammers derive energy for forging from potential energy of the ram, which is converted into kinetic energy.

Complex shapes can be forged with hammers. To complete forging several successive blows are made in the same die. Hammers are least expensive and versatile machines. They are classified as gravity drop hammers, power drop hammers, counter blow hammers and high energy rate hammers.

(A) Gravity Drop Hammers :

The main element from which energy is derived is free falling ram.

Energy = Ram's weight × Height of its drop

Ram weight ranges from 180 kg to 4500 kg. When mass production of identical articles is required by forging, drop hammers are used. Steel dies are made in two halves. One half is attached to the top while the other is fastened to the anvil block at the bottom. The top is raised to a suitable height by mechanical means and heated metal is placed on the lower die. Top then falls under its own weight from that height. This gives a blow and completes the job in a single operation. Many devices are used for raising the top of drop hammer. They are belt, rope, friction wheel and board, air, steam or oil.

(B) Board Drop Hammer :

In friction wheel and board drop arrangement, the drop is attached at the bottom of vertical board. The board is pressed between two rotating wheels and friction between the board and wheels moves the board up. This is shown in Fig. 4.17. The board is thus raised upward. At desirable height breaking shoes hold the board at position. When the blow is required, shoes are removed and board falls freely giving required blow.

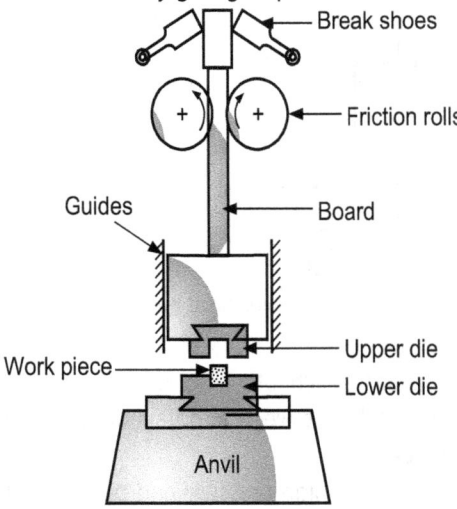

Fig. 4.17 : Board hammer

Other arrangements for lifting the tup like chain, belt, etc. are shown in Fig. 4.18. In drop hammers, falling weight varying from 300 to 600 kg with 60 to 80 strokes per minute are obtained.

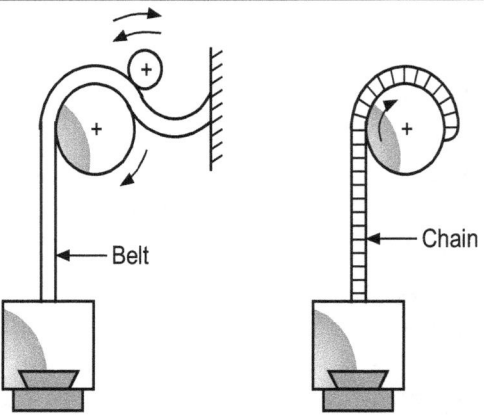

Fig. 4.18 : Lifting arrangements

(C) Power Drop Hammers :

The ram's downward stroke is accelerated by steam or air or hydraulic pressure at about 750 kPa. Ram weights range from 225 kg to 22500 kg (See Fig. 4.19).

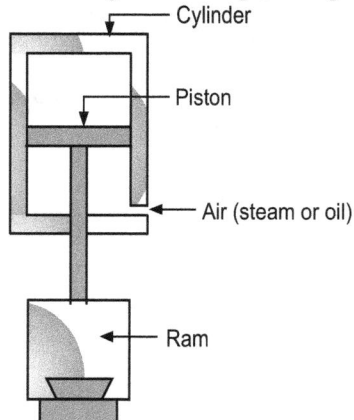

Fig. 4.19 Power drop hammer

(D) Counter Blow Hammers:

Two rams simultaneously approach each other, to forge part. They may act vertically or horizontally and job may be rotated in between to obtain desired shape.

(E) High Energy Rate Machines :

The ram is accelerated by inert gas at high pressure and part is finish forged in one blow at very high speed.

4.5.8 Forging Process Advantage:

Crankshaft for example made by forging saves material, fibres take contour of component, strength and corrosion and wear resistance of component will be better than machined component. Grains are continuous without cut (See Fig. 4.20).

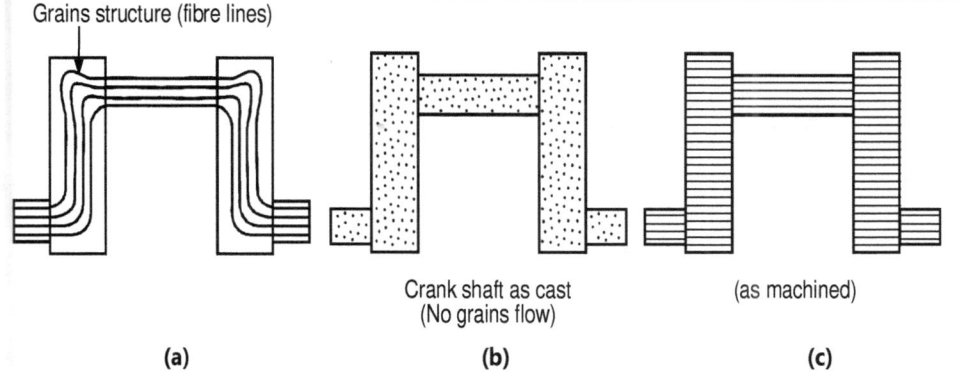

(a)   (b) Crank shaft as cast (No grains flow)   (c) (as machined)

Fig. 4.20 : Forged crankshaft

4.5.9 Other Operations

- **Roll Forging :**

In this process the cross-section of cylindrical or rectangular workpiece is reduced by passing it through a set of opposing rolls that have grooves matching the desired shape of the final part (see fig. 4.21). The rolls do not turn continuously in roll forging.

They rotate through only a portion of one revolution corresponding to the desired deformation to be accomplished on the part. Roll forged parts are stronger than machined parts.

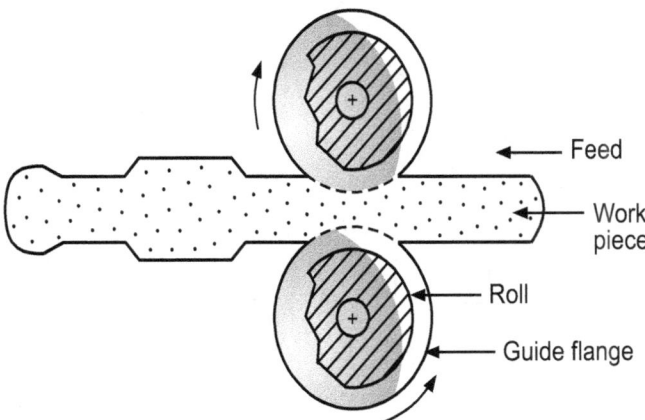

Fig. 4.21 : Roll forging or cross rolling

Roll forging is used to produce tapered shafts and leaf springs, table knives and hand tools (see fig. 4.22).

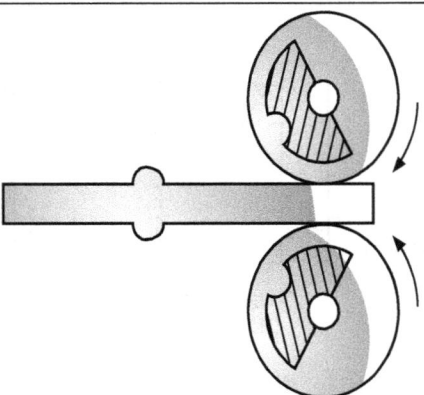

Fig. 4.22 Rroll forging for tapered shaft

- **Skew Rolling :**

This process is similar to roll forging. This is used for making ball bearings. (See Fig. 4.23). Round bar is fed into the roll gap and roughly spherical blanks are formed.

These balls are then finished in special machinery. It should be noted that rollers are arranged in cross axes.

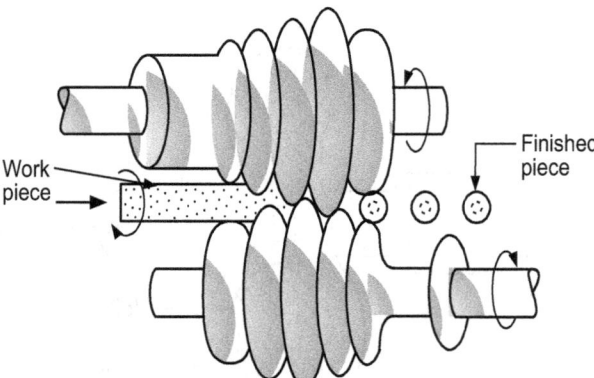

Fig. 4.23 Skew rolling

- **Orbital Forging :**

Also known as rotary, swing or rocking die forging. In this process (See Fig. 4.24), upper die moves along an orbital path. This is achieved by adjustable mechanical means. The part is formed gradually step by step. Bevel gears, conical parts, wheel, rings for bearings can be made by this process. The die contact with workpiece at any moment is small. Hence force required for forging is small.

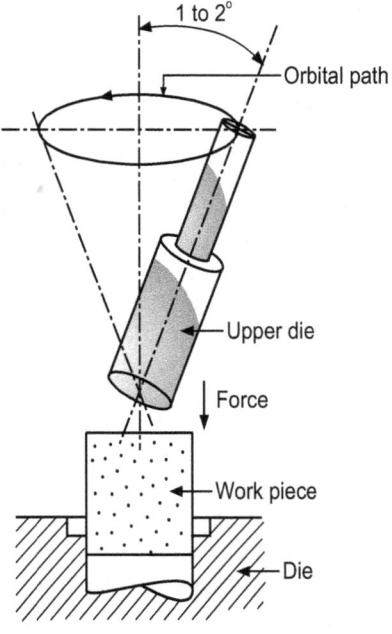

Fig. 4.24 Orbital forging

Upper die is slightly inclined to the vertical axis of machine. It imparts a high frequency circular rocking motion across the top surface of workpiece. This process is also called rota-forming process and is a cold working process.

- **Isothermal Forging :**

This process is also known as hot die forging. The dies are heated to same temperature as that of hot workpiece. Forging force is low because hot workpiece is prevented from getting cold by dies. Material flow in cavity is good because of maintained ductility of material. Complex parts with good dimensional accuracy can be produced. e.g. Nose wheel of air craft (Material Ti-6 Al-6V - 2Sn; a titanium alloy). The material of dies is nickel or molybdenum alloys. This is a slow process and is expensive.

- **Rotary Swaging :**

This process is also known as radial forging. A solid rod or tube is shaped by applying numerous, uniformly spaced, short hammer blows rapidly by rotating dies (see fig. 4.25). Thus bar is subjected to radial impact forces by reciprocating dies. Fig. 4.25 shows rotating backers contact rolls to close the dies. The dies reciprocate with high frequency due to the rotation of spindle in which they are mounted, thereby deforming the workpiece to conform to the shape of dies used. The workpiece is stationary and set of dies rotate, impacting the workpiece of rate of 20 strokes per second.

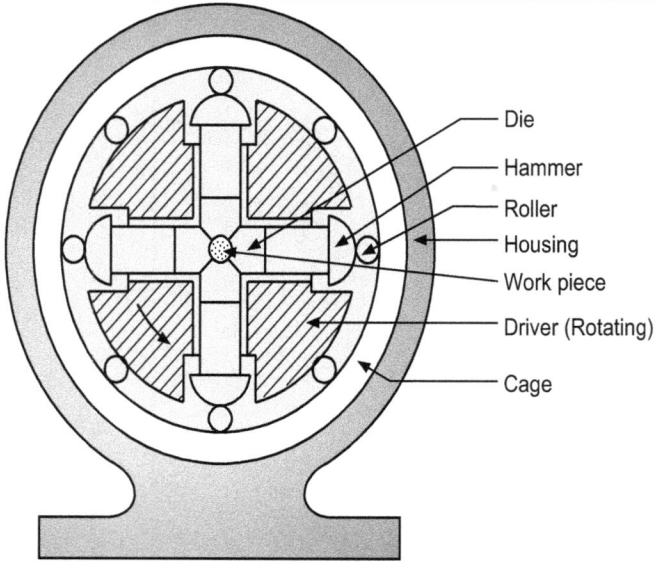

Fig. 4.25 Rotary swaging

The parts produced are screwdriver blades and soldering iron tips (See Fig. 4.26). Tube is swaged by using internal mandrels. Rifling in gun barrels is made by swaging a tube over a mandrel with spiral grooves. This process is used for assemble fittings over cables and wires, tapering tip of cylindrical part. Swaging is limited to stock diagram of 150 mm and small diameters of 0.5 mm. Tolerances are ± 0.05 mm to ± 0.5 mm.

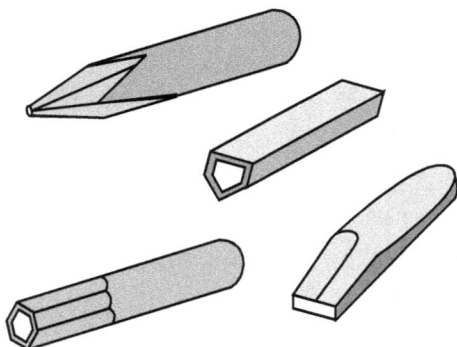

Fig. 4.26 Rotary swaging products

This process is limited to parts of symmetrical cross-section only.

- **Press forging :**

This is a slow action process. Not as drop forging where a fast action process is used. Press forging is done in process rather than with hammers. The action is relatively slow squeezing instead of delivering heavy blows and penetrates deeply because it gives the metal time to flow. Die may have less draft, and forgings come nearer to desired sizes. Press forgings are shaped at each impression with a single smooth stroke and they stick to the die impression

more rigidly. Unless same provision is therefore, made, the escape of air and excess die lubricant may be difficult. Thus press forging dies requires a mechanical means for ejection and venting for the escape of air and lubricant. Press forgings are generally moiré accurate dimensionally than drop forgings. Presses for closed die forgings can be of two classes:
(1) Hydraulic.
(2) Mechanical.

Difference between Press and Drop Forging :

No.	Press Forging	Drop Forging
1.	No hammering, slow squeezing.	Hammering, fast squeezing.
4.	Dimensionally accurate parts can be produced.	Dimensional accuracy lesser than press forging.
3.	Costly.	Cheaper.
4.	For large parts.	For small parts.
5.	High pressure required.	Works on low pressure.

- **High Energy Rate Forging :**

It is nothing but high energy rate forging. This is different from hammer forging because the blows are not repeated. A major contribution to conventional forging operations is their high impact velocity which is 2 to 10 times larger than conventional velocities. In the HERF, machines are vertical counterblow machines used principally for hot forging, although they can also be used for cold forming making powdered metal parts and deep forming sheet metal parts. It is also called as high velocity forming. HERF machines, except for one which uses exploded gas are operated by sudden release of nitrogen gas. This gas drives the ram which is pressed against a seal ring at the top. Enough high pressure is admitted to area inside the seal ring to dislodge the piston. The gas in high pressure cylinder then acts over the whole piston area and drives the ram down at a high velocity ranging between 9 to 20 m/s. Most parts are formed in a single blow.

4.6 ROLLING

Rolling is usually the first process used to convert material into a finished wrought product. Starting material for producing any product is in the form of thick stock, made by casting process. This stock is converted into bloom, billets or slabs by rolling process. Rolling is the process of reducing the thickness or changing cross-section of a long workpiece by compressive forces applied through set of rolls. This process involves plastic deformation of metal in which thickness of strip is reduced from h_i to h_f while length and width are increased. Rolling is shown in Fig. 4.27.

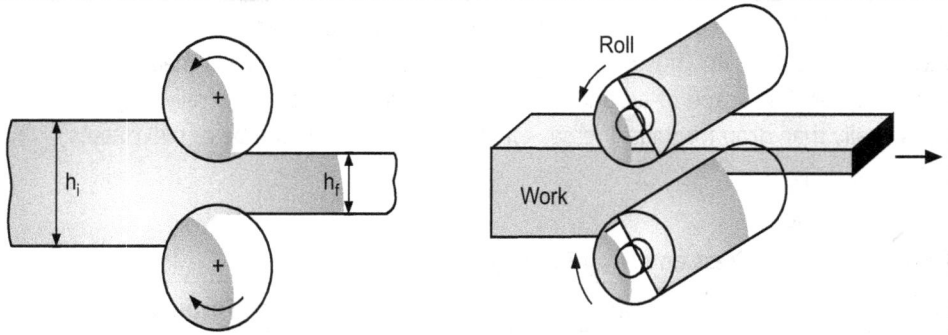

Fig. 4.27: Rolling process (Flat rolling)

The basic operation is flat rolling (rolling) where rolled products are flat plate or sheet. In addition to flat rolling various shapes can also be produced by shape rolling. They include straight and long structural shapes (i.e. solid bars having various cross-sections), channels, I-beams, rail road rails. Fig. 4.28 shows various flat and shape rolling processes.

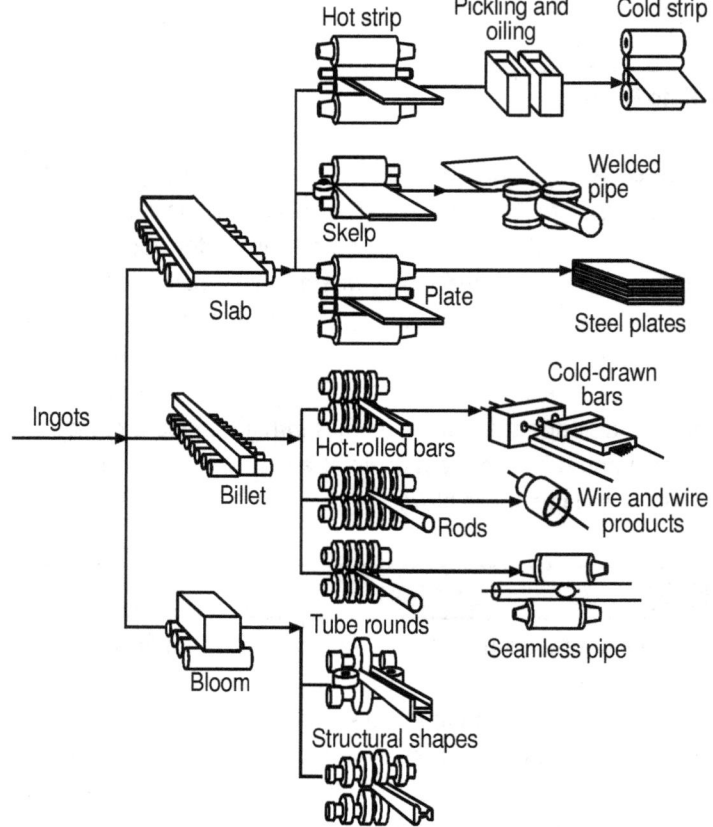

Fig. 4.28: Various rolling processes

Various raw material shapes and their dimensions with applications are as follows:

Name	Dimensions	Application / Use
1. Bloom :	Square or rectangular cross section. Thickness greater than 150 mm and width less than (2 × thickness) 150 × 150mm to 250 × 300mm.	Starting material that is further rolled to obtain different shapes. e.g. plates, structural shapes, rail roads, tracks.
4. Billet :	Smaller than bloom. Square or circular cross-section. (Side 37.5 mm or greater) 50 × 50 mm to 125 × 125 mm	To make shapes like rails, plates, bars, rods, etc.
3. Slab :	Rectangular solid, width is greater than twice the thickness. (Width 250 mm or more) 50 × 150 mm thick 600 to 1500 mm wide	To produce plate, sheet, strip, etc.
4. Plates :	Thickness greater than 6 mm	Structural applications e.g. ship hulls, boilers, bridges, girders, machine structures, nuclear vessels, battleship and tanks (125 mm thick)
5. Sheets :	Generally less than 6 mm thick	Automobile bodies, appliances, food and beverage containers, kitchen and office equipments. Aluminium foils used to wrap cigarettes is 0.008 mm thick.

4.6.1 Flat Rolling: Principle

As shown in Fig. 4.29, hot metal is passed between two rolls. Rolls rotate in opposite directions. The gap between rolls is less than thickness of entering metal. Rolls rotate with a surface velocity greater than speed of incoming material. Friction along contact interface acts to move metal forward. The metal is squeezed and elongates as a result of decrease in cross section area.

The amount of deformation that can be achieved in single pass between a given pair of rolls depends on friction conditions along surface. If very high reduction is required, rolls will stop advancing the material. If too little deformation per pass, cost of production will increase.

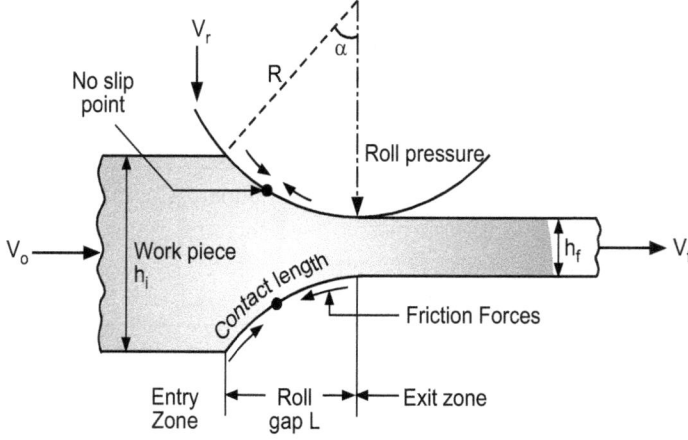

Fig. 4.29: Rolling principle

When rolls are rotated powered through shafts by electric motors, the surface speed of roll is V_r. The velocity of strip increases from V_o to V_{fi} as strip moves through gap. The velocity of strip is highest at the exit of roll gap and is denoted by V_f. Surface speed of roll is constant, there is relative sliding between the roll and strip along the arc of contact in the roll gap L. At one point along the contact length, the velocity of strip is the same as that of roll. This is called 'neutral' or 'No slip' point.

4.6.2 Rolling Temperature and Frictional Forces

Temperature control is crucial to the success of this process. If the temperature is not uniform, the subsequent deformation will not be uniform. While heating material prior to rolling, sufficient time must be provided. Otherwise outer hot portion will flow in preference to the cooler, stronger interior. If part cools prior to working, cooler surfaces will resist deformation. Cracking and tearing of the surface may result because of hotter, weaker interior tries to deform.

High volume producers use continuous casting process to produce starting material that is further rolled. Cooling from solidification is controlled, so as to enable direct insertion from continuous casting machine to hot rolling operation. This avoids additional handling and reheating. For small operations or secondary processing, the starting material (ingot, slab or bloom which at room temperature) is heated to rolling temperature in gas or oil-fired furnaces. For plain carbon and low alloy steels, the soaking temperature is about 1200°C. Induction furnace may be used for smaller cross-sections.

Hot rolling is stopped when temperature of material falls to about 50 to 100°C, above the recrystallisation temperature of the material. This helps in obtaining uniform grain size and prevents possibility of unwanted strain hardening. Rolls pull the material into the roll gap by a net frictional force on the material (see Fig. 4.30). Frictional force on the left of neutral point must be higher than the force on the right so that net frictional force directs to the right.

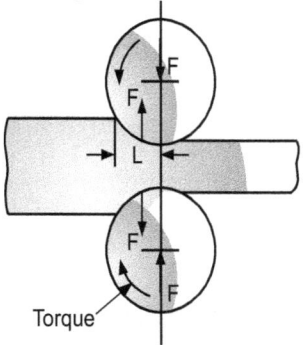

Fig. 4.30: Rolling forces

Increasing friction means increasing forces and power. High friction can damage surface of rolled product. Lubricants are used to obtain low coefficients of friction.

Draft :

It is defined as difference between the initial and final thickness ($h_i - h_f$). This is a function of coefficient of friction, μ, and the roll radius R.

$$h_i - h_f = \mu^2 R$$

Thus, higher friction and larger roll radius, greater is maximum draft and reduction in thickness is more.

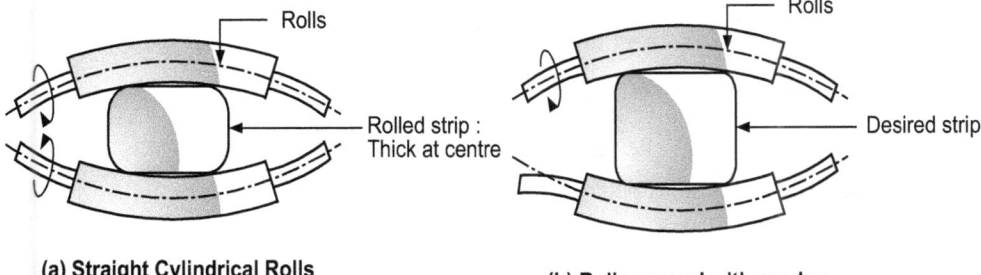

(a) Straight Cylindrical Rolls

(b) Rolls ground with camber

Fig. 4.31: Roll bending

High roll forces can cause deflection and bending of rolls. This adversely affects rolling process. Roll forces tend to bend rolls elastically during rolling [Refer Fig. 4.31 (a) and (b)]. Strip becomes thick at its centre than at its edges (known as crown). To avoid this, rolls are ground so that their diameter at centre is slightly larger than at their edges, giving them camber. Roll forces can be reduced by :

- Reducing friction,
- Using smaller diameter rolls to reduce contact area,
- Smaller reduction per pass,
- Increasing temperature of rolling.

4.6.3 Rolling Mills

The machines used to carry out rolling process, are known as rolling mills. The design, construction and operation of rolling mills require major investment. Many different types of rolling mills are built.

• **Types of Rolling Mills :**

The various types of rolling mill with their constructional details and working describe are as follows :

Two-High Mill :

This consists of two rolls between which is placed the bloom or sheet as shown in Fig. 4.32. two-High and three-High mills are used for primary roughing (or cogging) and diameter of rolls used is 600 to 1400 mm.

A two-High non-reversing mill is the simplest design. Material is passed through the mill in one direction only.

The workpiece is taken over the rolls and returned to the original position for re-rolling and the process is repeated. These mills are called 2-High pull over or drag over mills.

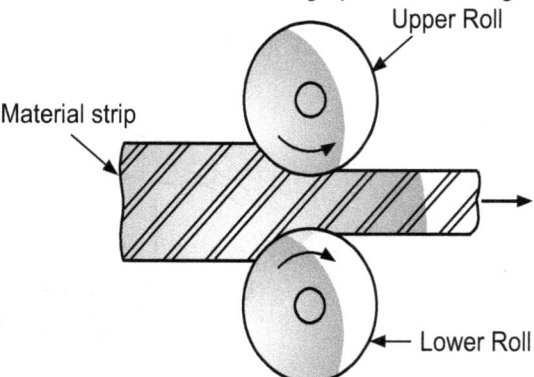

Fig. 4.32 : Two-High mill (non-reversing)

If the direction of rotation of the rolls is reversed, then it is called a two high reversing mill. (See Fig. 4.33).

Here the rolling is done in opposite directions alternatively, with workpiece travelling in both directions.

These mills are used for production of slabs, blooms, billets, rounds, plates and other semi-finished products.

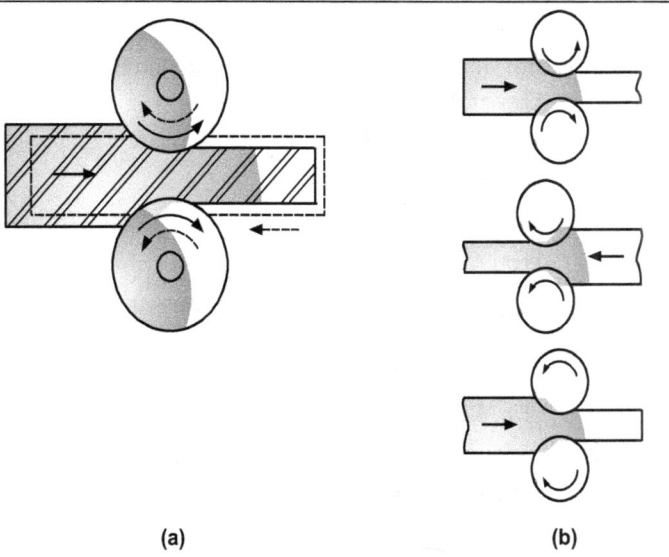

Fig. 4.33 : 2-High reversing mill

• Three-High Rolling Mill :

Heavy reduction is not possible in two-High mills. Increased load required for that cause bending and barrelling of rolls. In three-High rolling mill, the direction of material is reversed after each pass (See Fig. 4.34). The plate being rolled is repeatedly raised to the upper roller gap, rolled and then lowered to the lower roll gap by elevators and various manipulators.

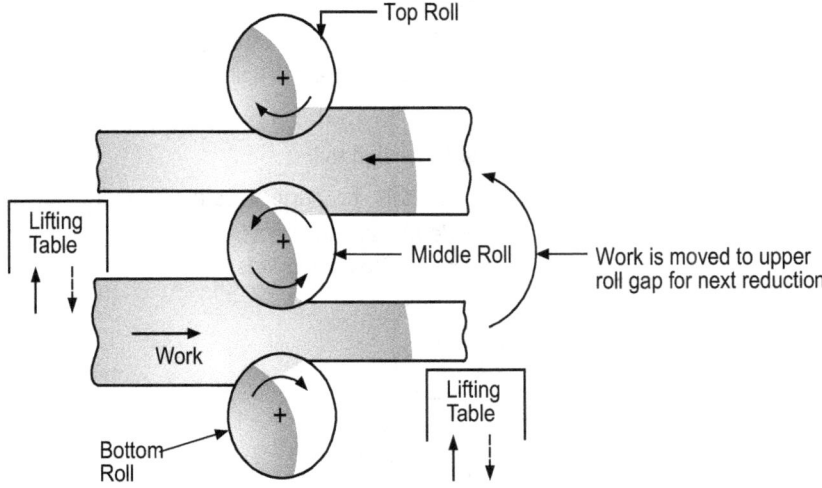

Fig. 4.34 : Three-High rolling mill

• Four-High Rolling Mill and Six-High or Cluster Mill :

Following figure (Fig. 4.35) illustrates that small diameter rolls produce less length of contact for a given reduction and hence require lower force and less energy to produce same shape. Heavy reduction requires larger forces and hence larger rolls. But increased roll diameter increases rolling load, also the spread and forward slip, so it is advisable to go in for small roll diameters. With this view, mills with smaller diameter rolls, more in number are developed.

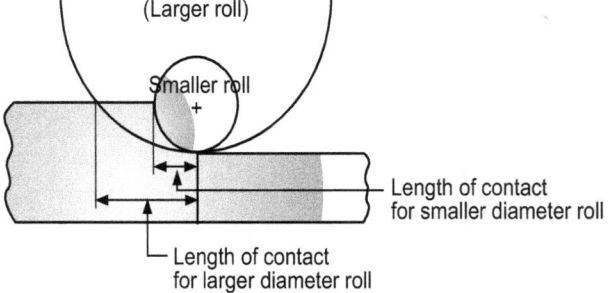

Fig. 4.35: Effect of small roll

Small rolls replacement also is economical. However, small rolls deflect more under roll forces and have to be supported by other rolls. This is done in Four-High and cluster mills. See Figs. 4.36 and 4.37.

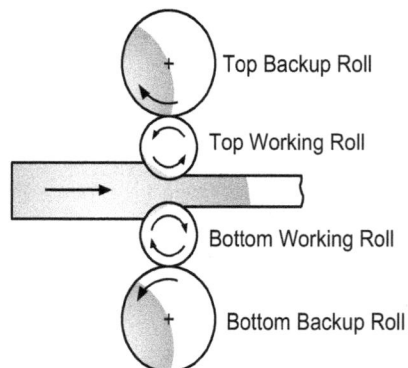

Fig. 4.36: Four-High mill

- **4-High** and **cluster mills** use back up rolls to support smaller work rolls. These configurations are used in hot working of wide plates and sheets.

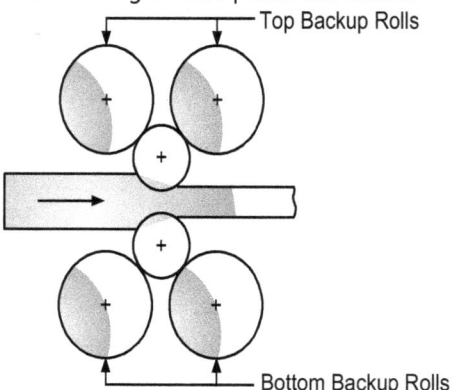

Fig. 4.37 : Six-High or Cluster mill

In cold rolling, where even small deflection of rolls can make variation in thickness of final part, the above mills are used. Foil is always rolled on cluster mills, since small thickness requires small diameter rolls.

• Sendzimir Cold Rolling Mill : (Twenty-High Rolling Mill) :

In this design each working roll is supported throughout its length by two first intermediate rolls, those in turn are supported by 3 second intermediate rolls and so on (See Fig. 4.38.). Only the outer rolls are driven. Working rolls get rotary motion from backup rolls. Rolling strips of various widths, thickness and hardness as well as very thin sheets (even in stainless steel) can be obtained. High carbon steel sheets of 5 to 50 microns thickness can be produced to accuracy of 1 to 5 microns.

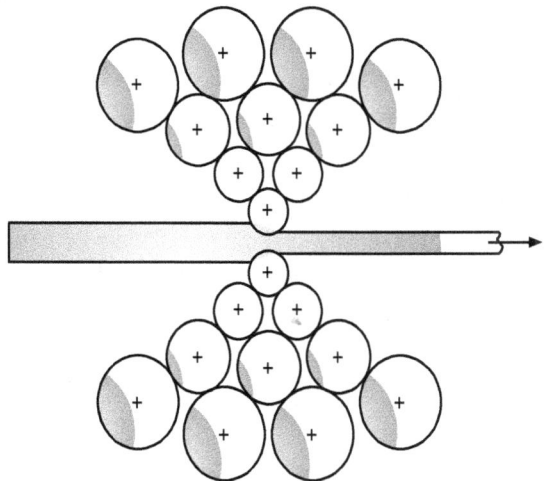

Fig. 4.38 : Sendzimir rolling mill

• Universal Mill :

This type is a combination of vertical and horizontal rolls, mounted in same roll stand (See Fig. 4.39). Vertical rolls give a perfect edge to the product. These mills are used for rolling of beams, H-sections, edge plated products, etc.

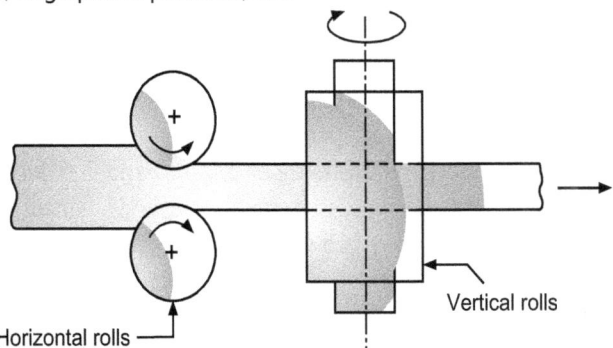

Fig. 4.39 : Universal Mill

• Planetary Mill :

To reduce slabs to coiled hot rolled strips in single pass, planetary mills are used. There are planetary assemblies and feed rolls push slab through a guide into planetary rolls where the main reduction takes place. (See Fig. 4.40).

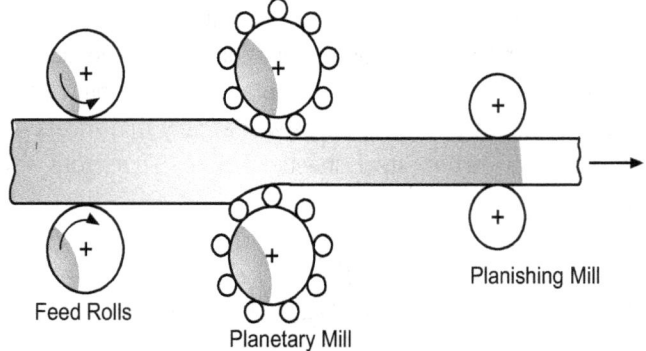

Fig. 4.40 : Planetary Mill

• Tandem Rolling (Continuous Rolling Mills) :

This mill is used in mass production. Billets, blooms or slabs are heated and fed through an integrated series of non-reversible stands (trains). Four high mills (approximately 4) are used for roughing and about 6 to 7 four high mills are used for finishing. The control and speed of sheet is critical. (See Fig. 4.41).

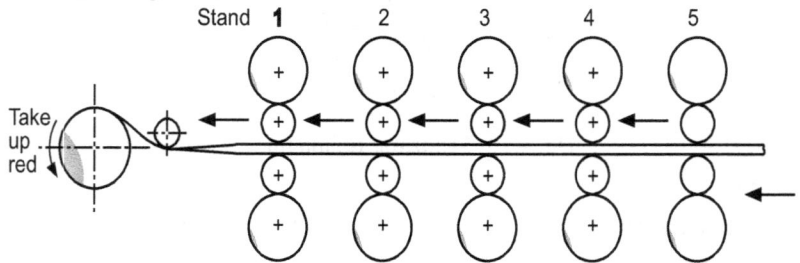

Fig. 4.41 : Tandem Rolling

• Shape-Rolling Operations :

Various shapes can also be produced by rolling process known as shape rolling. Structural shapes, channels, I beams and rail road rails, are rolled by passing the stock, through set of specially designed rolls (rolls having contoured grooves). To obtain final desired shape, the material is passed sequentially through rolls number of times and is reduced non-uniformly. Designing the sequence, number of passes, reduction etc., series of rolls requires considerable experience. This problem is known as problem of roll pass design. Proper roll pass design solution helps avoiding external and internal defects, hold tolerances, and reduce roll wear. Following example illustrates various stages in shape rolling of an 'H' section part. The material is passed through various contoured rolls before 'H' section is obtained. (See Fig. 4.42)

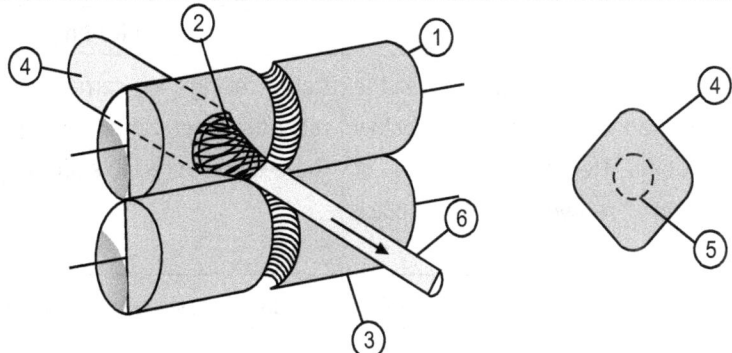

Fig. 4.42 : Shape-Rolling Operations

- **Ring Rolling :**

Ring rolling is a process of producing large diameter ring with reduced thickness. The ring is placed between two rolls (See Fig. 4.43). One is main roll (driven) and the other is idler roll. The rolls rotate and are brought close to each other. This applies force on ring and thickness of ring reduces and as a result hole in ring is expanded. Various shapes can be ring rolled using shaped rolls. Application of ring rolling are large rings for rockets and turbines, gear wheel rims, ball bearing races, flanges, etc.

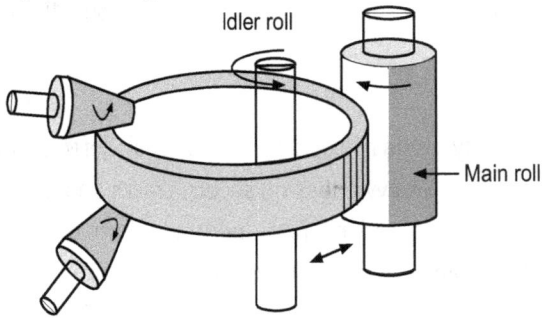

Fig. 4.43 : Ring rolling

Depending on size, ductility and strength of workpiece, ring rolling can be carried out at room temperature or higher temperature. Advantages are short production time, no material wastage, control on tolerance and grain flow in desired direction.

4.6.4 Forming Bars by Hot Rolling Process

When the metal is to be used for bars, blooms are reduced in size to billets by passing through a continuous series or rolls known as a billet mill. The billet is then cut into lengths which are reheated for further rolling in the bar mill. The blooming mill also feeds the rail mill with blooms and the plate mill with slabs. In the rail mill, the heavier structural sections and rails are made. So, it is from this mill that grinders, channels, angle irons are obtained. Aluminium, copper, magnesium and their alloys can be hot rolled.

No.	Hot Rolling	Cold Rolling
1.	Hot rolling is carried out above the recrystallization temperature and below melting point. Hence deformation of metal and recovery take place simultaneously.	Cold rolling is carried out below recrystallization temperature. As such, there is no appreciable recovery.
4.	No internal stresses are set up in metal.	Residual stresses are set up in metal.
3.	Close tolerance can not be maintained.	Close tolerance can be maintained.
4.	Surface finish is comparatively not good.	Surface finish is good.

- **Microstructure in Rolling :**

The structure of cast initial starting material before rolling is typically dendritic and includes coarse and non-uniform grains. This structure contains porosities and is brittle. Hot rolling converts cast structure into a wrought structure. This structure has finer grains. Brittle grain boundaries are broken down; internal defects (e.g. porosity) are removed. Hence ductility increases. Hot rolling temperature for aluminum alloys is about 450°C, for alloy steels is 1250°C.

- **Defects in Rolling Process :**

Rolled sheets and plates may contain external and internal defects. Scale, rust, scratches, cranks, pits are external defects. Weavy edges on sheets, cracks and alligatoring are shown in Fig. 4.44. Alligatoring may be caused by non-uniform deformation during rolling or by presence of defects in the original cast billet. Cracks are result of poor ductility of material at rolling temperature. These defects are removed by shearing and slitting operations.

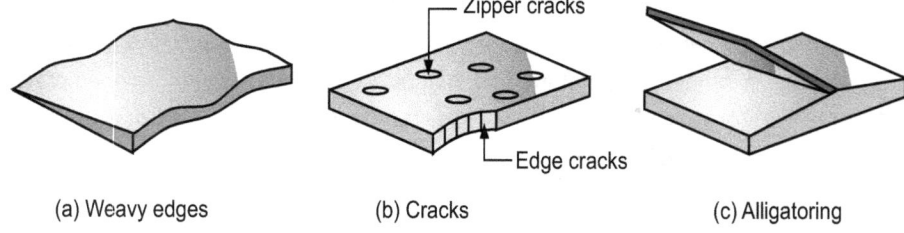

(a) Weavy edges   (b) Cracks   (c) Alligatoring

Fig. 4.44 : Defects in rolling

4.5.5 Flat Rolling Analysis

Rolling is the process of reducing the thickness of long work piece by compressive forces applied through a set of rolls as seen in Fig. 4.45.

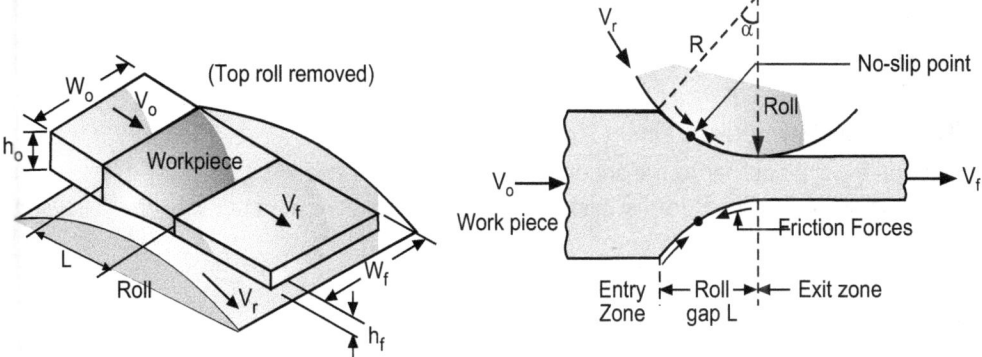

Fig. 4.45 : Flat Rolling Process

In flat rolling reduce to thickness hf by a pair of rotating rolls, each roll being powered through its own shaft by electric motors. The surface speed of the rolls is Vr. The velocity of the strip increases from its entry value, V0, as it moves through the roll gap. The velocity of the strip is highest at the exit from the roll gap. At one point along the contact length, called the neutral point or no-slip point, the velocity of the strip is the same as that of the roll. To the left of this point, the roll moves faster than the strip. To the right of this point, the strip moves faster than the roll.

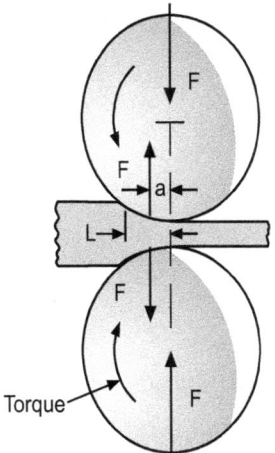

Fig. 4.46 rolling forces

Frictional Forces :

Increasing friction means increasing forces and power requirement. High friction damages the surface of the rolled product. However friction is necessary for rolling materials.

Draft is the difference between the initial and final thickness. Higher the friction and larger the roll radius, the greater the maximum possible draft

$$\text{Maximum possible Draft} = (h_0 - h_f)_{max} = \mu^2 R$$

Where

μ = the coefficient of friction

R = the roll radius

Roll Force and Power Requirement :

Since a force perpendicular to the arc of contact (Fig. 4.46) is needed, rolls apply pressure on the material in order to reduce its thickness. The **roll force** is estimated with the following formula:

$$F = LwY_{avg} *1.2$$

Where

L = roll strip contact length, $L = R\sqrt{h_o - h_f}$

w = width of the strip

Y_{avg} = average true stress of the strip

(Note that, higher the coefficient of friction between the rolls and the strip, the greater becomes the divergence, and the formula predicts a lower roll force than the actual force.)

The **roll power** formula:

$$\text{Power} = (\text{Torque})* (\text{angular speed})$$
$$= (F (L/2))* (2\pi N/60)$$
$$= 2\pi F L N/60{,}000 \text{ in [kW]}$$

Where

N = angular speed of roller in [rpm].

he Y_{avg} is obtained from the formula:

$$Y_{avg} = \frac{K*e^n}{1+n}$$

Where;

K = strength Coefficient

n = Strain Hardening Exponent

e = true strain = $\ln \frac{h_o}{h_f}$ K and n are material constants and they are obtained from the Table 4.1.

Table 4.1 : Typical Values for k and n at Room Temperature

	K (MPa)	n
Aluminium		
1100–O	180	0.20
2024–T4	690	0.16
6061–O	205	0.20
6061–T6	410	0.05
7075–O	400	0.17

(Contd.)

Brass		
70–30, annealed	900	0.49
85–15, cold-rolled	580	0.34
Cobalt-based alloy, heat-treated	2070	0.50
Copper, annealed	315	0.54
Steel		
Low-C annealed	530	0.26
4135 annealed	1015	0.17
4135 cold-rolled	1100	0.14
4340 annealed	640	0.15
304 stainless, annealed	1275	0.45
410 stainless, annealed	960	0.10

4.6 EXTRUSION

Extrusion is defined as a process in which metal is reduced in cross-section by forcing it through a die. This process is similar to squeezing tooth paste from a tube. Cylindrical bars and other complex solid shapes and hollow cross-sections (tubes) are produced by this method.

The starting material is cast or rolled billet. Extruded products have constant cross-section since the die geometry remains the same throughout the operation. Extrusion may be carried out at room or elevated temperature depending on ductility of material.

The products extruded are doors and window frames (in aluminium), railing for sliding doors, tubes, architectural shapes, door handles, brackets, etc. Commonly extruded materials are aluminium, copper, steel, magnesium and lead (Refer Fig. 4.47).

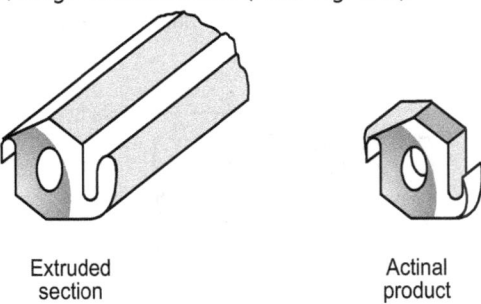

Extruded section   Actinal product

Fig. 4.47 Extruded parts

Extrusion can be classified as forward, backward and impact extrusion.

• **Forward or Direct Extrusion :**

A round billet is placed in a chamber (or container) portion of die. It is forced through a die opening by a hydraulically driven ram (Refer Fig. 4.48). Depending upon the shape of die opening, the product of a particular cross-section is produced. In this process, the direction in which material leaves the die is the same as that of punch motion, hence the name forward extrusion. In the case of hollow forward extrusion (Hooker Extrusion) the slug is hollow piece. In this case, the punch has a shoulder as shown in Fig. 4.49. Punch acts as a mandrel. The bottom of cup may be either opened or closed. During the forward stroke, metal is forced through the annular opening forming a cup. Flange that is produced in this process can be made thinner by having proper tool design.

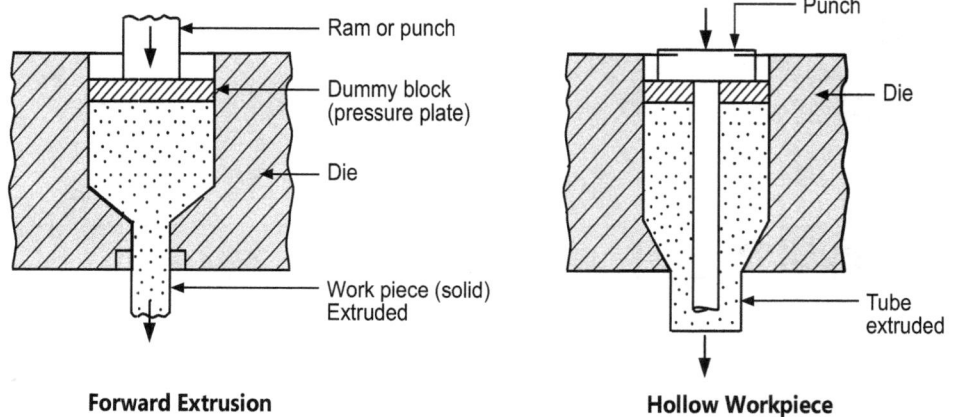

Fig. 4.48

• **Backward or Indirect Extrusion :**

In solid backward extrusion, the die is mounted on to the end of the hollow ram and enters the container (See Fig. 4.49). During stroke of ram, die applies pressure on billet (i.e. die moves towards the billet) and deformed metal flows through the die opening in the direction opposite to that of ram. In forward extrusion scrap produced is 18 to 20 % while in backward extrusion it is less (5 to 6 %) of the billet weight. In backward extrusion, force for extrusion is less by 25 to 30 %.

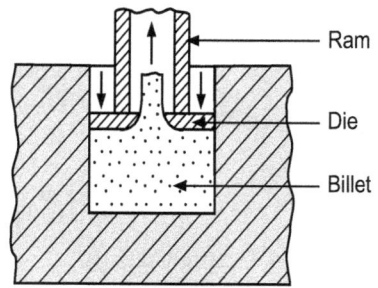

Fig. 4.49 : Backward extrusion

- **Side Extrusion : (Lateral Extrusion) :**

The movement of the material is in a direction perpendicular to that of ram motion. Refer Fig. 4.50. The force required for extrusion is very high. So it is used for non-ferrous metals or highly plastic metals like lead. Lateral extrusion is used for sheathing of wire and coating of electric wire with plastic.

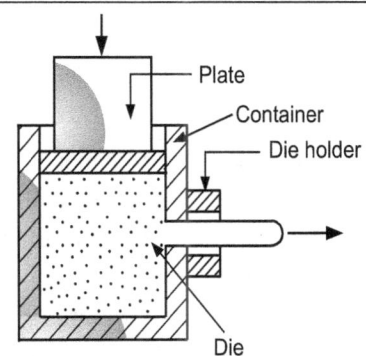

Fig. 4.50 : Side Extrusion

Fig. 4.51 shows details of die in extrusion. The geometric variables are die angle α, the ratio of cross-sectional area of billet to that extruded part A_0/A_f. (This is called extrusion ratio.)

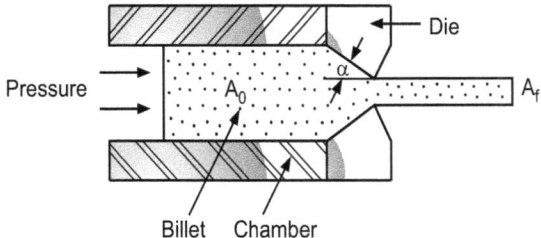

Fig. 4.51 : Forward Extrusion dies details

Extrusion process variables are temperature of billet, the speed at which the ram travels and type of lubricant used. Extruded products have an elongated grain structure in the preferred direction. Extrusion ratios range from 10 : 1 to 100 : 1. Tolerances in extrusion are ± 0.25 to 4.5 mm. The presence of die angle causes a small portion of the end of the billet to remain in the chamber after the operation has been completed. This piece called scrap or butt end, is removed by cutting off the extrusion at die exit.

4.6.1 Hot Extrusion

For metals having low ductility at room temperature or in order to reduce forces required for extrusion, the extrusion is carried out at elevated temperature. For lead 200 to 250°C, aluminium 375 to 475°C, copper 650 to 975°C, steels 875 - 1300°C and refractory alloys 975 to 2200°C are temperatures of extrusion for some metals.

Die wear can be excessive. Cooling of hot billet in cold container may cause problems and affect flow of metal in the die, producing non-uniform deformation. Extrusion dies may be heated to avoid this. Hot billet develops undesirable oxide films. To avoid this, dummy block (pressure plate) placed ahead of ram is made a little smaller in diameter than container. Thus after extrusion, a thin cylindrical shell is left in container which is later removed. Special considerations are given for die designing of dies for hot extrusion.

Lubrication is important in hot extrusion. Glass is used for steels, stainless steel and high temperature metals and alloys.

4.6.2 Cold Extrusion

This term denotes a combination of operations such as direct and indirect extrusion and forging. This is used for making tools and parts of automobiles, farm equipments.

Starting material is slug cut from cold finished or hot rolled bar, wire or plate. Cold extrusion has following advantages :

- Improved mechanical properties because of work hardening.
- Good control of tolerance. No subsequent machining is required.
- Improved surface finish.
- No billet heating.
- High production rate.

Disadvantages are magnitude of stresses on tooling in cold extrusion is very high. Lubrication is critical.

4.6.3 Impact Extrusion

This process is similar to indirect extrusion and is included in cold extrusion category shown in Fig. 4.52 (a) and (b) is a punch that comes down rapidly on the slug, which is extruded backwards.

The thickness of tubular extruded section depends on clearance between punch and die. Collapsible tubes used for tooth paste are made by this process. Non-ferrous metals can be rapidly impact extruded by presses.

Thin walled tubes with thickness to diameter ratio as small as 0.005 can be produced by this process.

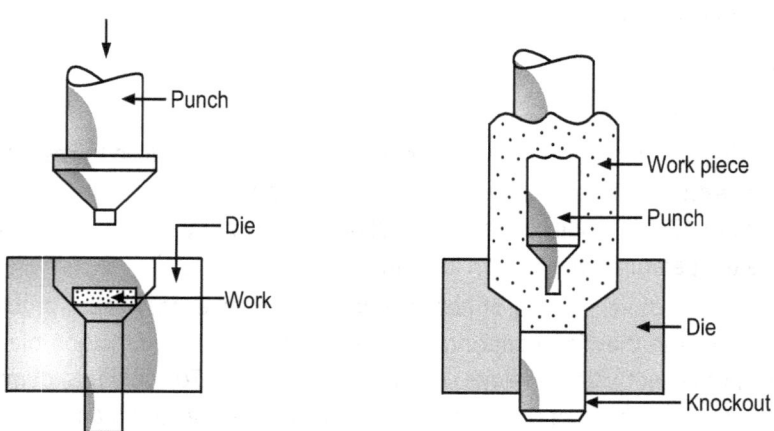

(a) Impact extrusion of collapsible tube

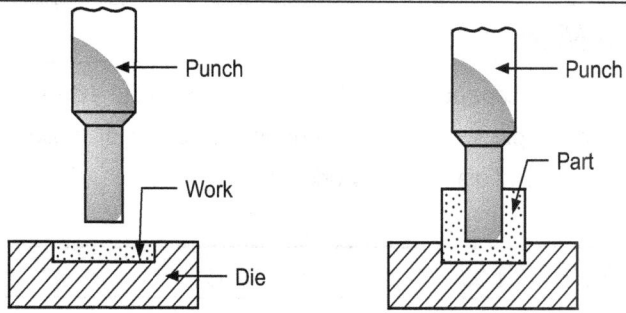

(b) Impact extrusion

Fig. 4.52 : Impact extrusion

4.6.4 Hydrostatic Extrusion

Here, liquid medium is used for transmission of the force to workpiece. Due to hydrostatic pressure, ductility of metals is increased and hence brittle materials like cast iron, tungsten can be formed. Pressurised fluid (vegetable oil) also acts as lubricant. Tooling is somewhat complex and long cycle times are required. See Fig. 4.53.

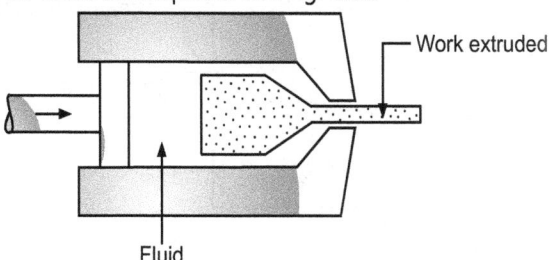

Fig. 4.53 : Hydrostatic Extrusion

4.6.5 Defects in Extrusion

Surface Cracking :

Surface cracking is a result of temperature, friction and too high speed. At low temperature, friction and too high speed. At low temperature, cracks may be produced by periodic sticking of extruded part along the die land.

Pipe :

Surface oxides and impurities are drawn into centre of the billet. This defect is known as pipe defect.

Cracks :

Cracks may get developed at the centre of product, called centre cracking. Tendency of centre cracking increases with increasing die angle and impurities and decreases with increasing extrusion ratio and friction.

4.6.6 Extrusion Machines

Hydraulic presses are used. Capacities as high as 120 MN. For cold extrusion vertical presses are used. They have less capacity. Crank and knuckle presses are also used. Choice of press depends on shape, weight and diameter of workpiece.

4.7 DRAWING PROCESS

This is a process of reducing the cross-section of a round rod or wire by pulling it through the die. Maximum reduction in cross-sectional area per pass is 63 percent. Various solid sections also can be produced (like extrusion) by drawing through dies with profiles. The wall thickness, diameter and shape of tubes produced by extrusion or other processes can be reduced by tube drawing process. Tubes as large as 0.3 metre in diameter can be drawn by this method (See Fig. 4.54).

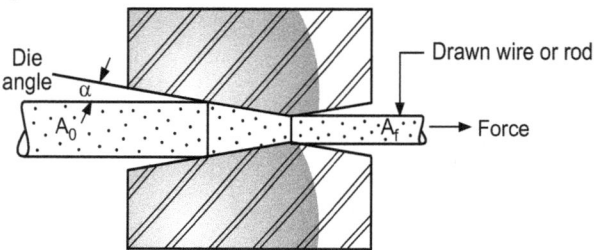

A_0 - original area, A_f - final area, · - die angle = 6 to 15°

Fig. 4.54 : Drawing operation

Drawing speeds vary from 1 m/s to 4.5 m/s for heavy sections to 50 m/s for very fine wire (used in electromagnets). Die material is tool steel and carbides and diamond for fine wire. Typical oils, emulsions of fatty or chlorinated additives, chemical compounds are used as lubricants. Defects are similar to those in extrusion.

- **Wire Drawing :** This involves pulling of metal through a die by means of a tensile force applied to the exit side of the die. Metal flow is caused by radial compression force. Fig. 4.55 (a) and (b) show the draw bench used for wire drawing. Metal can be drawn to very small diameters and to exact sizes.

The surface finish obtained in cold drawing is excellent. Wires for electrical and transformer industry, filaments and lead in wires for lamps, etc. are some applications of this process. Wire is generally defined as rod that has been drawn through a die at least once. Wires have diameter less than bar.

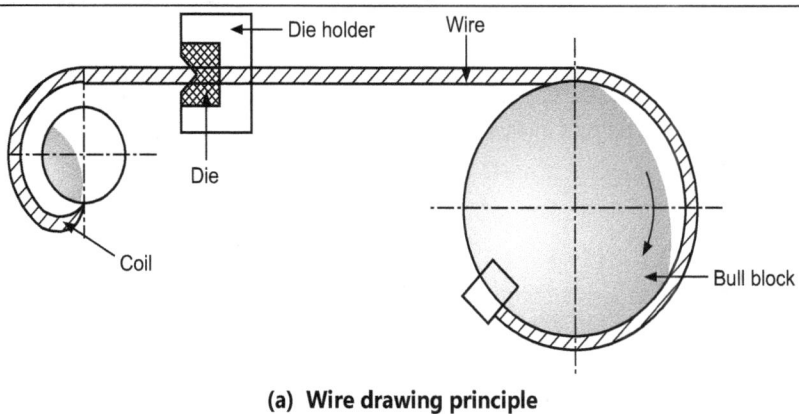

(a) Wire drawing principle

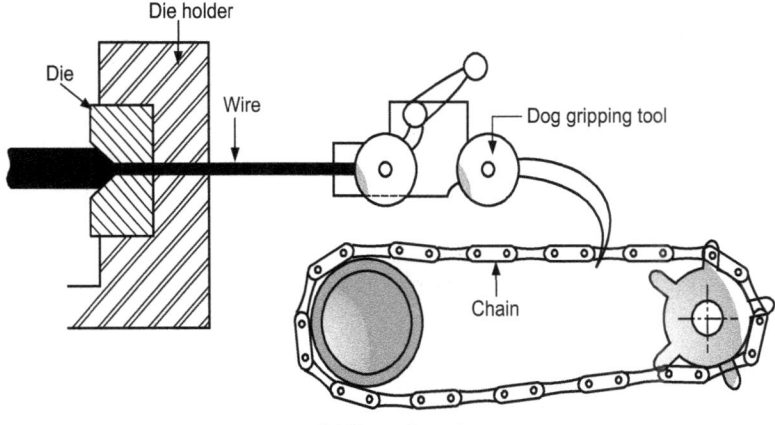

(b) Draw bench

Fig. 4.55 : wire Drawing

Tube drawing :

Tube drawing can be done with or without mandrel. Variety of diameters and wall thicknesses can be produced from the same initial tube stock (See Fig. 4.56). Drawing process mainly employed for hollow components. According to different material, thickness variation mandrel used in tube drawing. Drawing forces get reduced by using mandrel during production. Stress concentration also get reduced by using mandrel.

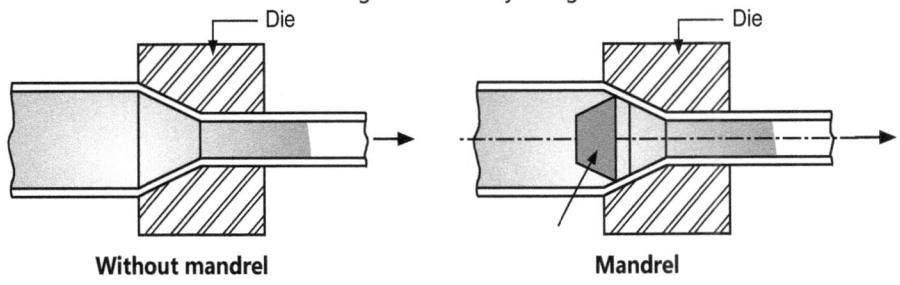

Fig. 4.56 : Tube drawing

QUESTIONS

1. Describe with the help of a neat sketch a board hammer used for drop forging.
4. Explain 'Rotary Swaging' process and state its applications.
3. Write a short note on Rolling mills
4. Describe spinning process. State its applications in manufacturing.
5. States the advantages and limitations of cold working process.
6. Describe the following processes.
   (i) Roll forging
   (ii) Tube drawing
   (iii) Extrusion
7. Describe with sketches only 3 high mill and cluster Rolling mills. State their relative merits.
8. Write a short note on Board Hammer.
9. Write a short note on spinning.
10. What is 'Impact Extrusion'?
11. Describe with the help of a neat sketch a Board-Drop hammer used for drop forging. State their relative merits.
14. Describe the following processes :
    (i) Shot peening
    (ii) Wire drawing.
13. What is roll forging ? What for is it used ?
14. How does direct extrusion differ from indirect extrusion ? Discuss their relative merits and demerits.
15. What is meant by 'cold working process' ? List different cold working processes along with their applications.
16. What is impact extrusion ? Explain the process and state its specific applications.
17. Describe the process of wire-drawing.
18. Describe with the help of a neat sketch a board hammer used for drop forging.
19. How direct extrusion differs from indirect extrusion ? Discuss their relative merits and demerits.
20. What is meant by 'cold-working process' ? List different cold working processes along with their applications.
21. How does Roll forming process differ from spinning process ?
24. Describe press forging process. How does it differ from drop forging ?

23. Explain the process of wire drawing.
24. Explain with the help of figure the process of 'Rotary Swaging'. Name the different components produced by it.
25. Write down difference between hot rolling and cold rolling.
26. Explain 'wire drawing' principle with suitable sketch.
27. Explain forward extrusion and backward extrusion process with figure.
28. Write short notes on the following :
    (i) HERF
    (ii) Roll forging.
29. Differentiate between hot working and cold working of metals.
30. Explain the following processes :
    (i) Metal spinning
    (ii) Tube drawing
31. Explain 'Rotary Swaging' process and state its applications.
34. Explain with the help of a neat diagram a "Deep drawing process". Give its product application.
33. Compare between rolling and forging as hot working process.
34. Explain drop forging process with suitable diagram.
35. Write down any four sample components manufactured by cold working and hot working process.
36. Explain basic principle of wire drawing with suitable sketch.
37. List different cold working processes along with their application and example.
38. Describe metal spinning process with neat diagram.
39. Explain with neat diagram, upset or machine forging process and mention any one sample component manufactured by upset forging process.
40. Draw only setup of tube drawing process and show the following main elements on it :
    (i) Mandrel
    (ii) Die.
41. Draw only sketch of principle of metal spinning cold working process and show main parts on it.
44. List any four sample components manufactured by hot working rolling process.
43. With the help of neat sketch, explain only basic principle setup of HERF cold working process.
44. Compare three high rolling and planetary rolling mill with respect to its diagram, application, nature of construction and material of roller.

45. Explain only operation principle of HERF (High Energy Rate of Forming) process with the help of neat sketch.
46. Explain only principle of operation of rotary swaging cold working process with suitable diagram.
47. Describe systematic sequence of steps in drop forging process in order to finish the forging component for application.
48. Explain the following defects in forging process with its causes and remedies:
    (a) Incomplete component
    (b) Cracks at the corner.
49. Metal cold spinning operation is possible on centre lathe. Comment on it with diagram.
50. Explain in brief drop forging technique. How does this technique vary from press forging technique?
51. Describe the operation of tube drawing.
52. Describe different types of rolling mills.
53. What is meant by 'Cold-working Processes'? List different cold-working processes along with their applications.
43. Explain the following processes:
    (i) Forward extrusion;
    (ii) HERF

Unit - V
JOINING PROCESSES

5.1 INTRODUCTION

Using 'Joining Processes', the required shape is obtained by adding metal or joining two or more parts together.

Materials can be assembled or joined by following various means. e.g.
- Mechanical fastening by screws, nuts and bolts or rivets.
- Joining of similar and dissimilar metals by welding, soldering and brazing techniques.
- Joining of materials by use of adhesives.

5.2 WELDING PROCESSES

Definition:

Welding is a materials joining process in which two (or more) parts are mixed (or joined) at their contacting surfaces by suitable application of heat and/or pressure. The final part that is obtained by joining is known as 'weldment'. Weldment results in homogeneous material and usually has same composition and characteristics as that of the two parts with which joining is done.

5.3 CLASSIFICATION OF WELDING PROCESSES

Some welding processes require only heat while some require heat and pressure. In some other processes, external filler material is required to obtain coalescence (or mixing). Various metals as well as plastics can be joined by welding methods.

Apart from technical factors, welding processes can also be classified on the fundamental approaches used for deposition of materials for developing a joint. Various positive processes involving addition or deposition of metal are first broadly grouped as welding process(see Fig. 5.1). Various welding processes can be categorized into two major groups; viz.

1. Fusion welding processes.
2. Solid state welding processes.

- **Fusion Welding :**

In these processes, heat is used to melt metals to be joined. Filler metal is generally used to add the metal and to facilitate the process and give strength to welded joint. Arc welding, resistance welding, gas welding are various processes in this group.

- **Solid State Welding :**

The process in this category make use of pressure or heat for welding purposes. Though heat is used, temperature in the process is below melting point of metals being welded. No filler metal is utilised in these processes. Diffusion welding, friction welding, ultrasonic welding are some examples. In the following descriptions, in this chapter, both fusion welding and solid state welding processes are studied.

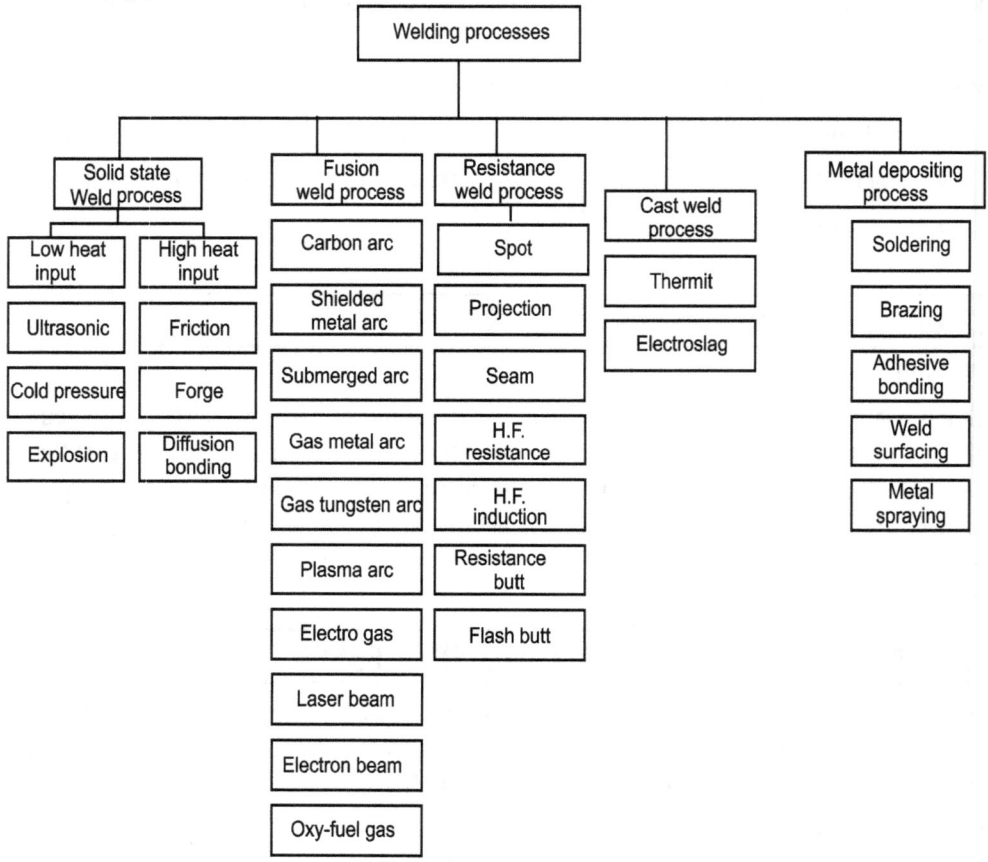

Fig. 5.1 : Classification of welding process

Advantages of Welding :

- Welding produces permanent joint.
- Welded joint can become stronger than parent metals if filler metal is used and it has superior properties.
- In terms of use of material and fabrication cost, welding is the most economical way of joining metals.
- Welding can be done in factory environment as well as in fields.
- Welding process can be mechanised.

Limitations of Welding :

- Skilled operator is required.
- High energy is used.
- No convenience of disassembly.
- Welded joint has certain defects of quality which are difficult to detect.
- Welding creates distortion and stresses in the joint. Also physical, chemical and structural changes occur.
- Radiations like light, fumes, spatters are harmful.

5.4 GAS WELDING PROCESS

A concentrated and controlled flame produced by burning a fuel gas with oxygen is a very convenient heat source for welding. Although a number of gases could be used for welding, only acetylene and liquefied petroleum gases are popular. The maximum possible flame temperatures for these gases are,

$$\text{Acetylene} \quad 3050° - 3150° \text{ C}$$
$$\text{LPG} \quad 2400° - 2500° \text{ C}$$

These temperatures are considerably lower than arc temperature (4000° C). Acetylene gives a higher temperature and is more commonly used. The burning of acetylene (C_2H_2) takes place in stages.

$$C_2H_2 + O_2 \rightarrow 2CO + H_2$$
$$2CO + O_2 \rightarrow 2CO_2$$
$$H_2 + 1/2\, O_2 \rightarrow H_2O$$

The reactions together produce about 1.3 MJ/mole. The flame has three distinct zones as shown in Fig. 5.2. Immediately near the tip of the burner (torch) is a small conical zone called as the inner cone. The cone contains partially decomposed gas with carbon particles. These particles glow with a bright luminescence. The middle zone is called as the reducing zone. Here the carbon particles get oxidized to carbon monoxide. The highest temperature occurs in this zone (~ 3000° C) and the region of highest temperature is located at about 3 – 5 mm from the tip of the inner cone. Here there is no ingress of atmospheric oxygen and the zone contains highly reducing carbon monoxide.

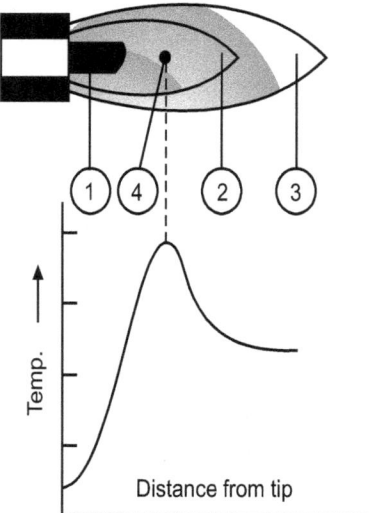

(1) Inner zone, (2) Reducing zone, (3) Outer zone, (4) Point of maximum temperature

Fig. 5.2 : Structure of oxy-gas flame

The complete burning of CO → CO_2 and H_2 → H_2O occurs in the outer most of the third zone. The burning is brought about by the ingress of oxygen from atmosphere. Hence the outermost zone is highly oxidizing. By adjusting the ratio of oxygen to gas a neutral, oxidizing or reducing (carburizing) flame can be produced.

Flame types in Gas Welding

Gas welding is a process of joining two metals by obtaining heat required for melting these metals by use of gas. The metals are melted and without application of pressure they are joined to each other. A filler metal is usually added. Oxyacetylene gas is most widely used and it produces flame temperature of 3500°C. This process can be used for welding of variety of ferrous and non-ferrous materials. There are three types of flames used.

- **Neutral Flame :**

$O_2 : C_2H_2$ = 1 to 1.2 – Neutral Flame :

This flame has well defined zones. Most welding operations are done with a neutral flame as it does not oxidize the metals.

When equal quantity of oxygen and acetylene are used to produce flame, it is known as neutral flame.

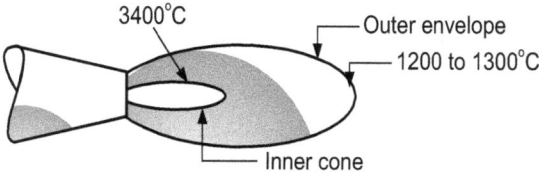

Fig. 5.3 : Neutral flame

This flame has two distinct visible zones as shown in Fig. 5.3 : (1) Outer envelope and (2) Luminous blue inner cone. This type of flame is used for welding of mild steel, stainless steel, copper, aluminium and their alloys.

- **Oxidizing Flame :**

$O_2 : C_2H_2 < 1.3$ – **Oxidizing Flame :**

Here the flame becomes slightly blue and the inner cone becomes shorter than that in the neutral flame. Oxidizing flame is not useful for welding. It has a decarburizing effect due to its oxidizing nature.

In this type of flame, volume of oxygen is more than volume of acetylene. This flame has two zones. The outer envelope is small and narrow while inner envelope is pointed. They are shown in Fig. 5.4.

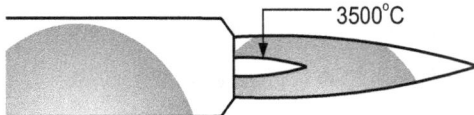

Fig. 5.4 : Oxidizing flame

This flame is harmful, it causes oxidation of steel. Only copper and copper base alloys are welded with this flame. This flame is used as a cutting flame or preheating the metals.

- **Carburising Flame :**

$O_2 : C_2H_2 < 1.0$ – **Reducing Flame :**

Here the inner cone is longer and the outermost zone is ill defined. The flame contains excess of carbon and is used for welding of cast irons, carbon steels, hard facing with carbides etc.

This is also known as reducing flame. It is produced when quantity of acetylene is more than that of oxygen. This flame consists of excess of carbon. This flame has three zones. Outer envelope, intermediate cone and inner cone as shown in Fig. 5.5.

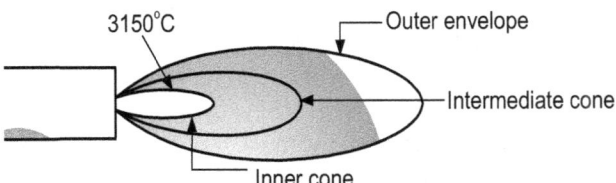

Fig. 5.5 Carburising flame

The temperature of this flame is lower. Processes and metals requiring low heat, such as brazing, soldering, flame hardening.

- **The Welding Torch :**

Gas welding is essentially a manual process. The gas and oxygen are burnt by using a hand held 'torch'. A typical welding torch is shown in Fig. 5.16.

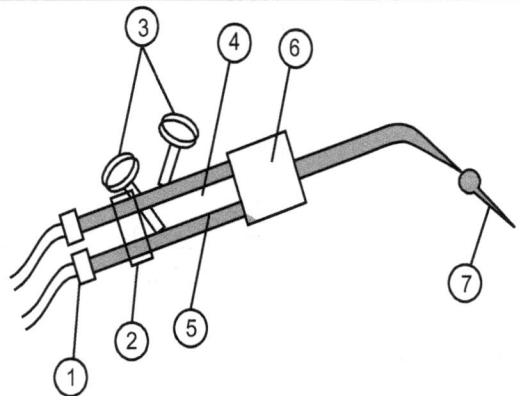

(1) Hose connection, (2) Non-return valves, (3) Gas/oxygen regulators, (4) Central oxygen passage, (5) Outer gas passage, (6) Miner/Injector, (7) Interchangeable tip or nozzle

Fig. 5.6 : A typical welding torch

The torch is made of brass or bronze fittings. At one end there are two pipe connections for oxygen and gas. These connections contain non-return valves which prevent the gases from going back. There are two separate regulating valves for adjusting the flow of air and gas. These valves give control over the flame. The gas and oxygen are mixed in the injector. The mixture flows forward to the tip where it is ignited.

Several types and sizes of tips are available. They can be interchanged to obtain a flame of required size.

- **Gas Welding Setup :**

Fuel gas LPG or Acetylene is available in cylinders. Under pressure, LPG is a liquid which vaporizes to a gas. Acetylene is highly explosive under pressure. It is dissolved in acetone. The acetylene cylinder contains acetone and a porous ceramic material. The porous medium increases the surface of dissolution. Oxygen (pure or mixed with air) is also available in cylinders.

The oxygen and acetylene cylinders are fitted with valves (generally two stage) and pressure gauges. The regulators and all other fittings for the gas connections have left hand threads, so that they can not be interchanged with other gas cylinders. Where portability is not a problem, acetylene can be generated in shop by reacting calcium carbide CaC_2 with water.

Several types of gas generators are available. They are based either on addition of controlled CaC_2 lumps to water or addition of controlled amounts of water to CaC_2. These generators are shown schematically in Fig. 5.7.

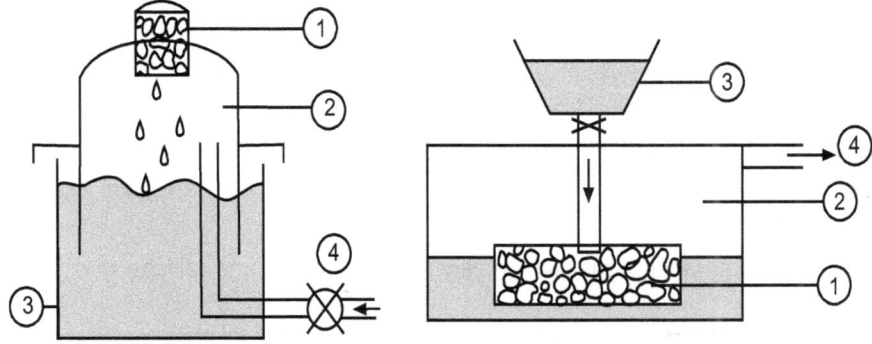

(1) Carbide lumps, (2) Gas chamber, (3) Water, (4) Gas outlet

Fig. 5.7 : Typical acetylene generators

- **Gas Welding Techniques :**

The welder manipulates the torch by one hand and feeds the filler metal wire to the pool with the other hand.

$$CaC_2 + H_2O \rightarrow CaO + H_2C_2 + Heat$$

In one technique called as fore hand welding, the torch moves from right to left and the filler is ahead (towards the left) of the flame. In the back hand technique, the torch is ahead of the filler. In either processes, it is necessary to hold the flame at an correct angle with the joint so as to get maximum heat transfer. Difference between is as follows :

	Forward Techniques	Backward Techniques
1.	Also called as leftward welding.	Also called as rightward techniques.
2.	Weld is made from right to left.	Weld is made from left to right.
3.	(diagram: Rod 30°–40°, Blowpipe 60° to 70°, Workpiece, Welding)	(diagram: Rod 30°–40°, Blowpipe 40° to 50°)
4.	Blowpipe should be given a small sideways movement.	No lateral movement given.
5.	60° to 70° is the angle made by blowpipe with the plane of weld.	40° to 50° is the angle made by blowpipe with the plane of weld.
6.	For plates having thickness upto 3 mm.	For plates with thickness more than 3 mm.

Advantages and Limitations of Gas Welding :

- No power supply is required, hence welding can be done in field or on site.
- Temperature available is lower than an arc.

- Heat transfer is slow, hence the welding speed is low.
- The flame is adjustable to give a neutral, oxidizing or reducing atmosphere as required. Hence the process can be used for all ferrous and non-ferrous materials.
- Due to low heat input, thin parts can be joined.
- There is a possibility of explosion if the equipments (the gases) are not properly handled.
- Because of portability, gas flame is very useful for repair and salvage work.

5.5 HEAT AFFECTS ZONES (HAZ) IN WELDING PROCESS

Before understanding HAZ, let us understand **Weldability of metals.** It is capacity of metals welded into inseparable joints to form a homogeneous structure after ensuring complete immiscibility of materials. There are physical, chemical, metallurgical changes produced in base metals being welded, resulting in number of defects. A good welded metal must perform its function satisfactorily. Heat affected zone is that portion of the base metal whose mechanical properties and microstructures have been altered by the heat of welding.

- **The Grain Growth Region :**

It is immediately adjustment to the weld metal zone. In this zone, parent metal has been heated to a temperature well above upper critical temperature. This resulted in grain growth or coarsening of the structure.

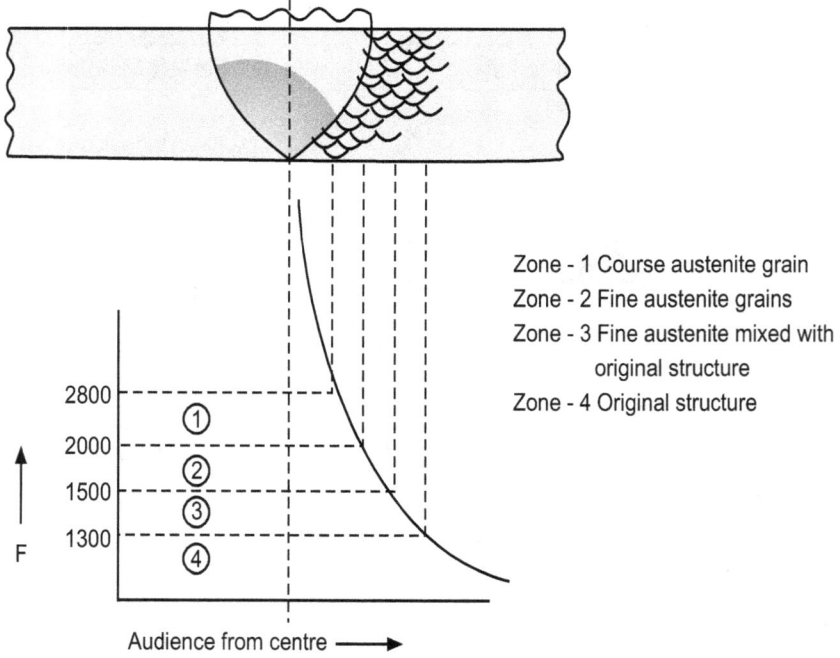

Zone - 1 Course austenite grain
Zone - 2 Fine austenite grains
Zone - 3 Fine austenite mixed with original structure
Zone - 4 Original structure

Fig. 5.8 : Heat affected regions

- **The Grain Refined Region :**

Adjustment to the grain growth region is the grain refined region. This zone indicates that the parent metal has been heated to just above the A_3 temperature where grain refinement is completed and the finest grain structure exists.

- **The Transition Zone :**

In the transition zone a temperature range exists between the A_1 and A_3 transformation temperature where partial allotropic recrystallisation takes place.

- **Unaffected Parent Metal :**

Outside the heat affected zone is the parent metal that was not heated sufficiently to change its microstructure.

5.6 TYPES OF WELD JOINT

Welding process can produces a 'weld joint', which is a junction of edges or surfaces. The types of joints are as follows:

- **Butt Joint :**

Parts lying in same plane are joined at their edges.

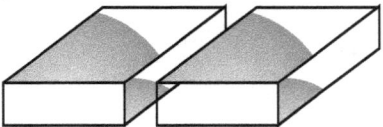

Fig. 5.9 : Butt joint

- **Lap Joint :**

Two parts are overlapping each other.

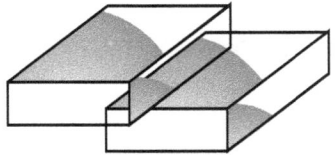

Fig. 5.10 : Lap joint

- **Tee Joint :**

One part is perpendicular to the other to resemble letter T.

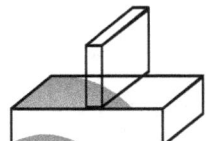

Fig. 5.11 : Tee joint

- **Edge Joint :**

One edge of each part is parallel and common.

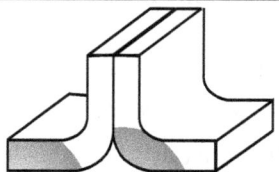

Fig. 5.12 : Edge joint

- **Corner Joint :**

Parts are joined at corner, as shown in Fig. 5.13.

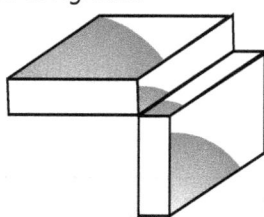

Fig. 5.13 : Corner joint

- **Fillet Weld :**

This is used to fill in the edges of plates created by corner, lap and tee joints.

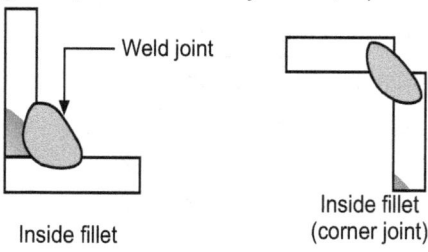

Fig. 5.14 : Fillet weld

- **Groove Welds :**

The edges of parts to be joined are prepared to have groove of shape like V, U or bevel etc. and filler metal is filled in it to obtain welding.

Single 'V' groove weld

Fig. 5.15 : Groove weld

Plug welds and slot welds are used for joining flat plates as shown in Fig. 5.16.

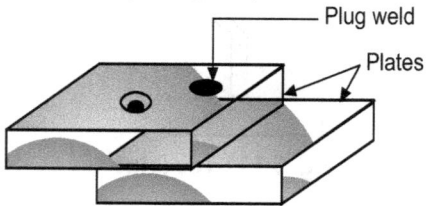

Fig. 5.16 : Plug weld

- **Spot Welds and Seam Welds :**

Spot weld is a small fused section between surfaces of two sheets or plates. Seam weld is similar to spot weld. It consists of a more or less continuously fused section between two sheets or plates.

5.7 WELDING PROCESSES

- **Arc Welding :**

Arc welding is a fusion welding process. The mixing of metals is achieved by heat from an electric arc between electrode and work. The process is shown in Fig. 5.17. The work materials to be joined form one electrode and the other electrode either consumable or non-consumable is held in the holder. Power supply of either AC or DC is

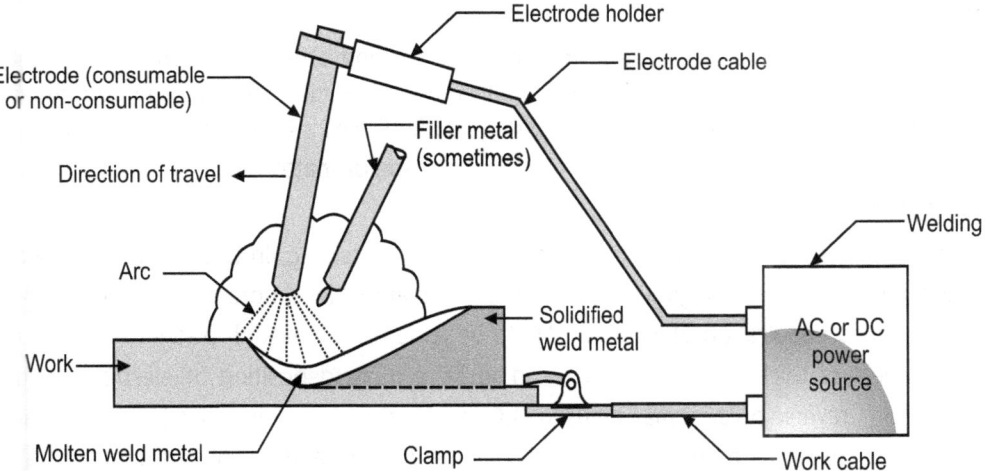

Fig. 5.17 : The basic configuration and electrical circuit of an arc welding process

Available between two above stated electrodes. To initiate arc, the electrode is brought into contact with work and then quickly separated from it by a short distance (3 to 6 mm). There is flow of electrons i.e. discharge of electric current across the gap in the circuit. The electric energy thus formed produces temperature of 5500°C or higher. This is sufficient to melt any metal. A pool of molten metal consists of base metals, filler metal and is formed near tip of electrode. In most arc welding processes, filler metal is added during operation to increase volume and strength of weld joint. The electrode is moved along ahead the joint and molten weld pool cools and solidifies at the back. This movement of electrode relative to work is either done by a human or by automatic means.

The welding circuit consists of a welding machine, lead cables, electrode holder, electrode and workpiece.

Electrodes :

These are classified as consumable and non-consumable electrodes. Consumable electrodes provide filler metal in arc welding. They are available in the forms of rods (sticks) and wire. Rods are 9.5 mm or less in diameter and 225 to 450 mm long. Non-consumable electrodes are made of tungsten. They do not melt by arc. The filler metal if required has to be supplied by separate wire of proper composition.

Arc :

The temperature after arc is formed is high. The metals at this temperature become reactive to oxygen, nitrogen and hydrogen in air. The mechanical properties are seriously affected by this reaction. To protect welding from this, the shielding around the arc is required. This is accomplished by covering electrode tip, arc, and molten weld pool with envelope of gas or flux or both, which prevent the exposure of weld metal to air.

Flux :

This is a substance to prevent the formation of oxides and other unwanted contaminants. Unwanted substances dissolve in flux and float in molten metal pool. They can be removed easily after solidification. This is known as slag tabili. Fluxes are also useful for protective atmosphere for welding, tabilization of arc and reduction of spatter.

Power Source :

Direct current as well as Indirect current are used in arc welding. In D.C. machines, work is positive and electrode is negative. This is straight polarity. Here more heat is generated at work and deep penetration of weld in parts to be joined is achieved. If plates that are to be joined have less thickness and it is desired to have more deposition of electrode in the welding joint, reverse polarity may be used. A.C. machines are less expensive to purchase and operate, but are restricted to welding of ferrous metals. D.C. equipment can be used on all metals with good results and is generally noted by better arc control.

Following is comparison between AC and DC welding.

AC Welding	DC Welding
1. A transformer contains no rotating parts.	1. Rotating parts are present in generator.
2. Maintenance cost is less.	2. Higher.
3. No problem of arc blow.	3. Arc blow occurs which is difficult to control.
4. Only ferrous metals are welded.	4. With change in polarity, both ferrous and non-ferrous metals are welded.
5. Arc is never stable.	5. Arc is stable.

6. No-load voltage is frequently too high (upto 70 V) that is why it is more dangerous.	6. No-load voltage is low, so it is safer.
7. An A.C. welding transformer is cheaper and simple in operation.	7. A D.C. generator set is costlier and more cumbersome in a operation.
8. Efficiency of transformer is high.	8. Efficiency of transformer is low so high cost of electrical energy.
9. Maintenance of transformer is easier because of no moving parts.	9. In D.C. it is easier to strike an arc even with thin electrodes.
10. Polarity concept is not present.	10. Polarity concept is present and can be used advantageously.
11. Welding of non-ferrous metal is not possible.	11. Welding of non-ferrous metals is possible.

5.8 ARC WELDING PROCESS

(1) Process Using Consumable Electrodes :

(a) (SMAW) : Shielded Metal Arc Welding :

Here, a consumable electrode, consisting of a filler metal rod coated with chemicals that provide flux and shielding, is used. The filler metal used in the rod must be compatible with the metal to be welded and its composition usually is very close to that of the base metal. The contents of coating are cellulose powder, oxides, carbonates and others held by silicate binder. Metal powders are sometimes included to have alloying effect. The coating is melted due to heat of welding and protective atmosphere is provided around arc. Slag formed is later removed. Stick is replaced after getting consumed.

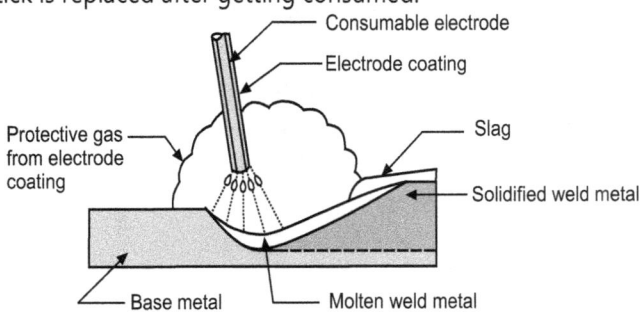

Fig. 5.18 : Shielded metal arc welding (SMAW)

For welding, the welding stick bare metal end is held in electrode holder and is connected to power source. The holder has an insulated handle so that it can be held and manipulated by a human welder. Currents used are 30 to 300 A and voltages from 15 to 45 volts.

This process is used for construction, pipelines, machinery structures, ship building, fabrication job shops and repair works. The equipment is versatile, portable and cheap.

(b) Gas Metal Arc Welding (GMAW) :

In this process, arc is struck between consumable bare metal wire and shielding is accomplished by flooding the arc with a gas. The bare wire is fed continuously and automatically from a spool through the welding gun. The diameter of wire is about 0.8 to 6.4 mm. This size depends on thickness of parts being joined and deposition rate required. Inert gases like argon, helium and active gases such as carbon dioxide are used for shielding purpose.

For welding mild steel, CO_2 is used while for aluminium and stainless steel, inert gases are used.

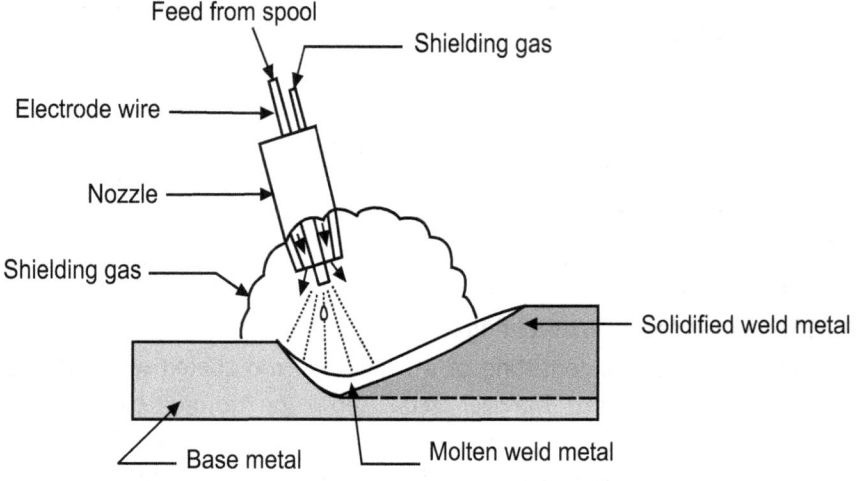

Fig. 5.19 : Gas metal arc welding (GMAW)

This process is also known as MIG welding, i.e. metal inert gas welding. Complete MIG welding set consists of source of power supply, MIG gas welding gun, inert gas cylinder, gas regulators, spool for electrode wire, filler metal electrode, wire feeding arrangement etc.

The process is faster, gives deeper penetration with strong and tough joints. The quality of welds is high and free from blow holes, porosity and gas contaminants. The cost of equipment is high and equipment is not easily portable. (Figs. 5.19 and 5.20)

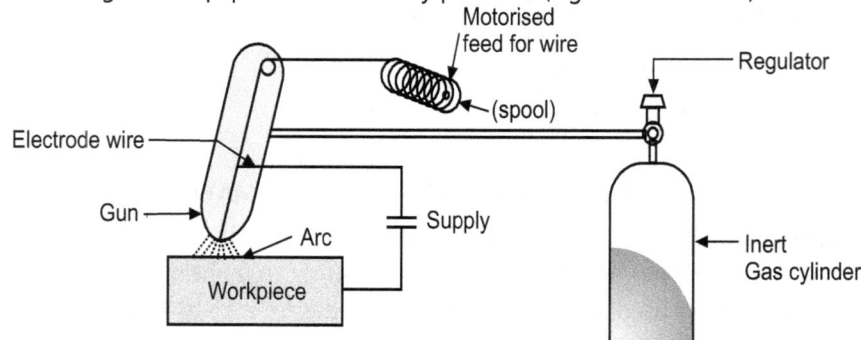

Fig. 5.20 : GMAW (or MIG) welding setup

(c) Flux-Cored Arc Welding (FCAW):

This is an adaptation of **SMAW** process. Here, electrode is a continuous tubing that contains flux and other ingredients in its core. This wire is flexible and is supplied in the form of coils and fed continuously. Shielding may be obtained either by flux core or in case of welding steels, shielding gases from outside are supplied like that of GMAW process. This is used for steels and stainless steels welding over a wide stock thickness range. High quality welds that are smooth and uniform are produced. (See Fig. 5.21)

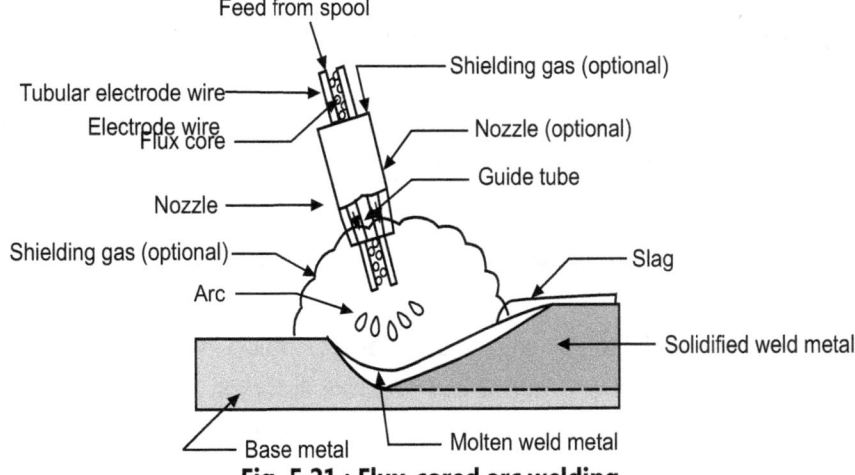

Fig. 5.21 : Flux-cored arc welding.

The presence or absence of externally supplied shielding gas distinguishes the two types : (1) self-shielded, in which the core provides the ingredients for shielding and (2) gas-shielded, in which external shielding gases are supplied

(d) Submerged Arc Welding :

This process uses a continuous, consumable bare wire electrode. Arc shielding is provided by a cover of granular flux. The electrode wire is fed automatically from a coil into the arc and flux is introduced to the joint slightly ahead of weld arc by gravity from a hopper (See Fig. 5.22). The flux completely submerges the arc, preventing spark, spatter and radiations.

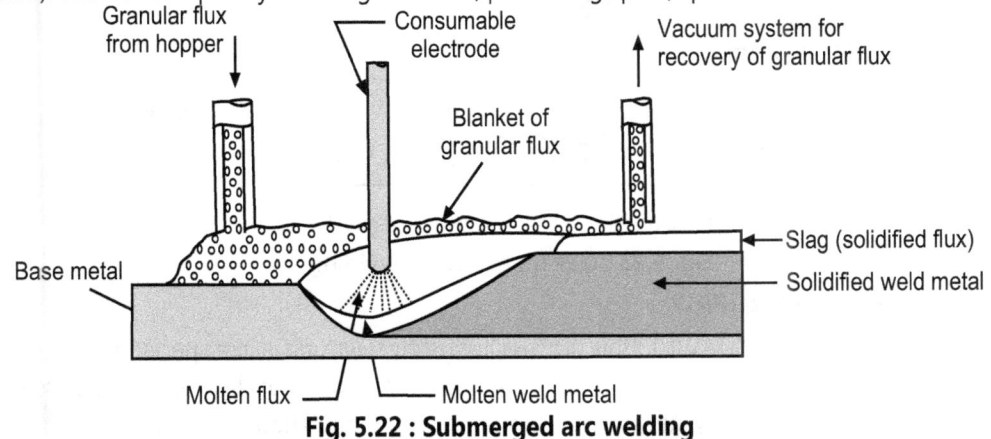

Fig. 5.22 : Submerged arc welding

This is widely used in steel fabrication for structural shapes, longitudinal seams for pipes, tanks, pressure vessels etc. Low carbon, low alloy and stainless steels are easily welded by this process.

(2) Processes Using Non-consumable Electrodes :

(a) Gas Tungsten Arc Welding (GTAW) :

Also known as TIG welding (Tungsten inert gas welding). In this process, arc is struck between a non-consumable tungsten electrode and workpiece. Inert gas is used for shielding purposes.

The filler metal may or may not be used. When filler metal is used, it is added to the weld pool from a separate rod or wire, being melted by heat or arc. Tungsten is good electrode and have melting point of 3410° C. Inert gases are argon, helium or mixtures.

Tungsten electrode is mounted centrally in a nozzle shaped hood through which an inert gas is passed. (See Fig. 5.23).

Generally, D.C. current of 500 to 950 amp. is used for most thicknesses. This is a very quick process. Welds produced are strong, ductile and free from distortion and corrosion resistant.

This process is specially used for welding light alloys and non-ferrous materials like copper, aluminium and magnesium.

It can also be used for joining various combinations of dissimilar metals. While stainless steel can be welded, cast iron, wrought iron, lead, tungsten are difficult to weld by this process.

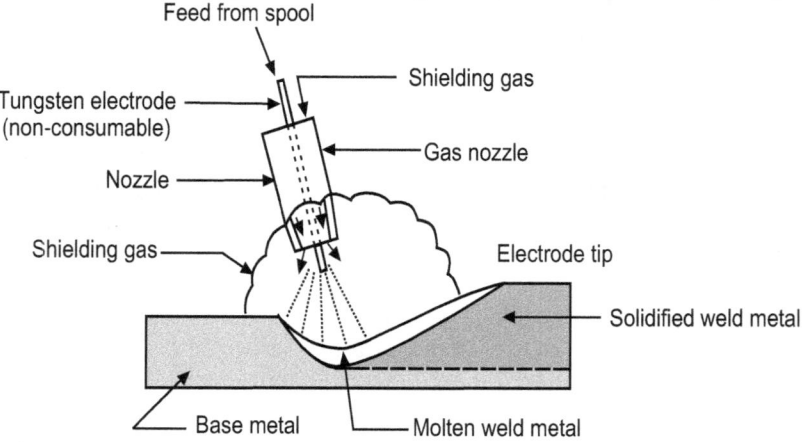

Fig. 5.23 : Gas tungsten arc welding

(b) Plasma Arc Welding (PAW) :

This is a special form of (GTAW). In this process, tungsten electrode is in a special nozzle. The arc is struck between tungsten and nozzle. When gases (argon, argon-hydrogen) are passed through arc and nozzle, they get ionised and become plasma. The nozzle directs the high velocity stream of plasma on the work to melt it. The temperature of about 28000°C can be obtained and is enough to melt any known metal.

The process is used for welding tube mills, rockets, motors, nuclear submarine plates. The arc produced is stable and quality of welds is excellent. The process is quick. Almost any metal can be welded including tungsten. Equipment is costly.

A plasma is thus ionised hot gas having electrons and ions. A concentrated plasma arc is produced and directed to the area where welding is to be done. The arc is struck between electron and nozzle and gas is ionised to become plasma. Heat is carried to workpiece by plasma gas. This is non-transferred method. In transferred arc method the arc is struck between electrode and workpiece. See Fig. 5.24 (a) and (b).

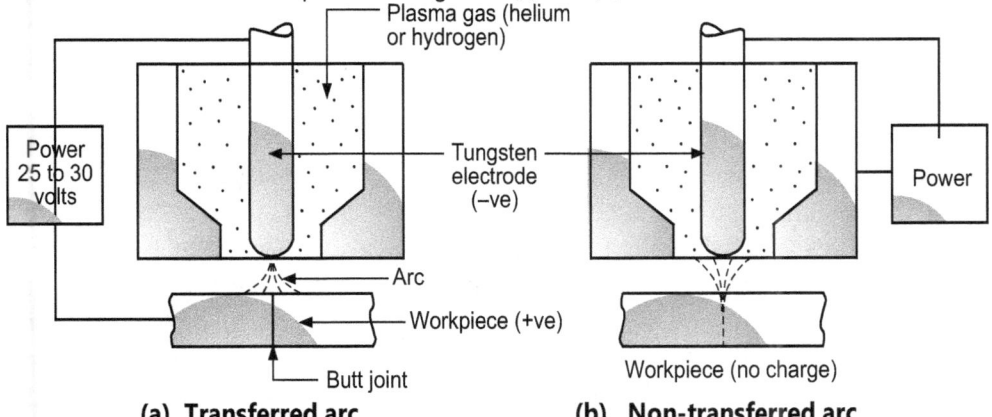

(a) Transferred arc (b) Non-transferred arc

Fig. 5.24 Plasma Arc Welding

Deeper and narrower welds can be obtained because of very high energy concentration. Higher welding speed (120 – 1000 mm/min), less distortion are advantages.

Some more Applications :

Welding of tube mills, rockets, S.S. tubes, nickel and titanium alloys.

(3) Other Arc Welding and Related Processes :

(a) Electro Slag Welding :

In this process, weld is produced by molten slag which melts the filler metal and surfaces of workpieces to be welded.

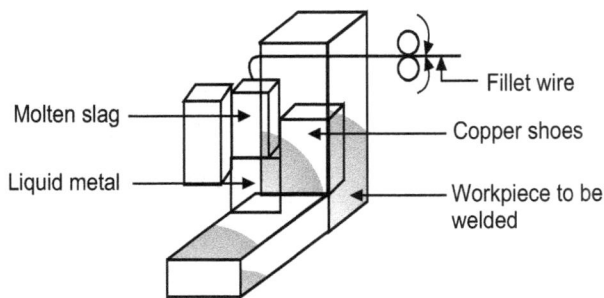

Fig. 5.25 : Electro Slag Welding

Initially arc is struck to melt metal and flux is added. Then arc is stopped and slag is maintained in molten state by resistance of electric current passing between electrode and work piece. Temperature inside the molten metal pool is 1950°C and outside is 1650°C. The temperature is sufficient to melt the base metal and filler metal to form weld.

The rate of metal deposition is high and no arc occurs during welding process. The process is used for larger depths and in welding bevels, V, U and J grooves.

(b) Thermit Welding :

Mixture of aluminium powder and iron oxide is known as 'Thermit'. When this mixture is ignited, heat is evolved through reaction. Thermit welding is a fusion welding process. Heat required for mixing is obtained by superheated molten metal made by chemical reaction of thermit.

Finely mixed powders of Al and Fe_3O_4 (1 : 3) when heated has following reaction :

$$8\ Al + 3\ Fe_3O_4 \rightarrow 9\ Fe + 4\ Al_2O_3 + Heat \uparrow$$

This heat creates temperature of 2500°C, resulting in superheated molten iron and aluminium oxide. In this process, superheated iron is contained in a crucible located above the joint to be welded as shown in Fig. 5.26. After the reaction is complete, the crucible is tapped and liquid metal flows into a mould built specially to surround the weld joint. The metal of reaction is hot and it melts the edges of base parts to be welded. Upon solidification, mixing and welding occurs. Aluminium oxide floats on the surface, protects iron from becoming oxide and is removed as slag after solidification. After cooling, the mould is broken away and gates and risers (the process seems to be similar to casting process) are removed by cutting.

Railroads joining, repairs of cracks in large steel castings and forgings, large diameter shafts, machine frames etc. are some applications of them it welding process.

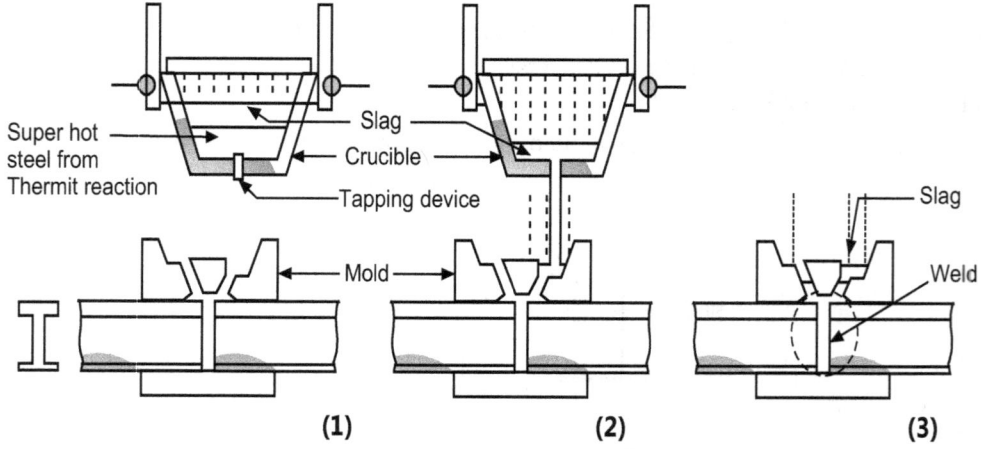

Fig. 5.26 : Thermit welding : (1) thermit ignited; (2) crucible tapped, superheated metal flows into mould; and (3) metal solidifies to produce weld joint

The heat required for joining of metals is produced by exothermic chemical reaction. This is a fusion welding process. Thermit is a registered trademark. Thermit mixture used in welding steel and cast iron is finely divided particles of iron oxide (Fe_3O_4) and aluminium oxide (Al_2O_3), iron and aluminium. The parts to be welded are aligned and gap is kept between two. Around the parts a sand or ceramic mould is built. The thermit mixture is then poured in the gap. The superheated products of the reaction are allowed to flow into the gap, melting the edges of the parts being joined. After weld cools, excess material is removed by machining. Copper, brass, bronze, nickel, chromium, magnesium are welded by this process.

Some More Applications :

This process is suitable for welding and repairing large forgings and castings. Rail road rails, broken frame of machines, spokes of driving wheels are some applications of thermit welding.

(c) Atomic Hydrogen Welding

Molecular hydrogen (H_2) dissociates to atomic state (H) at high temperature, according to the reaction

$$H_2 \quad 2H \pm 5.3 \text{ MJ}$$

On recombination to molecular state, the absorbed heat is released creating a heat source suitable for welding. An arc is created between two tungsten electrodes using AC power. Hydrogen is introduced (see Fig. 5.27) in the arc around the electrodes. At the high temperature of the arc, hydrogen dissociates. The arc is just above the joint area. Near the surface of metal, hydrogen recombines and the released heat heats the metal to the welding temperature.

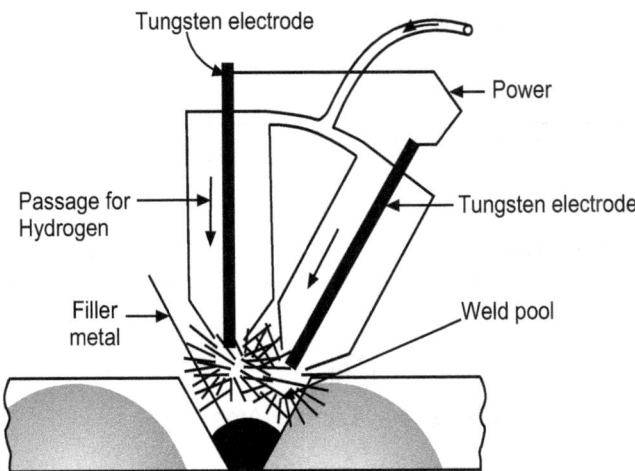

Fig. 5.27 : Atomic hydrogen welding

Because of the highly reducing atmosphere in the weld area, excellent welds are produced. The process is used for alloy steel and thick (upto 10 mm) plates. There is some hazard due to the explosive nature of hydrogen.

(d) Stud Welding (SW) :

This is a special version of arc welding and is automated to suit production needs. As the name suggests, the process is applied for joining fasteners (screws, studs, hooks etc.) to a flat surface.

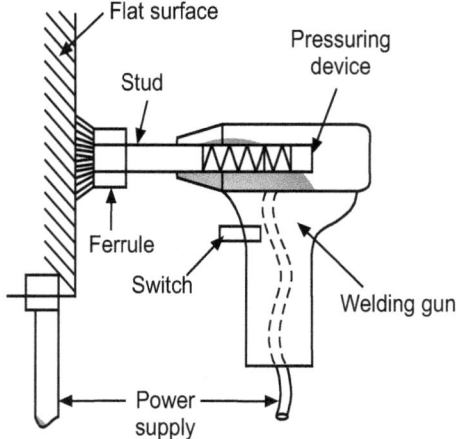

Fig. 5.28 : Stud welding

The stud to be welded is held in a pistol like device (see Fig. 5.28) or in a special chuck on a press. The stud and the flat surface are connected across a D.C. power supply. The stud is brought near the surface, when sufficiently close an arc is struck in the contact area. A small portion of the stud melts. On application of pressure, a firm joint is formed. The application of pressure is automatic. To concentrate the heat in contact area and to prevent damage from spatter, the welding end of the stud is fitted with a ceramic ferrule (ring). After welding the ferrule is broken away. Stud welding is highly automated and fast, no skill on the part of the operator is required.

5.9 ELECTRIC RESISTANCE WELDING (ERW)

- **Principle of ERW :**

If two metal parts, connected to an electric supply are short circuited, a heavy current will flow through the contact area. The current will generate heat at the contact area. This heat will be

$$H = I^2 Rt \qquad \ldots (5.1)$$

where, I = Current (Amp.)

R = Resistance of contact area, (m^2)

t = Time for which the current flows (sec.)

This heat will be sufficient to melt or to plasticize the contact area. If a pressure is applied on the contact, a sound joint restricted to the contact arc (the SPOT) will be obtained. This is the principle of electric resistance welding. Electric resistance welding processes are classified as below:

- Spot Welding (Lap)
- Butt Welding
- Seam Welding
- Projection Welding
- ERW Stud Welding

- **ERW Setup :**

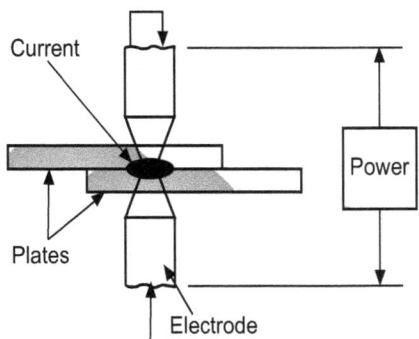

Fig. 5.29 : (a) Principle of ERW

A typical setup of ERW is shown in Fig. 5.29 (a) and (b). The surfaces to be joined are clamped between two water cooled copper electrodes. A low voltage high current power supply is connected across the electrodes. Pressure is applied by foot pedal in small manual machines or by a pneumatic or hydraulic mechanism on automatic machine. On switching the power ON for a predetermined time, a welded spot is created at the contact. By moving the job and repeating the cycle, a number of desired spots can be obtained. The spots can be overlapped to obtain a continuous joint. Continuous spot welding is called as 'Seam welding'.

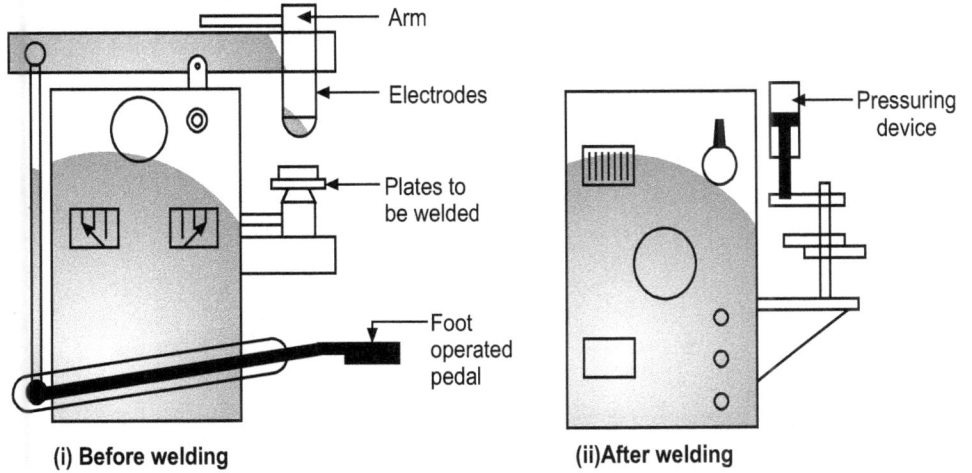

Fig. 5.29 (b) : Typical machines for ERW

In order to obtain a good joint the contact area must be free from dirt, greeze or oxides. The heat is required to be concentrated over the contact area, hence the electrical resistance of all the parts of the circuit should be extremely lower than the resistance of contact. The actual area of contact will be dependent upon the pressure applied. On manual machines there is no control on pressure. In automatic machines the pressure and its gradient can be precisely controlled and timed. See Fig. 5.29 (c).

Similarly, the delivery of current to the joint and the rate of rise and fall of the current during a cycle can be precisely controlled by using electronic circuits. As the current flows through the joint for a very small time (3 - 10 sec), the power supplies are rated in kVA and a duty cycle i.e. time for which maximum current can be drawn without damage. For regular production jobs, special resistance welding machines are built with facilities to handle a particular job.

- **Some Varieties of ERW :**

ERW can also be adopted for butt welding. The two parts to be joined are held horizontally on a lathe like machine. Collars attached to the parts carry the current. The parts (single or both moving) are brought in contact with a certain pressure and the current is switched ON to create a joint. If the parts to be joined (either one or both) have protruding tibs or 'projections', the spot is created at the contact between the projections. This is the principle of 'Projection Welding.' This process is extensively used in production.

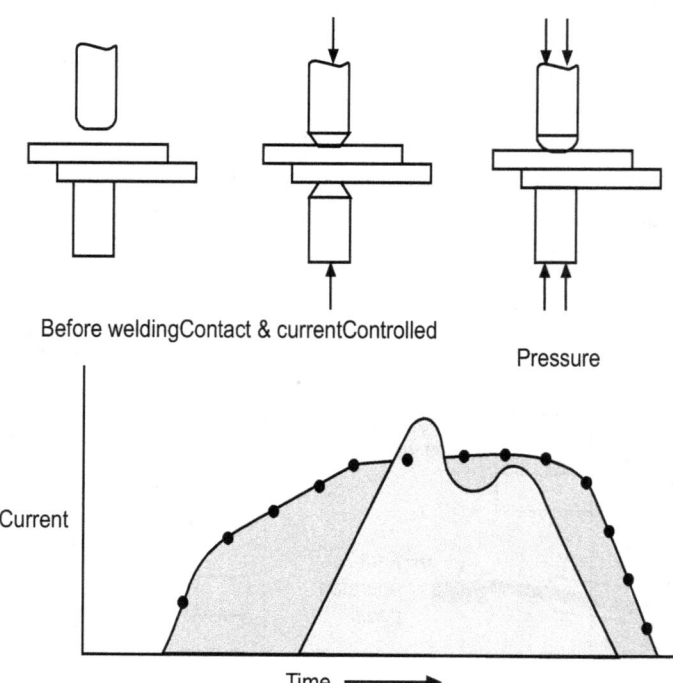

Fig. 5.29 (c) : **Typical spot welding cycle. Electric resistance spot welding**

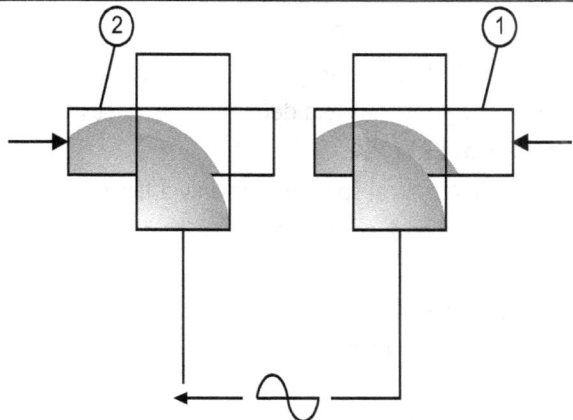

(1) Job, (2) Current carrying clamps

Fig. 5.30 (a) : ERW Butt Welding

Continuous welded 'seam' can be obtained if the job (joint) is moved between electrodes. This is the 'seam welding' process. It is used for making ERW tubes. A strip is longitudinally bent to form a open tube. The open sides are resistance welded by passing them continuously through electrodes and shaping wheels.

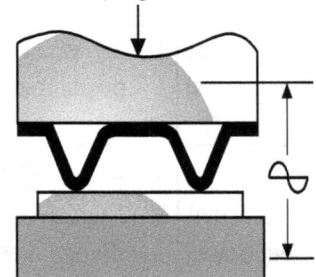

Fig. 5.30 (b) : Projection welding

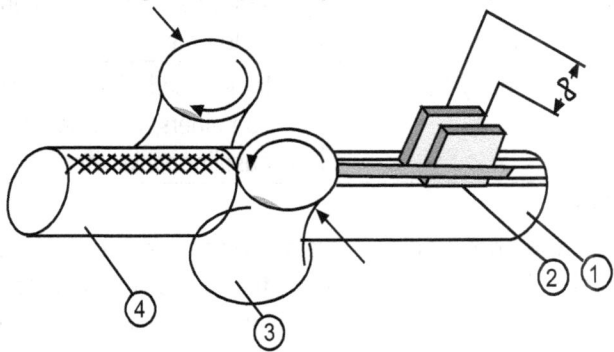

(1) Open pipe, (2) Electrodes, (3) Pressure wheels, (4) Welded tube

Fig. 5.30 (c) : Seam welding

Fasteners such as screws or nuts can be joined to a flat surface by making the fastener one of the electrodes. This is *ERW* stud *welding*.

Small hand-held spot welding guns can also perform small 'stitching' jobs in field.

In some ERW machines, the electrical energy (current) required is "*stored*" in a capacitor which is discharged through the joint to give a definite '*dose*' of current.

Advantages and Limitations of ERW :
- The process is very fast. A typical spot cycle is only a few seconds.
- If the surfaces are clean and correct pressure and current are used, the joint is extremely strong.
- The process can be automated.
- By using electronic and hydraulic power, the process parameters can be precisely controlled.
- Virtually any metal or combinations can be welded.
- There are no problems associated with filler or flux as in arc welding.
- Skilled operators are not required if process parameters are correctly chosen.
- Reliable and reproducible joints are consistently obtained.
- ERW machines are costly to buy and to maintain.

Spot Welding and Seam Welding :

	Spot Welding		**Seam Welding**
1.	In this two or more sheets of metal arc are held together between metal electrodes.	1.	It is continuous weld on two overlapping pieces of sheet metal.
2.	Pointed electrodes are used.	2.	Circular electrodes are used.
3.	A low-voltage current of sufficient amperage is passed between electrodes intermittently.	3.	The current passes through overlapping sheets kept under pressure continuously.
5.	Amount of heat is controlled by the speed of rotation of electrodes.	5.	Amount of heat is controlled by the weld time.
5.	This process is used for body building of vehicles.	5.	It is used for manufacturing metal containers, automobile mufflers, gasoline tanks, etc.

- **Precursion Welding :**

Precursion welding is a resistance welding process in which heat required is obtained from an intense discharge of electrical energy applied to the locality of the proposed weld for an extremely short time. The pressure is applied rapidly (precursively) during or immediately following the electrical discharge.

Precussion welding machine comprises of means for converting alternating current from the mains into direct current (transformer and rectifier), a storage medium and a suitable spot welder. Electrical capacitors are used to conserve the energy until it is required.

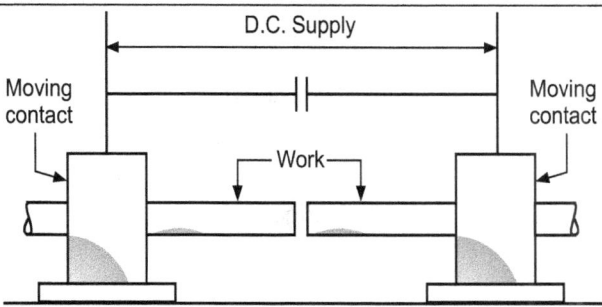

Fig. 5.31 : Precursion welding

The workpieces to be welded are cleaned and clamped into the machine. By application of force, the two workpieces are brought near each other and an arc is struck between the two, which heats the surfaces to be joined. At this point of time, pressure is applied which extinguishes the arc and holds the workpieces together till the weld cools. The advantage of this method is that there is extremely shallow depth of heating and time cycle is very short. The method is used for welding materials having low resistivity and for larger number of dissimilar metals.

- **Flash Welding :**

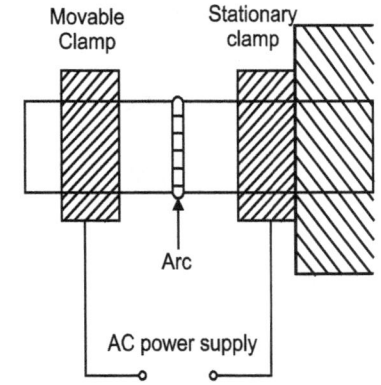

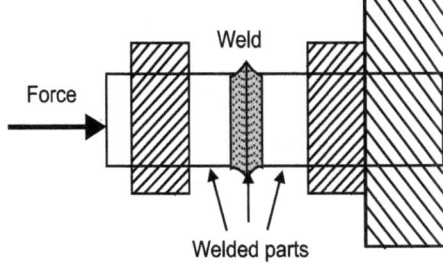

Fig. 5.32 : Flash welding

Flash welding is a type of resistance welding that involves pressing two ends together, while simultaneously running a current between them. This has the effect of forming a joint between the two metals that is free of oxides as the surfaces of the two joining parts is forced out the sides of the joint and is known as flash, hence the name.

Flash welding is a development of resistance butt welding and is particularly suitable for butt welding complex or larger sections. It is used for a wide range of component shapes and sizes from bicycle wheel rims to rails. More efficient energy input, and a more localized and evenly heated zone can be achieved, compared with resistance butt welding. In flash welding, the components are clamped between dies and brought together slowly with the current switched on, see Fig.5.32. Current flows through successive points of contact which heat rapidly melt and blow out of the joint giving the characteristic flashing action. After a pre-set material loss has occurred, sufficient to heat the material behind the interface to its plastic state, the components are forged together to expel melted material and contaminants.

This completes a solid phase forge weld. The joint is then allowed to cool slightly under pressure, before the clamps are opened to release the welded component. The weld upset may be left in place or removed, by shearing while still hot or by grinding, depending on the requirements.

Advantages	Disadvantages	Application
• Joint obtained is clean, as filler metal is not used in this process. • Produces defect free joint. Oxides, scales and other impurities are thrown out of the weld joint due to high pressure applied at elevated temperature.	• The process is suitable for parts with similar cross sectional area. • Joint preparation is must for proper heating of workpieces to take place.	Used for producing joints in long tubes and pipes

5.10 FRICTION WELDING

In this process heat required for joining two parts is generated through the friction at the interface of the two members being joined. See Fig. 5.33.

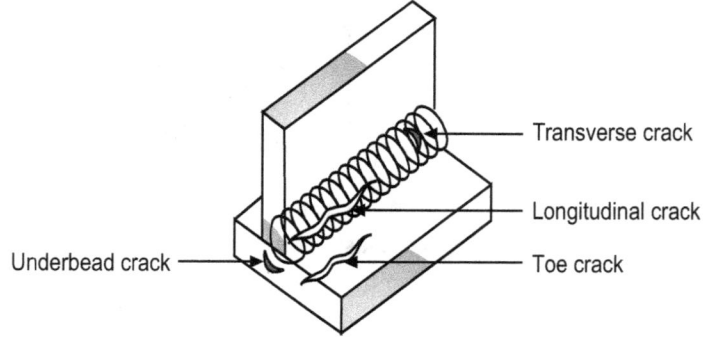

Fig. 5.33 : Friction Welding

One part out of two that are welded, is held in a chuck or collect and is rotated at high constant speed, while the other remains stationary. Axial force is then applied on the two pieces to be joined. After sufficient contact when the required heat is generated, the rotating member is quickly stopped. This helps to avoid destruction of weld by shearing. Then the axial force is increased. The pressure on workpieces friction provides heat for strong joint to be made. Weld zone is confined to narrow region.

Solid as well as tabular jobs can be made by this process. Surface speed of rotating member is as high as 900 m/min. At the joint, bulging takes place and flash is produced. This can be removed by grinding or machining. In inertia welding the energy required for welding is supplied by rotation of flywheels. As the friction at the interface slows the flywheel, axial force is increased. The weld is completed when the flywheel comes to a stop.

In another recently developed process, known as linear friction welding, the interface of the parts to be joined is subjected to linear reciprocating motion. Metals, plastic having shape other than round also can be welded. Friction welding is used for welding of steels, aluminium copper nickel etc.

5.11 FLAME CUTTING

Gas, a suitable burner and a steady hand are all that is needed for cutting mild steel. This principle has not changed since the beginning of the twentieth century. Flame cutting is a combustion process. It is not the heating flame itself that does the actual cutting but an oxygen jet, which burns the material during heat formation and transports the combustion products (slag) away from the cut (Refer section 5.4). When cutting, the purity of the oxygen is of huge importance to the cutting speed. The purer the gas, the higher the cutting speed and the better the productivity and cut quality. Iron is heated on one of its side to a kindling temperature (it is the temperature at which rapid oxidation of material takes place). Cutting torch is moved and the flow of oxygen is suddenly increased in the desired direction. The melting point of iron oxide is much lower than iron. So gas cutting is an oxidation process not a melting process. Aluminum cannot be cut by this process. Steel can be cut by this process. To cut any metal the following condition has to be full filled

- The kindling temperature should be lower than the melting temperature of the metal
- The melting point of the parent metal should have higher temperature than the metal oxide which is formed by reaction with oxygen and it should be fluid in molten state so as to blow out easily.
- It should have low thermal conductivity so that the material can be rapidly raised to its kindling temperature.

5.12 INSPECTION OF WELDS

To check quality of welds, various inspection methods and tests are conducted.

- **Visual Inspection :**

Human operator visually examines the weldment. He checks (a) conformance to the dimensions, (b) warpage, (c) cracks, cavities, incomplete fusion etc. Internal defects cannot be detected by visual inspection.

- **Non-Destructive Testing :**

These testing methods do not destroy the specimen while checking. Dye penetration and fluorescent penetration tests are used to detect cracks and cavities that are open to surface. Internal cracks, cavities and flaws are detected by radiographic and ultrasonic techniques.

- **Destructive Testing :**

Weld is destroyed in testing. Mechanical tests for tension, compression, shear etc. are performed on weld joint. (See Fig. 5.34) Metallurgical tests for microstructure, defects, heat affected zone etc. are performed on welded joint.

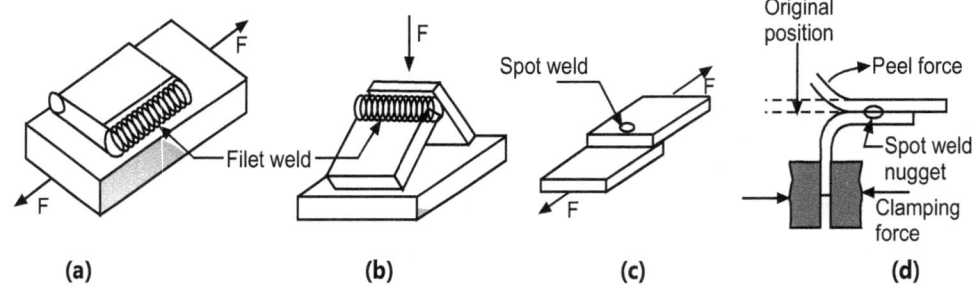

Fig. 5.34 : Mechanical tests used in welding : (a) tension-shear test of arc weldment,
(b) fillet break test, (c) tension-shear test of spot weld, and (d) peel test for spot weld

5.13 SOLDERING AND BRAZING

All welding techniques reviewed so far involved partial melting of base (parent) metal to form a homogeneous bond. In soldering and brazing processes, a joint is formed without melting of base metal. Both techniques have a certain similarity.

- **Process Characteristics :**

In soldering and brazing, the joint is filled by a liquid filler material. On solidification, the filler creates a bond. The melting temperature of the filler is much lower than the base metal. Hence at the process (soldering or brazing) temperatures, there is no melting of the base metal.

Soldering is a lower temperature process. The melting temperature of the filler metal is less than 400° C. Brazing is done at a higher temperature. The melting temperature of filler is higher than 400° C (soldering temperature) but is lower than 900° C. Both processes can be

performed manually or can be highly automated to suit large-scale production variety. The joint or bond is soldering and brazing is created by the filler metal which has :
- A composition which is generally quite different from the base metals.
- A melting temperature which is much lower than that of the base metals.

Hence to obtain a strong joint, it is necessary that the filler completely wets (spreads easily on) the joint surface. The wetting depends on :
- The surface tension and viscosity of the liquid filler material.
- The cleanliness of the joining surfaces.

- **Joint Preparation in Soldering and Brazing :**

Surfaces to be soldered or brazed are cleaned mechanically and chemically to assure a strong bond. During their manufacture the joining surface, come in contact with oil, grease, dirt etc. Some materials like steels easily develop an oxide layer. These surfaces are first cleaned by polishing or grinding to remove all dirt layers. Small articles are brushed and polished with sand or emery paper. Next the articles are cleaned chemically by using an acid and other corrosive chemicals such as chlorides etc. These chemicals react with the joining surface and clean them from foreign materials. If required, the articles are washed and dried.

Dirt and oxides on surfaces prevent the atomic bonding between the filler and the base metal, hence some kind of cleaning must be performed. The actual steps involved in cleaning will depend on the degree of contamination of base metal in their manufacture and handling prior to soldering or brazing. As the strength of joint depends upon wetting and filling of the joint by the filler material, it is necessary to design the joint to provide adequate clearances for the flow of the filler.

Production brazing usually involves the use of filler metal with a preform. The filler metal is in the form of a washer or sheet or wire. While assembling the joint, a preform is inserted in the joint. On heating, the preform melts and the filler metal flows in the joint clearance. For soldering the filler used has a much lower melting point. It is available as a wire or stick. In manual soldering the filler wire is melted and the melt applied to the joint. For large-scale production, the assembly to be soldered is dipped in a bath of molten filler.

Filler materials for both processes are frequently available with flux. The flux is included as a sandwiched layer in the preform or as a core material in filler wire.

- **The Flux Material :**

The general requirements of flux to be used for soldering and brazing are :
- They should have a good fluidity when melted so as to flow in the joint and wet the surfaces.
- Their melting temperature should be lower than that of filler material.
- There should be no residue or ash after they are consumed.
- They should dissolve or chemically remove any oxide or dirt on the joining surfaces.
- Reduce the surface tension of the filler metal.

Main ingredients of soldering flux are zinc and ammonium chlorides, resin and wax. Flux in paste form contains mineral oil, water, castor oil etc. Brazing fluxes are based on borax which can dissolve surface oxides. Other ingredients are sodium and potassium chlorides and fluorides, some wetting agents and oil or water.

- **The Filler Materials :**

Fillers for soldering and brazing should have the following properties :

- Impart adequate strength to the joint.
- They should easily spread and wet the base metal surfaces.
- Brazing and soldering is extensively used in electrical and electronic industries. The filler material used in such joints should have good electrical conductivity.
- Homogeneous structure and a melting point to suit the process.
- Good formability to acquire a wire or sheet form.
- As the filler has a composition different from the base, it should not corrode the base metal by forming a galvanic couple.

Based on these requirements, the following materials are commonly used.

- **Brazing Fillers :**

Copper Base :

These are alloys of copper with phosphorus 7-8 %, alloys of copper and silver and gold 5-30% and alloys of copper and nickel and chromium. Phosphorus in these alloys acts as a powerful deoxidizer and wetting agent.

Silver Base :

These alloys contain 40 – 60% silver, 15 – 25% copper and zinc and small additions of tin. These alloys have very good electrical conductivity and good fluidity. Brasses 50% Zn, Gold, Nickel gold alloys and aluminium silicon alloys are also used as fillers.

- **Soldering Fillers :**

Because of the requirement of low (< 300°) melting point, these materials are based on lead, tin, cadmium, indium etc.

- **Lead - Tin Alloys :** These contain 5 – 60% tin (tin based) and (95 – 40%) lead. These are cheapest and most widely used.
- **Tin - Zinc Alloys :** These are used for soldering aluminium and contain 30 – 90% tin and remainder zinc.
- **Lead - Tin - Antimony Alloys :** These contain lead, tin and 2 – 8% antimony.
- **Indium Alloys :** These contain 95% indium and 5% tin and used for soldering glass to metal.
- **Cadmium Alloys :** These contain about 90% cadmium, silver and / or zinc.

Lead-tin-antimony solders are more common. They are eutectic compositions with melting point of 230° - 250° C.

- **Brazing Operations :**

Manual brazing is performed with a gas flame. The filler is applied separately in the form of wire. The joining parts are first cleaned and then a flux is applied before brazing.

- **Production Brazing :**

This is generally performed with preformed fillers. The joints are cleaned, fluxed and assembled with preform around the joint. The assembled articles are arranged on a convair. Sometimes special fixtures are used to hold the joint, heating methods are used which leads to classification of brazing processes such as Furnace brazing, Vacuum brazing, Induction brazing etc. The assembled articles are heated in a convair furnace in special atmosphere or vacuum to prevent high temperature oxidation. In induction brazing, an induction coil surrounds the joint area and only the area in the shade of the coil gets quickly heated melting the filler material and filling the joint. The whole process takes a few seconds and can be automated. After brazing is over, the flux remaining on joint must be carefully removed.

Advantages and Limitations of Brazing :

- Small assemblies which are impossible to weld can be joined.
- The base metal or assembly is not heated and hence completely protected.
- Brazing gives strong joints which can withstand a temperature of 400° – 500° C.
- By choosing correct filler material, necessary physical properties can be imparted to the joint.
- The process can be automated to obtain high volume production. It can also be done manually to fabricate or repair single assemblies.
- There are no internal stresses or distortions.
- If they are metallized, ceramic parts can be joined to metallic parts (e.g. spark plug).
- Thin walled tubes, parts of widely different thickness, parts having different structures or parts of different metals can be easily joined.

Soldering Operations :

- **Manual Operation :**

For small jobs soldering is done manually by using an *'iron'* or a gas flame. The iron has a special tip made of iron coated copper. The iron is heated on a stove or by an electric heater. Flux and solder are applied separately. This method of soldering is extensively used in electronic circuit fabrication and in plumbing. Various types of tips are available to suit particular job. The manual process is slow as only one job is done at a time.

- **Wave Soldering :**

This is an automatic method developed for soldering assembled printed circuit boards. It should be noted that on a PCB there are large number of joints and all the joints are at one level. The PCB is held on a fixture and the liquid solder passes below it in the form of a wave. At the joints successively touch the *'wave'* and get soldered. This is a very fact method as all the joints are soldered in a minute.

• Dip Soldering :

The article to be soldered is dipped in a bath of liquid filler. This method can not be used for electronic fabrication. Difference between soft and hard soldering is as follows :

Sr. No.	Soft solder	Hard solder
1.	Involves comparatively less temperature.	Involves higher temperature.
2.	Comparatively weaker joint is formed.	The joint formed is stronger.
3.	The solder is composed of lead and tin.	The solder is composed of silver.
5.	The temperature in the process ranges from 150° to 350°C.	The temperature ranges from 600° to 900°C.

Advantages and Limitations of Soldering :

- Soldering is done at a low temperature and hence there is no damage to the joining materials and components.
- Because of low melting temperature, the liquid soldering of all can be easily handled.
- The joints cannot withstand elevated temperature.
- Unsatisfactory joints can be easily desoldered and resoldered.
- Manual soldering requires skill.
- Process can be operated both manually and automatically.

Comparing joining processes w.r. to principle, temperature and application :

	Soldering	Brazing	Braze welding
Principle	It is a joining process where in coalescence is produced by heating to a suitable temperature and by using filler metal.	It is a process where joint is produced by capillary action.	Here capillary action does not play any role. Simple welding helps. Joint produced by adhesion.
Temperature	600°C to 900°C	600°C to 850°C	< 250°C
Application	To join electronic components.	To join pipe fittings, carbide tips to tools.	To join dissimilar metals.

Difference between soldering and brazing is as follows :

Soldering	Brazing
1. The melting temperature of the filler metal is less than 400°C.	1. The melting temperature of the filler metal is between 400°C - 900°C.
2. The filler metal has much lower melting point.	2. Filler metal is used with preform i.e. high melting point.
3. On heating 'preform' melts and the filler metal flows in joint clearance.	3. Filler wire is melted and the melt applied to joint.
5. Main ingredients of soldering flux are zinc and ammonium chloride, rosin and wax.	5. Brazing flux is based on borax, sodium and potassium chloride and fluorides.
5. Soldering fillers are lead alloys, tin alloys, cadmium alloys or indium alloys.	5. Brazing fillers are copper base or silver base alloys.
6. Because of low melting temperature, the liquid soldering of all can be easily handled.	6. The base metal or assay not heated and hence completely protected.

5.14 WELDING DEFECTS

The common defects in welding are residual stresses and distortion in final assembly. Other than these, there are following defects found.

- **Cracks :**

These are interruptions of fracture type either in weld or in base metal. It is a serious defect. The welded joint becomes weak if cracks are present. Welding cracks (Ref. Fig. 5.35) are caused by embrittlement or low ductility of weld and base metal combined with high restraint during contraction.

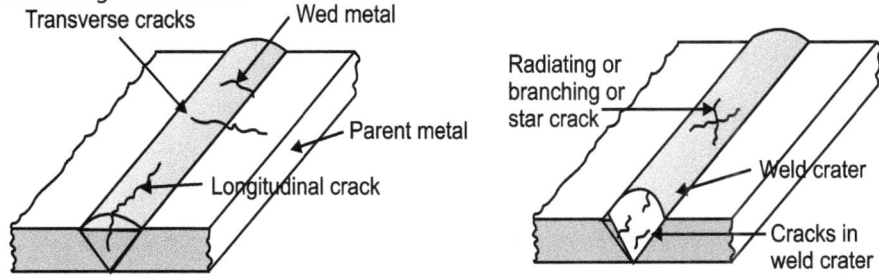

Fig. 5.35 : Various forms of welding cracks

- **Cavities :**

Porosity is present due to entrapped gases during solidification. The voids are spherical or elongated. Shrinkage voids are due to shrinkage during solidification.

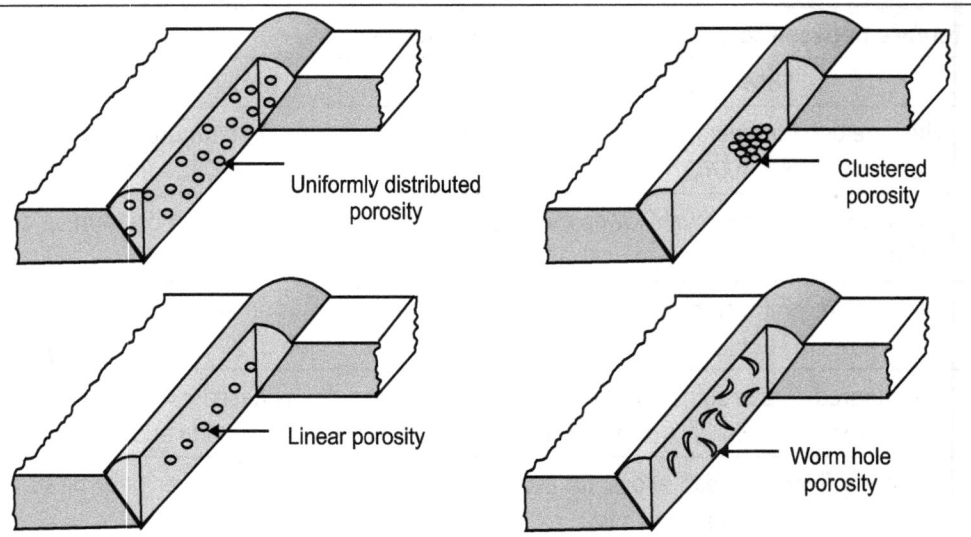

Fig. 5.36 : Different Forms of Porosities

- **Solid Inclusions :**

Non-metallic solid material gets entrapped in weld metal. The most common form is slag inclusions generated during various arc welding processes using flux. Ideally slag should float on top. But slag globules sometimes become encased during solidification and produce solid inclusions. Another form of inclusion is metallic oxides.

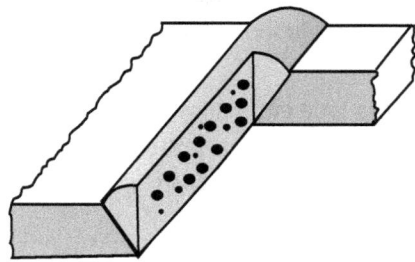

Fig. 5.37 : Slag Inclusion

- **Incomplete Fusion :**

In completed weld beads, fusion has not occurred throughout the entire cross-section of the joint and is shown in Fig. 5.38. This is lack of fusion. Lack of penetration is a defect that fusion has not penetrated deeply enough into root of joint relative to specified standard.

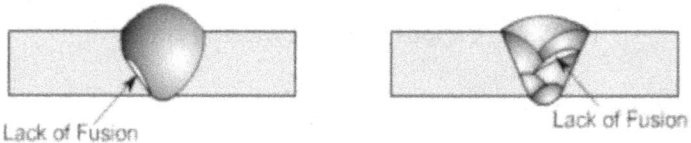

Fig. 5.38 : Several forms of incomplete fusion

• Improper Shape or Contour :

If the weld shape (e.g. 'V' shape) is proper then weldment has good strength. In Fig. 5.39 some defects of improper shape are given. Imperfect shape means the variation from the desired shape and size of the weld bead. During undercutting a notch is formed either on one side of the weld bead or both sides in which stresses tend to concentrate and it can result in the early failure of the joint. Main reasons for undercutting are the excessive welding currents, long arc lengths and fast travel speeds

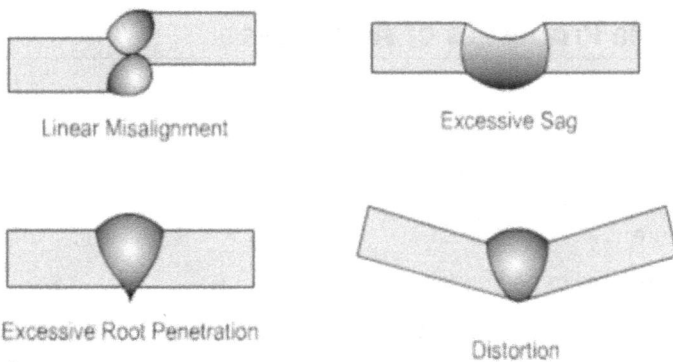

Fig. 5.39 : Various Imperfect Shapes of Welds

• Excessive Spatter :

Drops of molten metal splash on to the surface of base parts and is known as spatter.

5.15 ADHESIVE BONDING

Use of Adhesives for Joining:

Many components are joined now-a-days by using different adhesives. Packaging, labeling, home furnishings, footwear industries use adhesives to join the parts. Several layers of wood are joined by glue to form popular plywood. In manufacturing sector, adhesive bonding is gaining increased acceptance. Joints produced have adequate strength.

5.15.1 Adhesives

Types and Classification

1. Natural Adhesives : Starch, dextrin, soya flour and animal products.

2. Inorganic Adhesives : Sodium silicate, magnesium oxychloride.

3. Synthetic Organic Adhesives : Thermoplastics or thermosetting polymers. These have got better strength and are used where load bearing is required.

Synthetic organic adhesives are further classified as

- Chemically reactive : epoxies, silicones, polyurathanes acrylics : They are least expensive.

- Pressure sensitive : Natural rubber, nitrite rubber.
- Hot melt : Thermoplastics.
- Evaporative : Acrylics, polyurathanes, rubbers.
- Film and tape : Nylon expoxies, vinyl phenolics.

Adhesives are available in forms like liquids, pastes, solutions, emulsions, powder, tape and film.

5.15.2 Desirable Properties of Adhesives

- Strength,
- Toughness,
- Resistance to fluids and chemicals,
- Heat and moisture,
- Should wet the surfaces to be bonded.

Adhesive joints may have good shear, compressive and tensile strength but if peeling forces are present, joint may not be strong.

Table 5.1 gives different adhesives and their properties.

Table 5.1 : Typical properties and characteristics of chemically reactive structural adhesives

Sr. No.		Epoxy	Polyurethane	Modified Acrylic	Cyanoacrylate	Anaerobic
1.	Impact resistance	Poor	Excellent	Good	Poor	Fair
2.	Tension-share strength, MPa (10^3 psi)	15.4 (2.2)	15.4 (2.2)	25.9 (3.7)	18.9 (2.7)	17.5 (2.5)
3.	Peel strength N/m (ibf/in.)	< 525 (3)	14,000 (80)	5250 (3)	< 525 (3)	1750 (10)
5.	Substrates bonded	Most	Most smooth, non-porous	Most smooth, non-porous	Most non-porous metals or plastics	Metals, glass thermosets
5.	Service temperature range, °C (°F)	−55 to 120 (− 70 to 250)	− 160 to 80 (− 250 to 175)	− 70 to 120 (− 100 to 250)	− 55 to 80 (− 70 to 175)	− 55 to 150 (− 70 to 300)

6.	Heat curve or mixing required	Yes	Yes	No	No	No
7.	Solvent resistance	Excellent	Good	Good	Good	Excellent
8.	Moisture resistance	Excellent	Fair	Good	Poor	Good
9.	Gap limitations, mm (in).	None	None	0.75 (0.03)	0.25 (0.01)	0.60 (0.25)
10.	Odour	Mild	Mild	Strong	Moderate	Mild
11.	Toxicity	Moderate	Moderate	Moderate	Low	Low
12.	Flammability	Low	Low	High	Low	Low

5.15.3 Surface Preparation and Application

The important aspect of adhesive bonding is surface preparation of the parts to be joined. If dirt, oil, dust and other contaminants are present, joint strength is affected. Various compounds and primers are available to modify surfaces to increase adhesive bond strength. Liquid adhesives can be sprayed or applied by brushes. Different joints in adhesive bonding are given in Fig. 5.40.

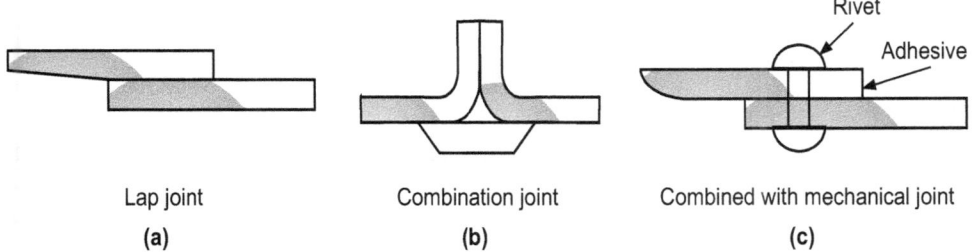

Lap joint
(a)

Combination joint
(b)

Combined with mechanical joint
(c)

Fig. 5.40 : Different joints in adhesive bonding

Good design requires large contact areas between the members to be joined. A wide variety of similar and dissimilar metallic non-metallic materials can be joined by adhesive bonding. Curing time of adhesives especially for thermosetting materials is very important. It may vary from few seconds to many hours. Adhesive bonds for structural applications are rarely suitable for service above 250°C. Adhesive bonding is used in aerospace, automotive appliances and building products.

Applications :

Attaching rear view mirrors to windshields, automotive brake lining assemblies, laminated wind shield glass, helicopter blades, sticking of abrasive sticks on shoes for honing etc.

Advantages :

- Very thin and fragile components can be joined.
- Porous materials can be joined.

- The joining is at interface, so localised stresses like in screws and bolts are not present.
- The process is carried at room temperature or low temperature, so distortion of components is absent.

Limitations :
- Long process time.
- Service temperatures are low.
- Testing of joints is difficult.

QUESTIONS

1. Write notes on :
   (i) Characteristics of different types of gas flames used in gas welding.
   (ii) Adhesives and their applications.
2. Compare gas welding with arc welding process.
3. Explain the principle of operation and advantages of the following welding processes.
   (i) Submerged arc welding.
4. Describe the characteristics of different types of oxy-acetylene gas flames and state their applications.
5. Write short note on Equipment used for arc welding.
6. Write short note on TIG welding.
7. Differentiate between forehand and backhand gas welding techniques.
8. Compare gas welding with arc welding process.
9. Describe the following welding processes stating their applications.
   (a) Submerged arc welding.
   (b) Seam welding.
   (c) Gas tungsten arc welding (GTAW)
10. Differentiate between soldering and brazing operations.
11. Describe the following welding processes stating their applications :
    (i) Submerged arc welding. (ii) Flash Welding
12. What is resistance welding ? Explain the types of resistance welding.
13. Compare A.C. Arc welding with D.C. Arc welding process.
14. Write a note on Adhesives and state their applications.
15. Enumerate the different types of flames used in gas welding.
16. What is resistance welding ? Explain the types of resistance welding.
17. Write a note on Adhesives and state their applications.

18. Enumerate the different types of flames used in gas welding.
19. Describe the following welding processes with their applications (any two) :
    (i) Projection welding
    (ii) Spot welding.
20. Differentiate between forward and backward gas welding techniques.
21. Explain submerged arc welding process with suitable sketch.
22. Describe the following resistance welding processes :
    (i) Spot welding
    (ii) Projection welding.
23. Write difference between 'TIG' and 'MIG'.
24. Describe different types of gas flames used in gas welding.
25. What is the purpose of coating on an arc welding electrode ?
26. Distinguish between "brazing" and "braze welding".
27. Explain the following electric arc welding processes with the help of neat sketches :
    (i) Flux - Corel Arc Welding [FCAW]
    (ii) Gas Metal Arc Welding [GMAW].
28. What are the special features of Resistance Projection Welding ?
29. Distinguish between "soft solder " and "hard solder".
30. Explain the following resistance welding processes with proper set up :
    (i) Spot welding
    (ii) Projection welding.
31. Explain in detail submerged arc welding process with neat diagram.
32. Describe the following resistance welding processes with proper set up.
    (i) Percussion welding;
    (ii) Seam welding.
33. Explain in detail Tungsten-Arc-Gas-Shielded (TAGS) welding process with suitable diagram.
34. Describe GMAW welding process with respect to principle, setup and its working and limitations.
35. Compare the following joining processes with respect to principle, temperature and applications :
    (a) Soldering
    (b) Brazing
    (c) Braze welding.

36. Describe Flux Cored Arc Welding (FCAW) with respect to principle, setup and its working with neat diagram.
37. List any two adhesive materials, also describe briefly reason for replacing other joining processes by adhesive material. State any two sample components joined by adhesive material.
38. Describe with the help of suitable working set-up, principle and operation of GMAW process.
39. Describe principle operation of GTAW process with suitable sketch.
40. Write down characteristics of three different types of flames used in gas welding process.
41. Explain the principle of resistance welding.
42. Explain the different types of flames used in gas welding with application of each flame.
43. Describe various types of adhesives and their applications.

Unit - VI
SHAPING OF PLASTICS

6.1 INTRODUCTION

Being that today plastic is one of the most used materials on a volume basis in the world. One can realize that the benefits of plastic manufacturing are numerous: light weight, corrosion resistance and additional style and color to name a few. Plastics are broadly integrated into today's lifestyle and make major, irreplaceable contributions to virtually all product areas. Plastics and plastic manufacturing play a prominent role in industries such as Aerospace, Building & Construction, Electronics, Packaging, and Transportation. In this unit, important plastic processing methods are discussed.

6.2 BLOW MOLDING

Blow Molding is a manufacturing process by which hollow plastic parts are formed. The blow molding process begins with melting down the plastic and forming it into a heated hollow thermoplastic tube (parison or perform). The parison is a tube-like piece of plastic with a hole in one end through which compressed air can pass. The air pressure then pushes the plastic out to match the mold. Once the plastic has cooled and hardened the mold opens up and the part is ejected.

- The most widely used materials for Blow Molding are: Low Density Polyethylene (LDPE), High Density Polyethylene (HDPE), Polypropylene (PP), Polyvinyl Chloride (PVC), Polyethylene Terephtalate (PET)
- Disposable containers of various sizes and shapes, drums, recyclable bottles, automotive fuel tanks, storage tanks, globe light fixtures, toys, tubs, small boats are produced by Blow Molding method.
- There are three principal techniques of Blow Molding, differing in the method by which parisons are prepared are 1. Extrusion Blow Molding, 2. Injection Blow Molding, 3. Stretch Blow Molding

6.2.1 Extrusion Blow Molding

- Extrusion Blow Molding involves manufacture of parison by conventional extrusion method using a die similar to that used for extrusion pipes.
- Extrusion Blow Molding is commonly used for mass production of plastic bottles. The production cycle consists of the following steps:
  - **Step 1:** The parison is extruded vertically in downward direction between two mold halves.

Extrusion Blow Molding

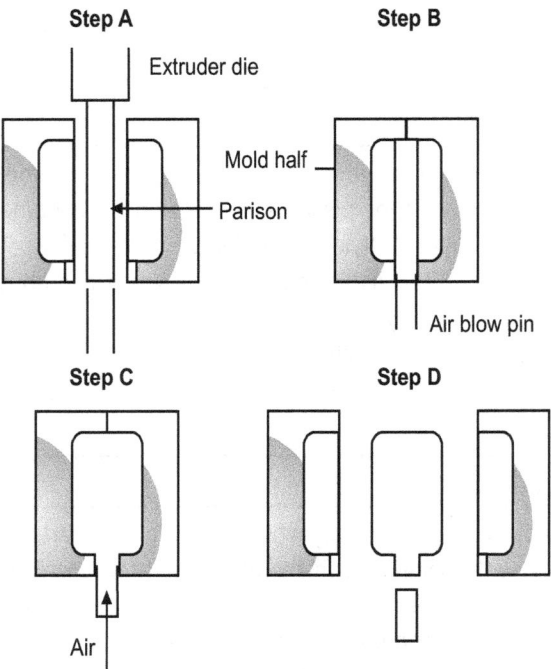

Fig. 6.1 : Extrusion Blow Molding

- **Step 2:** When the parison reaches the required length the two mold halves close resulting in pinching the top of parison end and sealing the blow pin in the bottom of the parison end.
- **Step 3:** Parison is inflated by air blown through the blow pin, taking a shape conforming that of the mold cavity. The parison is then cut on the top.
- **Step 4:** The mold cools down, its halves open, and the final part is removed.

6.2.2 Injection Blow Molding

The process of **blow molding** is used for the production of hollow glass and plastic objects in large quantities. In the IBM process, the polymer is injection molded onto a core pin; then the core pin is rotated to a blow molding station to be inflated and cooled. This is the least-used of the three blow molding processes, and is typically used to make small medical and single serve bottles. The process is divided into three steps: injection, blowing and ejection. The production cycle consists of the following steps:

- **Step 1:** The injection blow molding machine is based on an extruder barrel and screw assembly which melts the polymer. The molten polymer is fed into a hot runner manifold where it is injected through nozzles into a hollow, heated preform mold. The preform mold forms the external shape and is clamped around a mandrel (the core rod) which forms the internal shape of the preform. The preform consists of a

fully formed bottle/jar neck with a thick tube of polymer attached, which will form the body.
- **Step 2:** The preform mold opens and the core rod is rotated and clamped into the hollow, chilled blow mold.
- **Step 3:** The core rod opens and allows compressed air into the preform, which inflates it to the finished article shape.
- **Step 4:** After a cooling period the blow mold opens and the core rod is rotated to the ejection position. The finished article is stripped off the core rod and leak-tested prior to packing.

- The preform and blow mold can have many cavities, typically three to sixteen depending on the article size and the required output. There are three sets of core rods, which allow concurrent preform injection, blow molding and ejection.
- Injection Blow Molding is more accurate and controllable process as compared to the Extrusion Blow Molding.
- It allows producing more complicated products from a wider range of polymer materials.
- However production rate of Injection Blow Molding method is lower than that of Extrusion Blow Molding.

6.2.3 Stretch Blow Molding

Stretch Blow Molding is similar to Injection Plow Molding. In this type of blow molding process, the plastic is first molded into a "preform" using the injection molding process. These preforms are produced with the necks of the bottles, including threads (the "finish") on one end. These preforms are packaged, and fed later (after cooling) into a reheat stretch blow molding machine. Material, commonly used in this method is Polyethylene Terephtalate (PET). The production cycle consists of the following steps:

- **Step 1:** The preforms are heated (typically using infrared heaters) above their glass transition temperature, then blown using high pressure air into bottles using metal blow molds.
- **Step 2:** The preform is always stretched with a core rod as part of the process. In the single-stage process both preform manufacture and bottle blowing are performed in the same machine.
- **Step 3:** The stretching of some polymers, such as PET (polyethylene terephthalate) results in strain hardening of the resin; which is allowing the bottles to resist deforming under the pressures. The main applications are

- In this method biaxial molecular orientation is produced. The specific molecular orientation provides higher mechanical strength, rigidity and transparency of the material.
- Stretch Blow Molding is used for manufacturing bottles, jars and other containers viz. carbonated beverages.

6.2.4 Advantages of Blow Molding

- Advantages of blow molding include: low tool and die cost; fast production rates; ability to mold complex part; produces recyclable parts

6.2.5 Limitations of Blow Molding

- Limitations of blow molding include: limited to hollow parts, wall thickness is hard to control.

6.3 INJECTION MOLDING

Injection molding is a manufacturing process for producing parts by injecting material into a mold. Injection molding can be performed with a host of materials, including metals, glasses, elastomers, confections, and most commonly thermoplastic and thermosetting polymers.

- After a product is designed, usually by an industrial designer or an engineer, molds are made by a mold-maker (or toolmaker) from metal, usually either steel or aluminum, and precision-machined to form the features of the desired part.
- Injection molding is widely used for manufacturing a variety of parts, from the smallest components to entire body panels of cars. Material for the part is fed into a heated barrel, mixed, and forced into a mold cavity where it cools and hardens to the configuration of the cavity. This process is discussed in detail stepwise next.
- **Step 1:** Granulated or powdered thermoplastic plastic is fed from a hopper into the Injection Moulding machine (refer figure Fig. 6.2).
- **Step 2:** The Injection Moulding machine consists of a hollow steel barrel, containing a rotating screw (Archemidial Screw). The screw carries the plastic along the barrel to the mould. Heaters surround the barrel melt the plastic as it travels along the barrel.
- **Step 3:** The screw is forced back as the melted plastic collects at the end of the barrel. Once enough plastic has collected a hydraulic ram pushes the screw forward injecting the plastic through a sprue into a mould cavity. The mould is warmed before injecting and the plastic is injected quickly to prevent it from hardening before the mould is full.
- **Step 4:** Pressure is maintained for a short time (dwell time) to prevent the material creeping back during setting (hardening). This prevents shrinkage and hollows, therefore giving a better quality product. The moulding is left to cool before removing (ejected) from the mould. The moulding takes on the shape of the mould cavity. The fig. below shows an Injection Moulding machine.

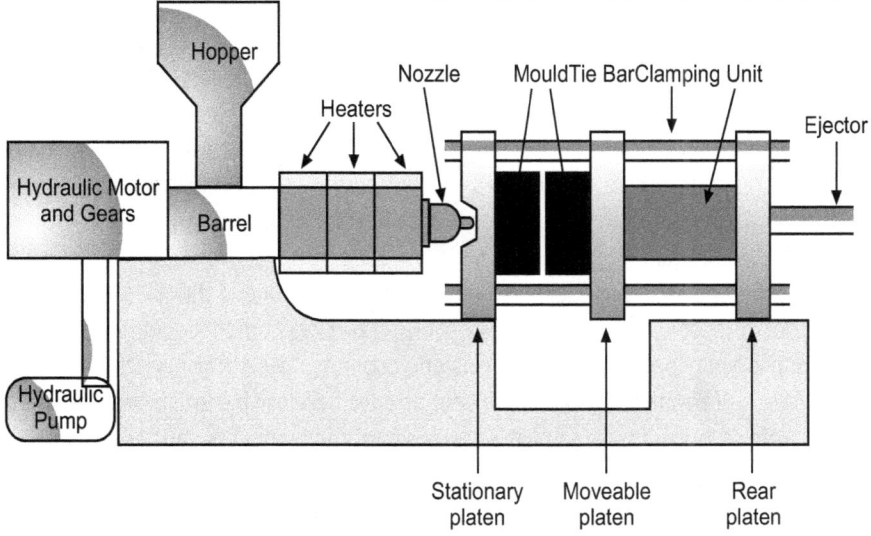

Fig. 6.2 : Scematic diagram of Injection Molding Machine

6.3.1 Advantages of Injection molding

- More precise control of material mixing and flow resulting in better part quality and consistency.
- Fewer cavities are used in this process compared to transfer molding resulting in less dimensional variation among parts produced from a given mold.
- Lower unit cost (for larger order quantities) due to faster curing and cycle times and higher production rates.
- Less reject material (vs. the transfer process where some material is lost in the transfer pot)
- Is more cost effective when molding onto metal inserts.
- Molds may be less expensive since you are not making a separate ram and pot.

6.3.2 Limitations of Injection molding

- Injection molding is a complex technology with possible production problems.
- Limitations can be caused either by defects in the molds, or more often by the molding process itself.
- When filling a new or unfamiliar mold for the first time, where shot size for that mold is unknown, a technician/tool setter may perform a trial run before a full production run.
- The initial cost is high; however the per-piece cost is low, so with greater quantities the unit price decreases.

6.3.3 Applications of Injection molding

- Injection molding is the most common modern method of part manufacturing; it is ideal for producing high volumes of the same object.
- Injection molding is used to create many things such as wire spools, packaging, bottle caps, automotive dashboards, pocket combs, some musical instruments (and parts of them), one-piece chairs and small tables, storage containers, mechanical parts (including gears)
- Most other plastic products available today viz. pipe fittings, battery casings, toothbrush bases, bottle lids, disposable razors, automobile bumpers and dash boards, power-tool housing, television cabinets, electrical switches, telephone handsets, automotive power brake, automotive fascias, transmission, and electrical parts, mirror housings, steam irons, washer pumps, spoilers, butter tubs, moisture vaporizers, yogurt containers, toilet seats, cell-phone housings, cradles or bases for personal digital assistants, case of a notebook-computer, computer mouse, electrical connector housings, lawn chairs, automotive ashtrays, and cookware appliance handles and knobs, aerosol caps, household items, bottle caps, toys.

6.4 EXTRUSION OF PLASTICS

Extrusion of **Plastics** is a high volume manufacturing process in which raw plastic material is melted and formed into a continuous profile. Extrusion produces items such as pipe/tubing, weather stripping, fence, deck railing, window frames, plastic films and sheet, thermoplastic coatings, and wire insulation.

6.4.1 Plastics Extrusion Process

Plastics extrusion process is discussed insteps; which is as follows.
- **Step 1:** In the extrusion of plastics, raw thermoplastic material in the form of nurdles (small beads, often called resin in the industry) is gravity fed from a top mounted hopper into the barrel of the extruder. Additives such as colorants and UV inhibitors (in either liquid or pellet form) are often used and can be mixed into the resin prior to arriving at the hopper. (See Fig. 6.3.).
- **Step 2:** The process has much in common with plastic injection moulding from the point of the extruder technology though it differs in that it is usually a continuous process. While pultrusion can offer many similar profiles in continuous lengths, usually with added reinforcing, this is achieved by pulling the finished product out of a die instead of extruding the fluid raw material through a die.
- **Step 3:** The material enters through the feed throat (an opening near the rear-side of the barrel) and comes into contact with the screw. The rotating screw (normally turning at up to 120 rpm) forces the plastic beads forward into the barrel which is heated to the desired melt temperature of the molten plastic (which can range from 200 °C to 275 °C depending on the polymer).

- [Note: In most processes, a heating profile is set for the barrel in which three or more independent PID controlled heater zones gradually increase the temperature of the barrel from the rear (where the plastic enters) to the front. This allows the plastic beads to melt gradually as they are pushed through the barrel and lowers the risk of overheating which may cause degradation in the polymer.
- Extra heat is contributed by the intense pressure and friction taking place inside the barrel. In fact, if an extrusion line is running certain materials fast enough, the heaters can be shut off and the melt temperature maintained by pressure and friction alone inside the barrel. In most extruders, cooling fans are present to keep the temperature below a set value if too much heat is generated. If forced air cooling proves insufficient then cast-in heater jackets are employed, and they generally use a closed loop of distilled water in heat exchange with tower or city water.
- At the front of the barrel, the molten plastic leaves the screw and travels through a screen pack to remove any contaminants in the melt. The screens are reinforced by a breaker plate (a thick metal puck with many holes drilled through it); which serves to create back pressure in the barrel for uniform melting and proper mixing of the polymer, and also does the function of converting "rotational memory" of the molten plastic into "longitudinal memory".]
  - **Step 4:** After passing through the breaker plate molten plastic enters the die. The die is what gives the final product its profile and must be designed so that the molten plastic evenly flows from a cylindrical profile, to the product's profile shape.

[Note: The product must now be cooled and this is usually achieved by pulling the extrudate through a water bath. Plastics are very good thermal insulators and are therefore difficult to cool quickly. Compared with steel, plastic conducts its heat away 2000 times more slowly. In a tube or pipe extrusion line, a sealed water bath is acted upon by a carefully controlled vacuum to keep the newly formed and still molten tube or pipe from collapsing. For products such as plastic sheeting, the cooling is achieved by pulling through a set of cooling rolls.]

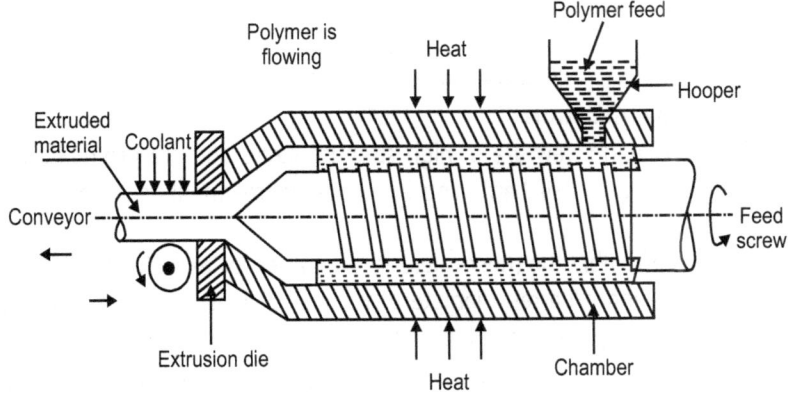

Fig. 6.3 : Extrusion of plastic

6.4.1.1 Types of Plastic Extruders

As discussed in earlier section, the extruder drive is electrical in operation and is geared via a thrust bearing to produce the rotational movement of the extruder screw. The polymer feed to the screw is from the feed hopper and the feed may be by gravity, metering screw or simple conveying spiral. The extruder screw has the following basic functions:

- To bring the feedstock into the extruder and to move the material along the screw whilst at the same time compressing it and removing volatiles.
- To soften the melt by heating it (both from internally generated shear forces and externally applied heat).
- To mix the melt and produce a homogeneous melt without impurities.
- To apply the constant pressure (free of pulsation) required to force the material through the die.

These functions, at least for the single screw extruder, are generally achieved at different sections of the extrusion screw as the material progresses along the barrel and the functions. There are many different types of extruders and the illustration shown in Fig. 6.4 attempts to divide these into a logical order.

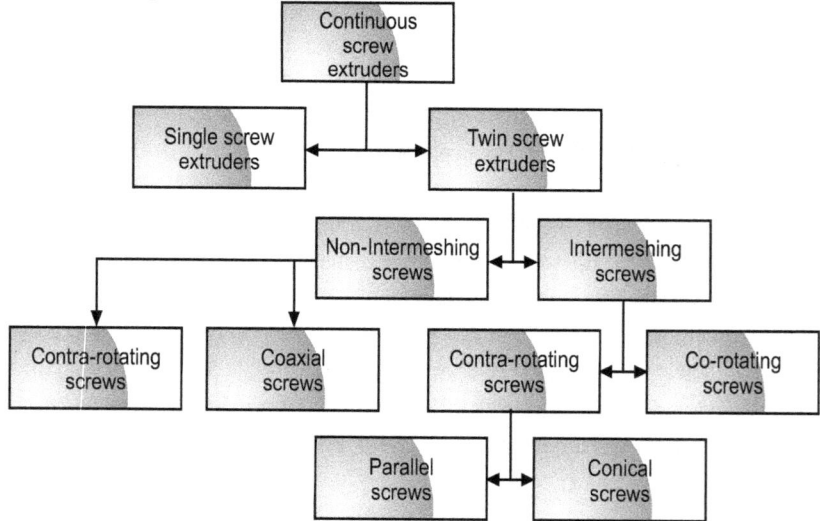

Fig. 6.4 : Basic extruder types

6.4.1.2 Extruder Specifications

- The extruder barrel and screw are of high strength steels and are protected from wear and corrosion by a variety of hardening and coating treatments such as nitriding and hard chroming.
- In absolute terms probably the most referenced number for extruder specification is the L/D ratio (barrel length/barrel diameter) as this defines many of the operating characteristics of the extruder for all types of extruders(refer figure Fig. 6.5).
- For most extruder types the L/D ratio has increased as technology has advanced and have steadily increased from L/D's of around 15 to up to 30.

Most screws have these three zones:

- **Feed zone:** Also called solids conveying. This zone feeds the resin into the extruder, and the channel depth is usually the same throughout the zone.
- **Melting zone:** Also called the transition or compression zone. Most of the resin is melted in this section, and the channel depth gets progressively smaller.
- **Metering zone:** Also called melt conveying. This zone, in which channel depth is again the same throughout the zone, melts the last particles and mixes to a uniform temperature and composition.

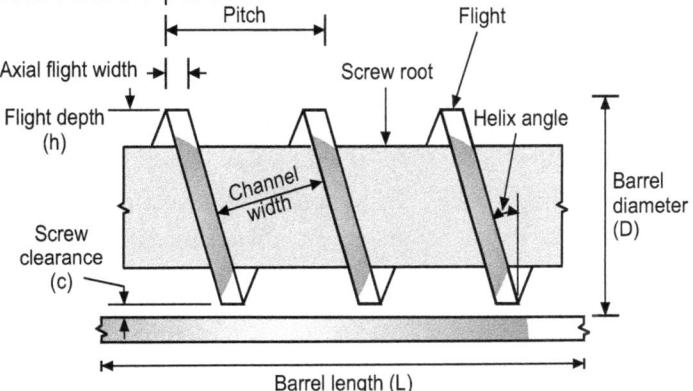

Fig. 6.5 : Extruder specification

In addition, a vented (two-stage) screw will have:

- **Decompression zone:** In this zone, about two-thirds down the screw, the channel suddenly gets deeper, which relieves the pressure and allows any trapped gases (usually moisture or air) to be drawn out by vacuum.
- **Second metering zone:** This zone is like the first metering zone, but with greater channel depth, and repressurizes the melt to get it through the resistance of the screens and the die.

6.4.2 Advantages of Plastics Extrusion Process

- The production capabilities of plastic extrusion technology allows you to manufacture high volumes.
- Compared to steel, plastic is a cheap material. The production process of plastic extrusion is also designed to offer low cost tooling and short lead times. This means you could produce a high volume of products relatively quickly.
- Plastic extrusion is extremely versatile. It allows you to create products of complex shapes with different sizes, thicknesses, hardnesses, textures and colours.
- The co-extrusion process enables manufacturers to incorporate different plastic materials and compounds into one product. Multiple layers are created which are then 'fused' into one. This allows manufacturers to tailor a product to meet different function or market requirements - **something with monolayer extrusion you cannot do.**

6.4.3 Limitations of Plastics Extrusion Process

- Uneven flow at this stage would produce a product with unwanted stresses at certain points in the profile. These stresses can cause warping upon cooling.
- Limited complexity of parts
- Uniform cross-sectional shape only

6.4.4 Applications of Plastics Extrusion Process

- There are many geometrical possibilities when using extrusion.
- Thin film (flat or tubular) is the most common product.
- Other extruded products include pipe and tubing, coated paper or foil, monofilaments and textile fibers, flat sheet (anything over 0.010 inch (0.25 mm)), wire and cable covering, and a great variety of profiles such as window frames, gaskets and channels, and house siding. The products can be cut to length or rolled up as needed. Processes for the said product are discussed in brief as follows.

6.4.4.1 Sheet/Film Extrusion

- For products such as plastic sheet or film, the cooling is achieved by pulling through a set of cooling rolls (calender or "chill" rolls), usually 3 or 4 in number.
- Running too fast creates an undesirable condition called "nerve"- basically, inadequate contact time is allowed to dissipate the heat present in the extruded plastic. In sheet extrusion, these rolls not only deliver the necessary cooling but also determine sheet thickness and surface texture (in case of structured rolls; i.e. smooth, levant, haircell, etc.).
- A common post-extrusion process for plastic sheet stock is thermoforming, where the sheet is heated until soft (plastic), and formed via a mold into a new shape. In food packaging plastic film is sometimes metallised, see metallised film.

6.4.4.2 Pipe/Tubing Extrusion

- Extruded tubing process, such as drinking straws and medical tubing, is manufactured the same as a regular extrusion process up until the die.
- Hollow sections are usually extruded by placing a pin or mandrel inside of the die, and in most cases positive pressure is applied to the internal cavities through the pin.
- Tubing with multiple lumens (holes) must be made for specialty applications. For these applications, the tooling is made by placing more than one pin in the center of the die, to produce the number of lumens necessary.
- In most cases, these pins are supplied with air pressure from different sources. In this way, the individual lumen sizes can be adjusted by adjusting the pressure to the individual pins.

6.4.4.3 Overjacketing/Wire/Cable Extrusion

- In a wire coating process, bare wire (or bundles of jacketed wires, filaments, etc.) is pulled through the center of a die similar to a tubing die.
- Many different materials are used for this purpose depending on the application. Essentially, an insulated wire is a thin walled tube which has been formed around a bare wire.
- There are two different types of extrusion tooling used for coating over a wire. They are referred to as either "pressure" or "jacketing" tooling.
- The selection criteria for choosing which type of tooling to use is based on whether the particular application requires intimate contact or adhesion of the polymer to the wire or not. If intimate contact or adhesion is required, 'pressure tooling' is used. If it is not desired, 'jacketing tooling' is chosen.
- The main difference in jacketing and pressure tooling is the position of the pin with respect to the die. For jacketing tooling, the pin will extend all the way flush with the die.
- When the bare wire is fed through the pin, it does not come in direct contact with the molten polymer until it leaves the die. For pressure tooling, the end of the pin is retracted inside the crosshead, where it comes in contact with the polymer at a much higher pressure.

6.4.4.4 Extrusion Coating

- Extrusion coating is using a blown or cast film process to coat an additional layer onto an existing rollstock of paper, foil or film.
- For example, this process can be used to improve the characteristics of paper by coating it with polyethylene to make it more resistant to water.
- The extruded layer can also be used as an adhesive to bring two other materials together. A famous product that uses this technology is tetrapak.

6.6 THERMOFORMING

Thermoforming is a process in which a flat thermoplastic sheet is heated and deformed into the desired shape. The process is widely used in packaging of consumer products and to fabricate large products such as bathtubs, contoured skylights, and internal door liners for refrigerators. Thermoforming consists of two main steps: heating and forming. Heating is usually accomplished by radiant electric heaters, located on one or both sides of the starting plastic sheet at a distance of roughly 125 mm (5 in.). Duration of the heating cycle needed to sufficiently soften the sheet depends on the polymer, its thickness and color.

The methods by which the forming step is accomplished can be classified into three basic categories: (1) vacuum thermoforming, (2) pressure thermoforming, and (3) mechanical thermoforming. In our discussion of these methods, we describe the forming of sheet stock; in the packaging industry, most thermoforming operations are performed on thin films.

6.5.1 Vacuum Thermoforming

In case of thermoforming process, a negative pressure is used to draw a preheated sheet into a mold cavity. The process is explained using schematic diagram shown Fig. 6.6. The holes for drawing the vacuum in the mold are on the order of 0.8 mm (0.031 in.) in diameter, so their effect on the plastic surface is minor.

Referring Fig. 6.6 of vacuum thermoforming;

- **Step 1:** a flat plastic sheet is softened by heating
- **Step 2:** the softened sheet is placed over a concave mold cavity;
- **Step 3:** a vacuum draws the sheet into the cavity; and
- **Step 4:** the plastic hardens on contact with the cold mold surface, and the part is removed and subsequently trimmed from the web.

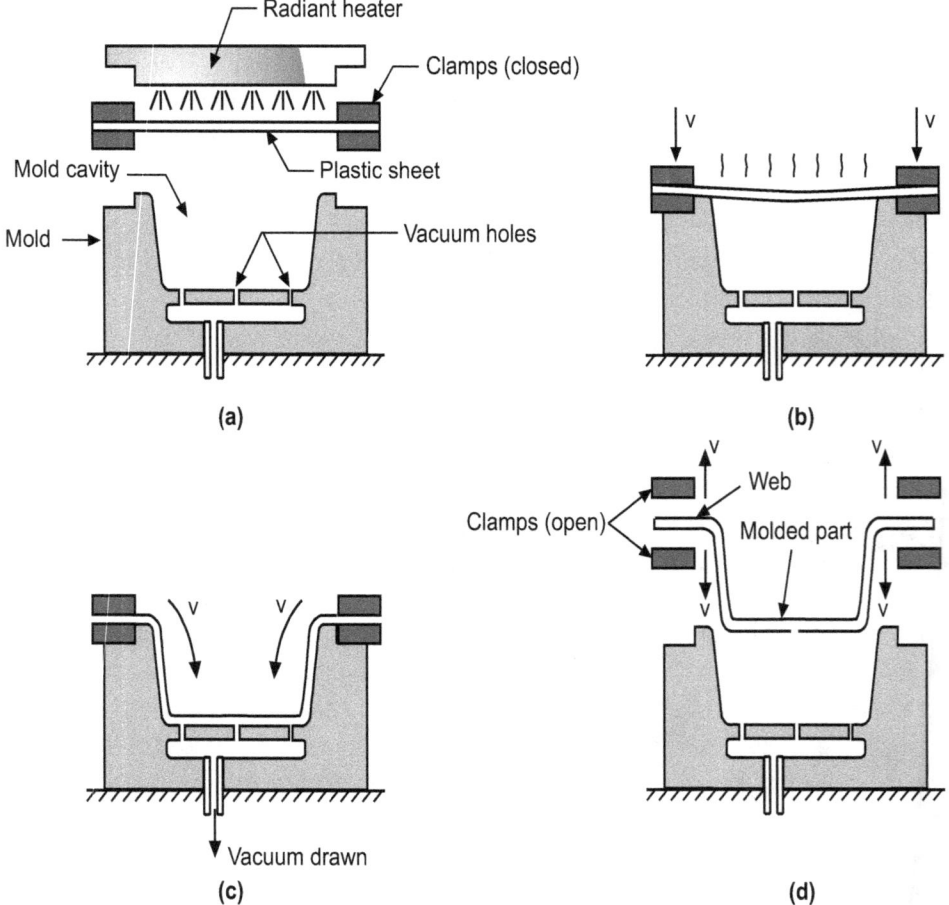

Fig. 6.6 : Vacuum-Thermoforming

6.6.2 Pressure Thermoforming

An alternative to vacuum forming involves positive pressure to force the heated plastic into the mold cavity. This is called **pressure thermoforming** or **blow forming** its advantage over vacuum forming is that higher pressures can be developed because the latter is limited to a theoretical maximum of 1 atm. Blow-forming pressures of 3 to 4 atm are common. The process sequence is similar to the previous, the difference being that the sheet is pressurized from above into the mold cavity. Vent holes are provided in the mold to exhaust the trapped air. The forming portion of the sequence (steps 2 and 3) being differences are: (2) sheet is placed over a mold cavity; and (3) positive pressure forces the sheet into the cavity, which is illustrated in Fig. 6.7.

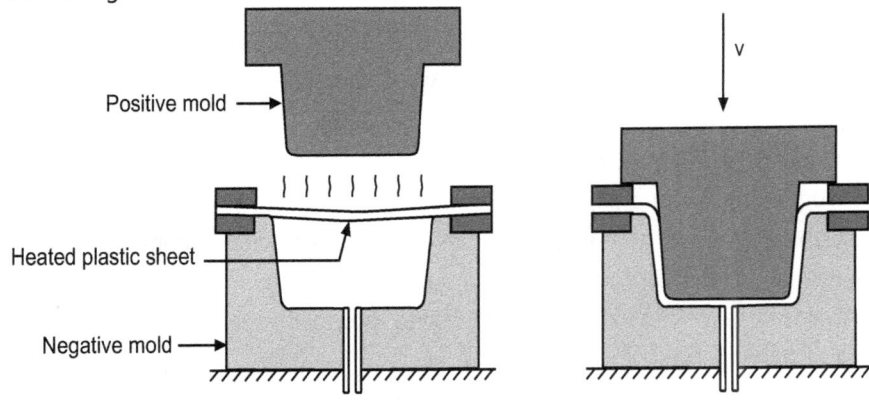

Fig. 6.7 : Pressure-Thermoforming

At this point it is useful to distinguish between negative and positive molds. The molds shown in Fig. 6.7 are **negative molds** because they have concave cavities. A **positive mold** has a convex shape shown in figure 3.10.

Both types are used in thermoforming. In the case of the positive mold, the heated sheet is draped over the convex form and negative or positive pressure is used to force the plastic against the mold surface. The positive mold is shown in below for the case of vacuum forming.

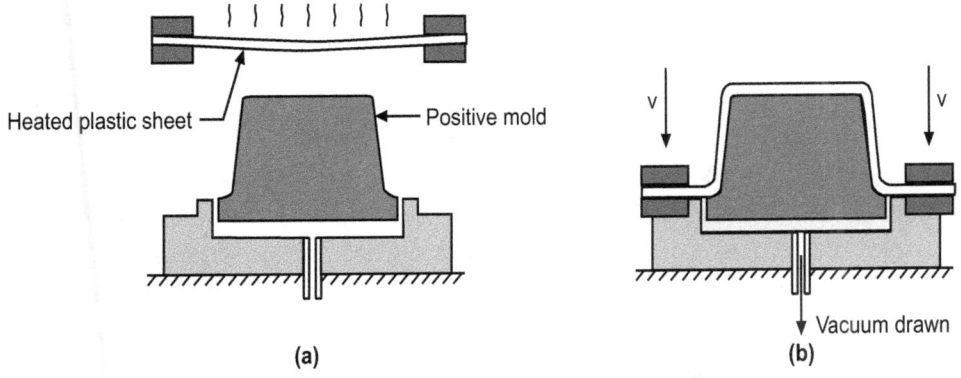

Fig. 6.8 : Pressure-Thermoforming with positive mold

6.5.3 Mechanical Thermoforming

The third method, called **mechanical thermoforming**, uses matching positive and negative molds that are brought together against the heated plastic sheet, forcing it to assume their shape. In the pure mechanical forming method, air pressure (positive or negative) is not used at all. The forming sequence (steps 1 and 2) are :

(1) sheet is placed over a mold cavity; and

(2) positive mechanically forces the sheet into the cavity.

6.5.4 Advantages of Thermoforming Process

- Its advantages are better dimensional control,
- Better opportunity for surface detailing on both sides of the part.

6.4.5 Limitations of Thermoforming Process

- Main limitation is that two mold halves are required,
- The molds for the other two methods are therefore less costly.
- Only thermoplastics can be thermoformed, since extruded sheets of thermosetting or elastomeric polymers have already been crosss-linked and cannot be softened by reheating. [Common thermoforming plastics are polystyrene, cellulose acetate and cellulose acetate butyrate, ABS, PVC, acrylic (polymethylmethacrylate), polyethylene, and polypropylene.]

6.5.6 Applications of Thermoforming Process

- Thermoforming is a secondary shaping process, the primary process being that which produces the sheet or film.
- Mass production thermoforming operations are performed in the packaging industry. The starting sheet or film is rapidly fed through a heating chamber and then mechanically formed into the desired shape.
- The operations are often designed to produce multiple parts with each stroke of the press using molds with multiple punches and cavities. In some cases, the extrusion machine that produces the sheet or film is located directly upstream from the thermoforming process, thereby eliminating the need to reheat the plastic. And for best efficiency, the filling process to put the consumable food item into the container is placed immediately downstream from thermoforming.
- Thin film packaging items that are mass produced by thermoforming include blister packs and skin packs. They offer an attractive way to display certain commodity products such as cosmetics, toiletries, small tools, and fasteners (nails, screws, etc.).
- Thermoforming applications include large parts that can be produced from thicker sheet stock. Examples include covers for business machines, boat hulls, shower stalls, diffusers for lights, advertising displays and signs, bathtubs, and certain toys.

6.6 CLAENDARING

The fig shows the calendaring process, which is used to produced sheet. The polymer is first mixed with the plasticizers and other additives such as coloring agents. The mix is then heated for short time to produce a rough sheet which is fed through a series of rolls. The thickness is gradually reduced, and at the same time a smooth surface, as required, is produced. The finish thickness is determined by the setting of the gap between the last paired of rolls.

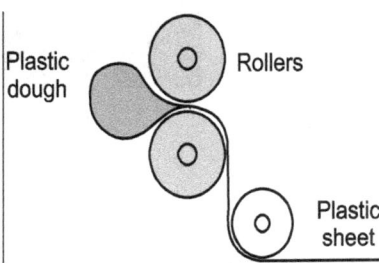

Fig. 6.9 : Calendaring Process

6.7 COMPRESSION MOLDING

Compression molding is an old and widely used molding process for thermosetting plastics. Its applications also include thermoplastic phonograph records, rubber tires, and various polymer matrix composite parts.

Compression molding is a method of molding in which the molding material, generally preheated, is first placed in an open, heated mold cavity. The mold is closed with a top force or plug member, pressure is applied to force the material into contact with all mold areas, while heat and pressure are maintained until the molding material has cured. The process employs thermosetting resins in a partially cured stage, either in the form of granules, putty-like masses, or performs. The process, is illustrated in Fig. 6.10. It consists of

- **Step 1**: Loading a precise amount of molding compound, called the *charge*, into the bottom half of a heated mold;
- **Step 2**: Bringing the mold halves together to compress the charge, forcing it to flow and conform to the shape of the cavity;
- **Step 3**: Heating the charge by means of the hot mold to polymerize and cure the material into a solidified part; and
- **Step 4**: Opening the mold halves and removing the part from the cavity.

Materials that are typically manufactured through compression molding include: Polyester fiberglass resin systems (SMC/BMC), Torlon, Vespel, Poly(p-phenylene sulfide) (PPS), and many grades of PEEK.

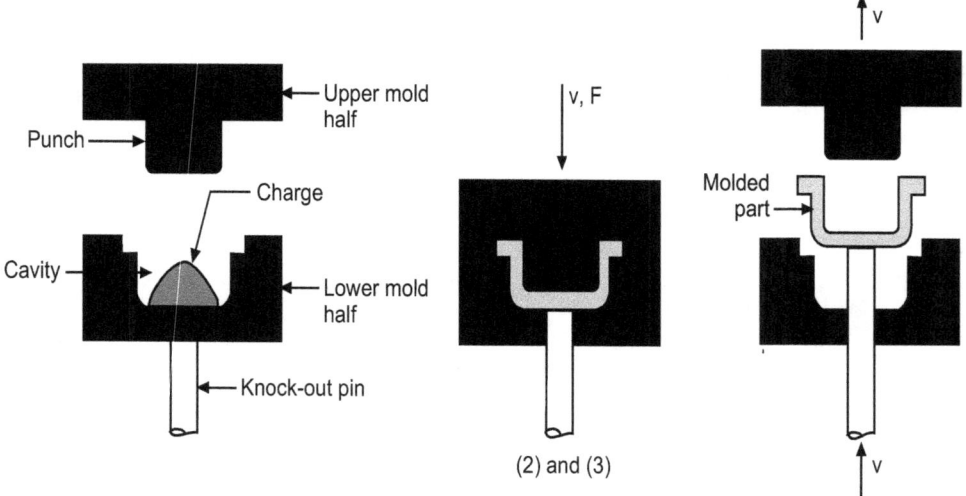

[Compression molding for thermoplastics: (1) charge is loaded, (2) and (3) charge is compressed and cured, and (4) opening the mold halves and removing the part from the cavity.]

Fig. 6.10 : Schematic diagram of Compression molding

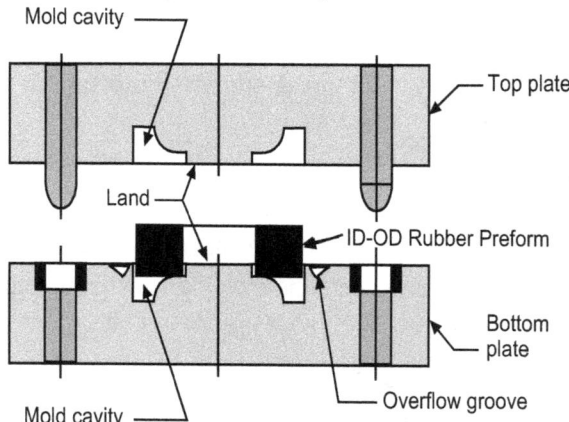

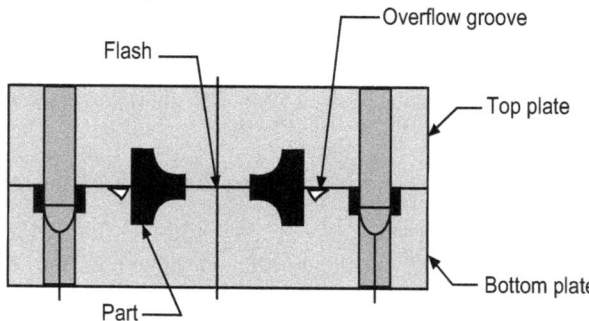

Fig. 6.11 : Schematic diagram of Open and Closed Compression mold

In case of compression molding, there are some important process parameters that an engineer should determine, viz. determining the proper amount of material, determining the minimum amount of energy required to heat the material, the minimum time required to heat the material, the appropriate heating technique, predicting the required force, to ensure that shot attains the proper shape, the mold for rapid cooling after the material has been compressed into the mold.

6.7.1 Advantage of compression molding

- The advantage of compression molding is its ability to mold large, fairly intricate parts.
- It is working with short cycle time (typically 1-6 minutes) resulting in high volume production
- It is one of the lowest cost molding methods compared with other methods such as transfer molding and injection molding; moreover it wastes relatively little material, giving it an advantage when working with expensive compounds.
- It could produce class A (high quality) surfaces.

6.7.2 Limitations of Compression Molding

- However, compression molding often provides poor product consistency and difficulty in controlling flashing,
- It is not suitable for some types of parts.
- Fewer knit lines are produced and a smaller amount of fiber-length degradation is noticeable when compared to injection molding. Compression-molding is also suitable for ultra-large basic shape production in sizes beyond the capacity of extrusion techniques.

6.7.3 Applications of Compression Molding

This process is a high-volume, high-pressure method suitable for molding complex, high strength fiberglass reinforcements.

Compression molding was first developed to manufacture composite parts for metal replacement applications; compression molding is typically used to make larger flat or moderately curved parts. This method of molding is greatly used in manufacturing automotive parts such as hoods, fenders, roofs, scoops, spoilers, air deflectors, lift gates, battery trays as well as smaller more intricate parts.

Advanced composite thermoplastics can also be compression molded with unidirectional tapes, woven fabrics, randomly oriented fiber mat or chopped strand.

The material to be molded is positioned in the mold cavity and the heated platens are closed by a hydraulic ram. Bulk molding compound (BMC) or sheet molding compound (SMC), are conformed to the mold form by the applied pressure and heated until the curing reaction occurs. SMC feed material usually is cut to conform to the surface area of the mold. The mold is then cooled and the part removed.

6.8 TRANSFER MOLDING

Transfer molding is closely related to compression molding, because it is utilized on the same polymer types (thermosets and elastomers). One can also see similarities to injection molding, in the way the charge is preheated in a separate chamber and then injected into the mold. This type of molding process, a thermosetting (plastic) charge (preform) is loaded into a chamber immediately ahead of the mold cavity, where it is heated; pressure is then applied to force the softened polymer to flow into the heated mold where curing occurs.

- A transfer mold setup is comprised of the part cavity, and a transfer pot and piston. The pot is connected to the cavity via sprues [refer Fig. 6.12 (a)] which allow rubber to flow from the pot as the rubber is forced out by the piston into the cavity.
- Since the mold cavity is completely closed just before the material enters the cavity, there is less flashing and better control of the "closure" dimensions of the mold.
- It is also used commonly whenever rubber has to be molded onto a metal or ceramic insert since the mold is closed prior to transferring the rubber into the cavity. This prevents the insert from moving or being displaced due to the forces of the rubber that are generated during mold closure.

6.8.1 Types of Transfer Molding Process

- There are two variants of the process (refer figure Fig. 6.12):

(i) **Pot transfer molding:** In this process, the charge is injected from a "pot" through a vertical sprue channel into the cavity; and

(ii) **Plunger transfer molding:** In this process, the charge is injected by means of a plunger from a heated well through lateral channels into the mold cavity.

Cycle in both processes is

- **Step 1:** charge is loaded into pot;
- **Step 2:** softened polymer is pressed into mold cavity and cured; and
- **Step 3:** part is ejected.

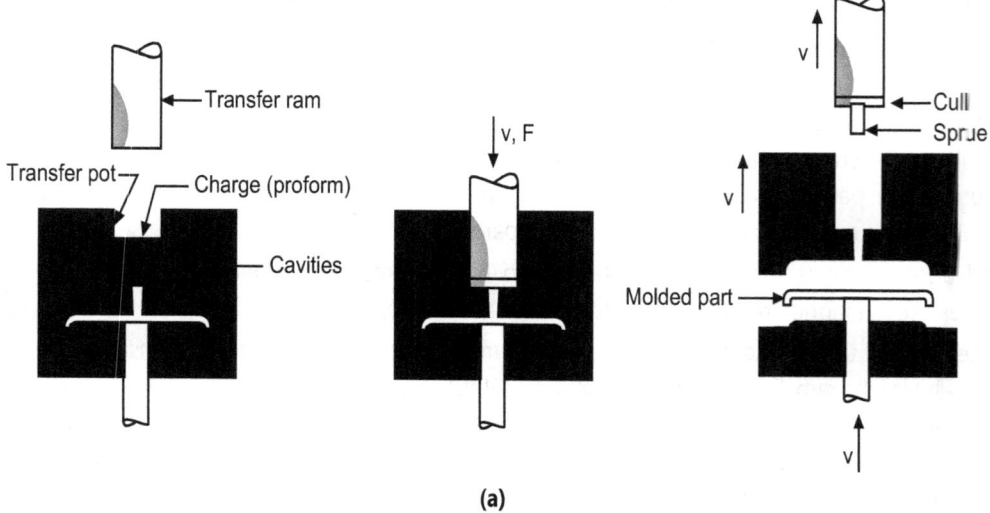

(a)

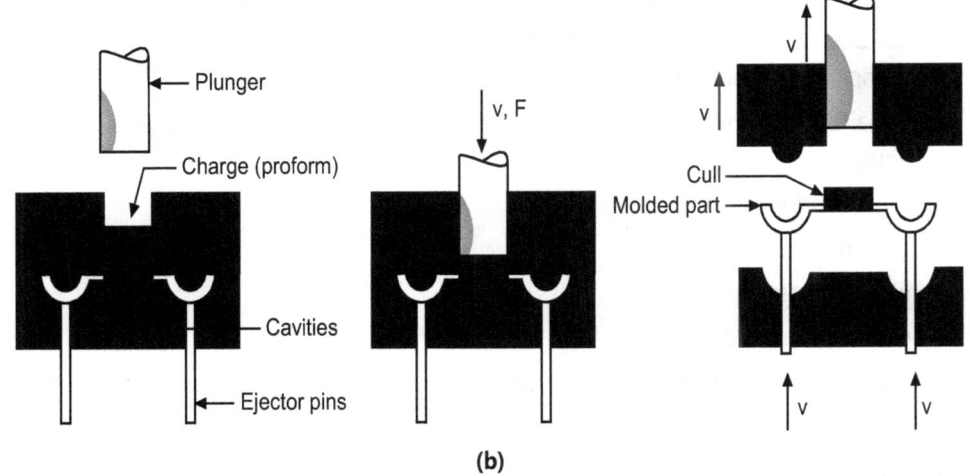

Fig. 6.12 : Schematic diagram of (a) Pot transfer molding, and (b) plunger transfer molding

6.8.2 Advantage of Compression Molding

- It can produce parts of better dimensional quality and larger quantities than produced with the compression molding process.
- Cycle times are generally faster than with compression method.
- Lower unit cost than with compression usually, due to shorter cycle times
- Less part flashing
- Since mold is completely closed before the rubber is transferred into the cavity inserted parts are more easily produced

6.8.3 Limitations of Compression Molding

- In both (types) cases of transfer molding, scrap is produced each cycle in the form of the leftover material in the base of the well and lateral channels, called the '**cull**'.
- In addition, the sprue in pot transfer is scrap material. Because the polymers are thermosetting, the scrap cannot be recovered.

6.8.4 Applications of Compression Molding

- Transfer molding is capable of molding part shapes that are more intricate than compression molding but not as intricate as injection molding.
- In the semiconductor industry, package encapsulation is usually done with transfer molding due to the high accuracy of transfer molding tooling and low cycle time of the process.
- Some common products are utensil handles, electric appliance parts, electronic component, and connectors.
- Transfer molding is widely used to enclose or encapsulate items such as coils, integrated circuits, plugs, connectors, and other components.

QUESTIONS

1. Compare thermoplastic and thermosetting plastics.
2. Explain the construction and working of Compression molding Process and equipment.
3. Write short note on:
   (i) Transfer molding,
   (ii) Blow molding,
   (iii) Injection molding
4. Explain the construction and working of Injection molding Process and equipment.
5. Explain working principle of screw type injection molding process
6. Explain the construction and working of Extrusion of Plastic.
7. Discuss the type of extruder.
8. Explain with neat diagram how extruders are specified?
9. Discuss how pipe, cable and sheet are produced?
10. List Thermoforming process and explain any one in detail.
11. Compare pressure forming and vacuum forming.

www.ingramcontent.com/pod-product-compliance
Lightning Source LLC
Chambersburg PA
CBHW062128160426

43191CB00013B/2237